THE INDONESIAN REVOLUTION AND
THE SINGAPORE CONNECTION

Dedicated to
Siao Hui, Khai Ern, Khai Wern and Khai Si

VERHANDELINGEN
VAN HET KONINKLIJK INSTITUUT
VOOR TAAL-, LAND- EN VOLKENKUNDE

208

YONG MUN CHEONG

THE INDONESIAN REVOLUTION AND THE SINGAPORE CONNECTION

1945-1949

KITLV Press
Leiden
2003

Published by:
KITLV Press
Koninklijk Instituut voor Taal-, Land- en Volkenkunde
(The Royal Netherlands Institute of Southeast Asian and Caribbean Studies)
P.O. Box 9515
2300 RA Leiden
The Netherlands
website: www.kitlv.nl
e-mail: kitlvpress@kitlv.nl

Cover: Creja Ontwerpen, Leiderdorp

ISBN 90 6718 206 0

© 2003 Koninklijk Instituut voor Taal-, Land- en Volkenkunde
No part of this publication may be reproduced or transmitted in any form or by any means, electronic or mechanical, including photocopy, recording, or any information storage and retrieval system, without permission from the copyright owner.

Printed in the Netherlands

Contents

Acknowledgements	vii
Note on spelling and currency	ix
Abbreviations and acronyms	xi
Glossary	xiii
Maps	
Indonesia and Singapore	xiv
Riau archipelago and Singapore	xv
Singapore – locations and placenames	xvi
I The Singapore connection	1
An introduction	
II Context of the Indonesian Revolution	13
III Constituents of the Singapore connection	25
IV Competition between Indonesians in Singapore	67
V Contest for influence	81
VI Clandestine activities	101
VII Commercial relations, or the 'Singapore squeeze'	139
VIII Conclusion	175
Curtains for the Singapore connection	
Bibliography	199
Index	205

Acknowledgements

In my attempt to explore connections, I have benefited from many associations and liaisons developed over many years with colleagues and institutions.

I am grateful to friends and supporters in Singapore, Indonesia, the Netherlands, and England. I was privileged to discuss the ideas developed in this book with colleagues from diverse parts of the world at conferences and other meetings. They are too numerous to be identified, but they can all claim a share in the outcome. Of course they are not responsible for the book's shortcomings.

My home institution was also most generous. The National University of Singapore provided sabbatical leave and a research grant (R-110-000-003-112) during the years that were required to complete the book. Everybody was most patient and indulgent. They seldom asked difficult questions about my target schedule while the research was in progress. Meanwhile, the deanship of the Faculty of Arts and Social Sciences at the National University of Singapore, as well as the headship of the Department of History, changed hands, but the new Dean and the new Head continued to give me space to pursue my scholarly interests at my own pace. To all of them, a hearty 'thank you'.

This book was written using source materials, archival and non-archival, obtained from Singapore, Indonesia, the Netherlands, and England. These are identified in the bibliography. The book benefited from comments of referees appointed by KITLV Press. I also wish to thank Chee Min Fui and Tan Li Kheng for helping in preparing the manuscript for publication.

An essential ingredient that made this book possible was family support. In addition to the 'Singapore connection' studied in this book, my family was the connection between research and everyday life in Singapore. This book is dedicated to them.

Note on spelling and currency

Spelling

Invariably, authors writing about Indonesia have to contend with the changes in spelling systems. In archival materials, the spelling of names is often different from the ones used in later years. Place names are often entirely different.

In this study, the current spellings of Indonesian geographical names are used. The names of persons and organizations are given in their contemporary spellings. As for the capital city of Indonesia, 'Batavia' is retained when referring to Dutch authority but 'Jakarta' is used when discussing control exercised by the Republic of Indonesia.

Currencies

At various times from 1945 till 1949, several different kinds of monetary units circulated in Indonesia. They included the Straits dollar, the Netherlands guilder, the Indonesian rupiah, Japanese army notes, and the Netherlands Indies Civil Authority (NICA) guilder. The last-named currency was the successor to the Netherlands East Indies (NEI) guilder, sometimes called the Java guilder. The Indonesian rupiah, the currency unit issued by the Republic of Indonesia, bore the initials 'ORI', for Oeang Republik Indonesia. For convenience, the Straits dollar will carry the symbol '$', unless indicated otherwise.

Abbreviations and acronyms

ATC	Atjeh Trading Corporation
BNI	Bank Negara Indonesia
BTC	Banking and Trading Corporation
CCC	Chinese Chamber of Commerce
ECAFE	Economic Commission for Asia and the Far East
FEBS	Far Eastern Broadcasting Service
GLU	General Labour Union
Hiwarni	Himpoenan Warga Negara Indonesia
MCP	Malayan Communist Party
NEFIS	Netherlands Forces Intelligence Service
NICA	Netherlands Indies Civil Administration
OCBC	Overseas Chinese Banking Corporation
Perkabim	Persatoean Kaoem Boeroeh Indonesia Melayu
PI	Persatoean Indonesia
PKBI	Persatoean Kaoem Boeroeh Indonesia
SBTC	Sumatra Banking and Trading Corporation
SEAC	South East Asia Command
SERTA	Sarikat Rahasia Tanah Air
SOCIEA	Singapore Overseas Chinese Importers and Exporters Association
TNI	Tentera Nasional Indonesia
TRI	Tentera Repoeblik Indonesia
USI	United States of Indonesia

Glossary

chinchew	supercargo/ Chinese chief clerk
chinchew palsu	bogus chinchew
kelong	fishing stakes
kongsi	business firm
oom	uncle
pemuda	youth group
perjuangan	armed struggle
picul	weight measurement equivalent to about 62.5 kg
prauw	small boat
sampan	small boat
tongkang	barge
wedana	head of a district

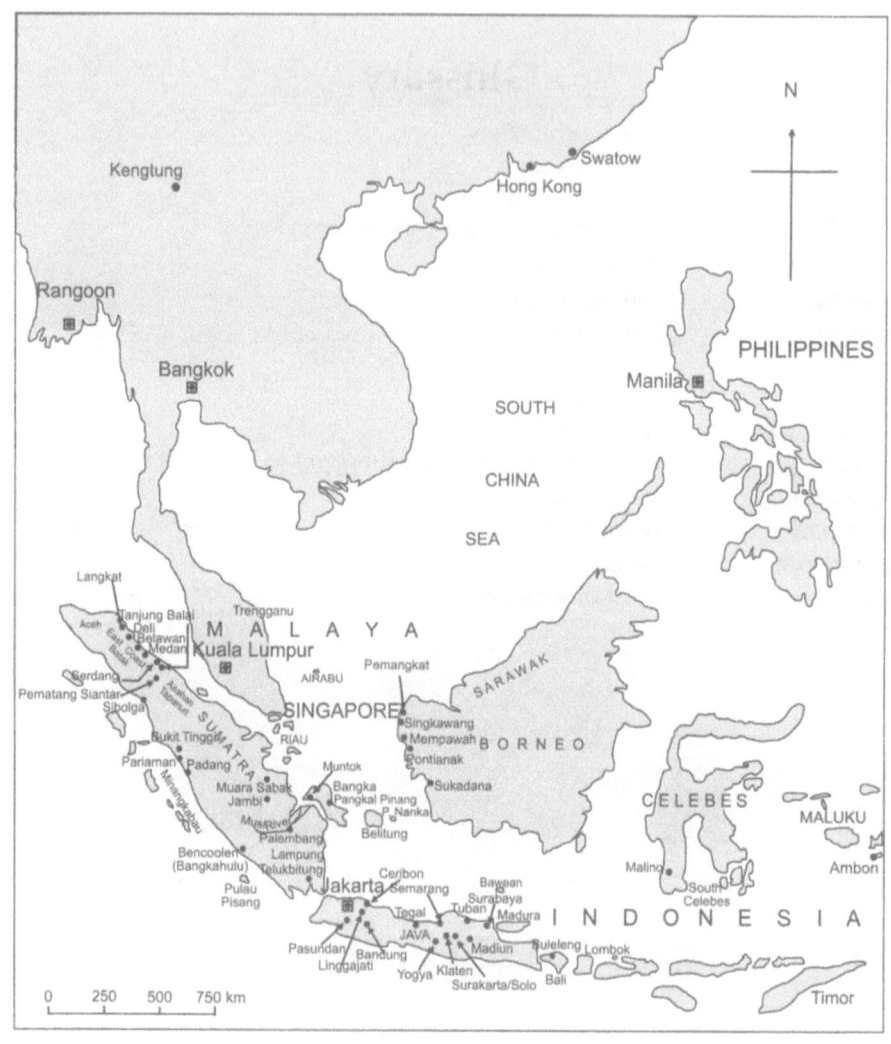

Map 1. Indonesia and Singapore

Map 2. Riau archipelago and Singapore

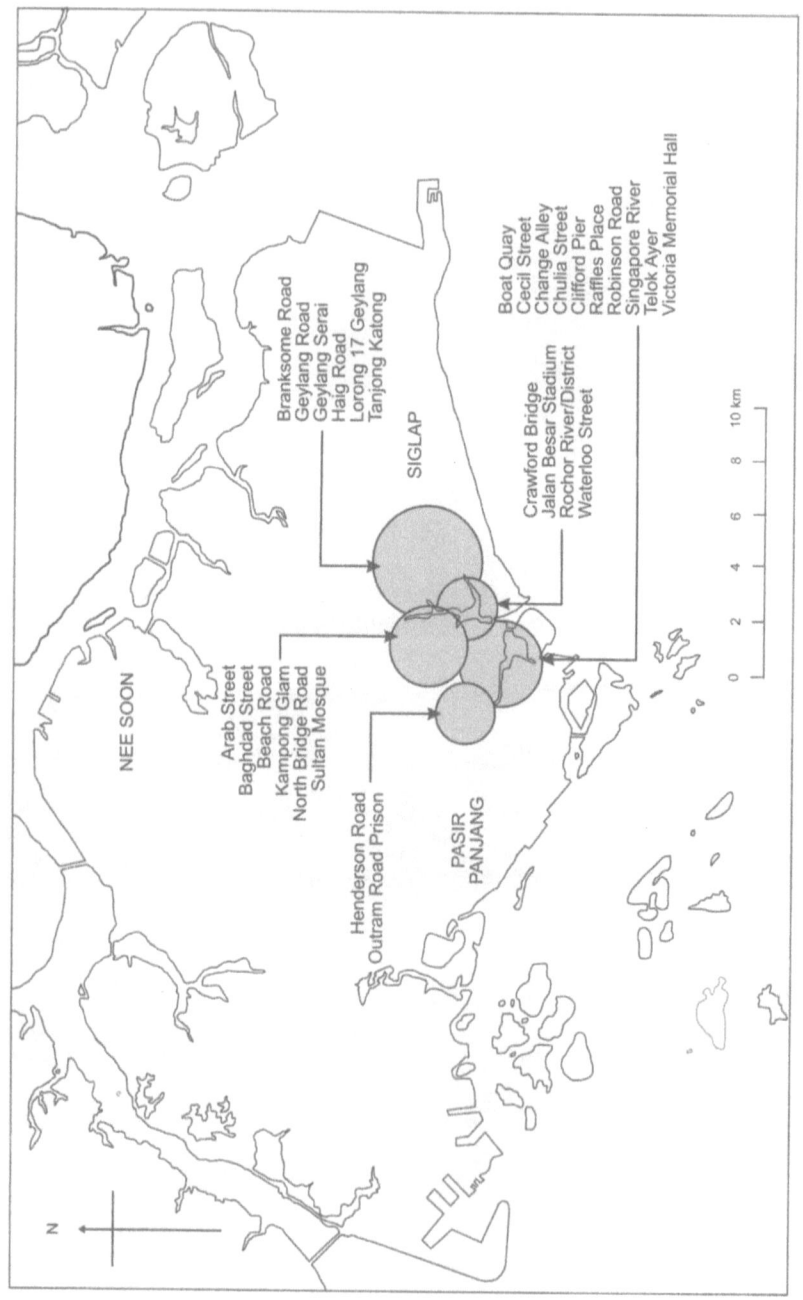

Map 3. Singapore – locations and place-names

CHAPTER I

The Singapore connection
An introduction

Since the founding of Singapore, the island has played host to many visitors from Indonesia. These visitors were of various types. Most of them were traders and pilgrims. Some decided to settle, after working for a time. There were also criminals on the run, and smugglers who carried opium or weapons. Indeed, the Singapore connection was busy and thriving.

What is meant by the 'Singapore connection'? Specifically, it refers to the secret operations between Indonesia and Singapore going on from 1945 to 1949. These operations were clandestine because the Republic of Indonesia was then engaged in a nationalist struggle for independence with the colonial power, the Netherlands. Ships from the Netherlands navy patrolled the high seas to prevent trade in contraband, for example weapons. The Republican navy was equally interested in the weapons trade, using Singapore as a base of operations. However, the Singapore connection was not confined to trade in weapons. It extended to all kinds of goods deemed by the Dutch to be contraband or vital for the survival of Indonesia. The Singapore connection was also described as a 'third front' of the Indonesian revolution.[1] (The first front was diplomacy and the second front was guerrilla resistance.)

Moreover, the connection was an open door drawing all kinds of visitors to Singapore. Along with the naval or military officials came diplomats, journalists, and private businessmen. Many of the private businessmen were smugglers with contacts among the Chinese traders of Singapore. Others were Indonesian visitors devoted to nationalist ideals of an independent Republic of Indonesia. Some of these were adventurers, and not all were Indonesian in origin or nationality. The list could be extended indefinitely.

Their arrivals and departures were not always recorded in history, especially when they did not fall foul of the law. To give an impression of the kind of traffic, I will give three examples of visitors. The first visitor was strictly serious and businesslike. He journeyed to Singapore to promote the cause of

[1] Darusman 1992, see preface by Mochtar Kusumaatmadja.

independence for the Republic of Indonesia. The second wavered between the serious business of independence and the romantic ideals of nationalism. The last visitor was an adventurer wanted by the Republic of Indonesia government for mass murder.

Our first visitor, Sjahroedin, was a journalist in Jakarta during the Japanese occupation (1942-1945). He worked as an editor for Domei, the Japanese news agency. Upon the surrender of the Japanese in August 1945, he was one of those responsible for broadcasting the news throughout Indonesia. Very quickly, the journalists working at Domei seized control from their Japanese bosses and renamed it the Antara news agency. The Antara is still in business, but in those early days, the leading journalists felt it was essential to establish branches outside Jakarta. Singapore was immediately identified as an important site and Sjahroedin was the journalist chosen to set up the new branch. It was in February 1946 that Sjahroedin made his way to Singapore.

In those days, most Indonesians did not fly to Singapore, arriving at Kallang airport. That mode of travel was reserved for dignitaries. Most entered Singapore by boat (*sampan*), landing at Clifford Pier, or undetected, at Pasir Panjang, Beach Road, or the Rochor area. Sjahroedin did not even possess a passport recognized by the British colonial authorities in Singapore. (The Republic of Indonesia was not recognized as a government; the Dutch Netherlands East Indies was.) Sjahroedin did not even have money to rent premises and set up a branch of Antara. All he had was the conviction that the pen was as mighty as the sword. If soldiers and weapons were needed to fight the Dutch colonialists, he would use his writing skills on behalf of the Republic.

Sjahroedin's mission to Singapore was never in doubt. Even ordinary people like Oom (Uncle) Djakman, an antiques dealer in Jakarta, urged him to go: 'Young people must fight with courage. Don't get worried even before you start. Don't be concerned about how you will survive in Singapore, whether your money will run out. Neither should you worry about where you will sleep, how to get a visa, and other nuisances.' In short, if Sjahroedin felt it was important to go to Singapore, just go! Nevertheless, as a parting gift, Oom Djakman gave Sjahroedin a silver urn that could be sold in Singapore for cash.

Sjahroedin's journey to Singapore made use of an indirect route. It was not a simple affair of jumping into a boat in Jakarta bound for Singapore. Apart from the need to evade Dutch patrol ships, he thought it prudent to seek support from Indonesians with contacts in Singapore. With Sofyan, his companion and colleague for the trip, he therefore first made his way to Palembang to seek the help of A.K. Gani, the Republican governor of South Sumatra.

Gani was an ideal person for Sjahroedin to meet. He maintained a vast network of trade and business with Singapore Chinese. He was also a strong supporter of the Republic of Indonesia government, sharing the ideals of independence. Through Gani's help, Sjahroedin was introduced to Mawardi, a boatman of Indonesian origin residing in Singapore. Mawardi operated a 100-ton boat sailing between Palembang and Singapore. He knew the seas very well. He was familiar with the winds, the currents, the shallows, and above all, he had experience in how to evade the Dutch patrol boats.

For three nights, Sjahroedin sailed. The journey to Singapore was uneventful. After arriving, he moved into Mawardi's house in a Malay settlement. This was a nearly perfect hiding place for migrants without papers. An Indonesian could easily blend in with the Malay population of Singapore, living as one of them. What is more, Mawardi's father-in-law was a policeman. With this newly found freedom, Sjahroedin was soon busy contacting other Indonesians and like-minded journalists who had made Singapore their abode even before the Japanese occupation. With the help of Gani and other Indonesians sympathetic to the Republic of Indonesia, it was not long before the new branch of the Antara news agency was up and running.[2] This success story, however, had a tragic sequel, which will be taken up later.

The second visitor arrived in January 1947. Smuggled into Singapore without papers by her Indonesian friends, she was an ardent supporter of the Republican cause. K'tut Tantri or 'Surabaya Sue' was her name. This was an American woman forty years of age with a Balinese name showing her affection for and identification with things Indonesian. She was nicknamed 'Surabaya Sue' because her voice over radio had become familiar to thousands of British and Dutch soldiers as she vituperated against the Dutch and earnestly pressed the Republican cause for independence. Her anti-colonial diatribes were so strident that even the Republican leaders were embarrassed. On the pretext that the Dutch would arrest her at the first opportunity, they smuggled her out of Indonesia to Singapore.[3]

K'tut Tantri's journey to Singapore took an indirect route. She left Tegal, the Republican harbour on the north coast of Java, in a boat bound for the Bangka Straits before crossing the waters to Singapore early one morning. Then, without proper documents, she had to fake her way through immigration, assuming the identity of an intoxicated woman hanging on the arms of her Chinese partner after spending a night with him. Her arrival in January 1947 was not the end of the story. K'tut Tantri re-entered Indonesia and returned to Singapore on secret missions for the Republic on a number of occasions (Lindsey 1997:193).

---

[2] For the story of Sjahroedin, see *Memoar pejuang* 1992, Chapters II-IV.
[3] 'Sourabaya Sue in Singapore', *Straits Times*, 31-1-1947, p. 1. K'tut Tantri has published her own account; see Tantri 1960.

Some time in February 1950, a very colourful figure entered Singapore via the Johore causeway. He had not applied for an entry permit but he was known to have been in contact with smugglers operating between Sumatra and the coast of Malaya.[4] He landed by boat at Pontian in Johore. As he made his way to Singapore, he met a few Chinese soldiers (most likely communist guerrillas) who did not stop him after he claimed that he was a British army deserter who quit because 'he did not like the way things were going'. Using the forged passport of a Dutch man who died in 1943, he crossed three or four police roadblocks, arrived at the Johore causeway, and entered Singapore. Undisguised, he walked about freely in the amusement parks, and spent his weekends at coffee shops and hotels.[5]

He was R.P.P. Westerling, a former Dutch army commando holding the rank of captain and nicknamed 'The Turk' or 'Turko' because he was of Dutch-Turkish parentage. The Republic of Indonesia placed a price on his head for mass murder in South Celebes, where he was responsible for applying harsh measures to 'pacify' the region by getting rid of Republican supporters. Unhappy with the Republic of Indonesia's attempts to overthrow Dutch rule and impatient with the Dutch decision to negotiate with their opponents, he made himself leader of the unofficial 'army of the heavenly host' in West Java. Then only thirty years old, he demanded recognition for his 'army' as the official military force in the autonomous West Java state of Pasundan. His 'army' counted ten thousand to fifteen thousand followers. They were recruited from the former Netherlands Indies army (the KNIL in Dutch), and among Ambonese and Timorese who were generally unsympathetic to the Javanese and Sumatrans occupying leading positions in the Republican-led uprising against the Dutch.[6] With this force, he captured Bandung and held it for several hours before his forces retreated into the surrounding areas. Fearing the worst, he fled to Singapore to escape arrest.

In Singapore, Westerling checked into the Empress Hotel in Middle Road, identifying himself as R. Willem. For three days, he wandered around Singapore, visiting the entertainment spots. He was only arrested on 26 February 1950 for illegal entry.[7] At first he was detained at the Central Police Station and made to share a cell with an Indonesian by the name of Haris

[4] 'Westerling may try to come to Singapore', *Straits Times*, 21-2-1950, p. 1.
[5] '"Turko" talks to the Tribune', *Malaya Tribune*, 27-2-1950, pp. 1 and 12.
[6] 'Westerling says, U.S.I. has plans to invade New Guinea', *Malaya Tribune*, 23-1-1950, p. 1.
[7] 'Westerling arrested at Singapore house', *Straits Times*, 27-2-1950, pp. 1 and 7; 'Singapore deportation order against Westerling', *Straits Times*, 1-3-1950, p. 1; '"Turko" discussed by Dutch cabinet', *Straits Times*, 2-3-1950, p. 1; 'Mrs Westerling in Jakarta', *Straits Times*, 2-3-1950, p. 1; 'An embarrassing guest', *Straits Times*, 2-3-1950, p. 8; '"Turk" gaoled for illegal Singapore entry', *Straits Times*, 9-3-1950, pp. 1 and 9. See also comments by C.R. Dasaratharaj, *Straits Times*, 18-3-1950, p. 9; 'Turko's gaol term query out of order', *Straits Times*, 22-3-1950, p. 7; 'Colony can decide on "Turko"; USI told "repeat extradition plea"', *Straits Times*, 8-4-1950, p. 5.

Porkas. The next morning when Porkas was cleaning his teeth, Westerling approached him and introduced himself, 'I am the Turk. You have heard of me. Shake hands.' Porkas refused and Westerling said, 'You have insulted me'. Thereupon, he punched the Indonesian, breaking his jaw. After the brawl, Westerling was transferred to Changi Prison, where he was placed in solitary confinement. He had a deportation order made out against him, and a further charge of assault hung over his head. Under the prevailing regulations, any other charges against him could be ignored if he was deported.[8]

I do not intend to place Sjahroedin on a par with the likes of Westerling and K'tut Tantri. They were as different as night and day. Yet, seen together, they capture the variety of characters that took part in the performance called the Singapore connection. They showed how that connection could be put to use by serious people as well as criminals and adventurers. The connection benefited some and disadvantaged others. It was all things to all people.

What was Singapore like when Sjahroedin, K'tut Tantri, and Westerling arrived? Living conditions were anything but pleasant or easy. Like all places that survived the Japanese occupation, there was a shortage of food and insufficient accommodation; industrial disputes were the order of the day; political unrest was brewing even as attempts were made to establish administrative structures suitable for a post-war world.

However, as always, discontent was relative. To the Indonesians across the waters, Singapore after the Japanese surrendered was still a peaceful haven compared to the deprivations they suffered at home. Singapore offered something for everyone. Indonesian traders and businessmen came to Singapore because of the commercial possibilities. Smugglers found in Singapore a supply centre for all kinds of goods needed in Indonesia. Government and semi-government agencies despatched their representatives to Singapore. They came with impressive-sounding missions, for example to acquire weapons or to gather information.

The attraction of Singapore, of course, was not a new development. Since its founding in 1819, Singapore had created controversies while pursuing the mundane business of managing its entrepot role that was the reason for its existence in the first place. It injected a 'fizz', a 'buzz', to the Indonesian archipelago that has since been a staple of historical research. A survey of the relations maintained between Singapore and the different parts of the Indonesian archipelago during the nineteenth and twentieth centuries will substantiate the claim that Singapore was more than just a convenient and strategically located port to tranship goods. The story begins with opium.

---

[8] 'Turko in solitary confinement; Cell-mate is found with broken jaw', *Malaya Tribune*, 1-3-1950, p. 1. Westerling's memoirs were published as Raymond ('Turk') Westerling, *Challenge to terror* in 1952, see especially Chapters XXXII and XXXIII.

Singapore, a haven for opium smugglers

One of the commodities transacted in early Singapore was opium. The trade in this drug was carried out both legally and illegally. An exploration of Singapore's role as an opium supply base can start with the court case in which a Chinese trader was prosecuted for opium smuggling. This case was heard before the Council of Justice in Surabaya in 1889. It concerned one The Toan Huat who was accused of carrying opium from Singapore to the island of Bawean off Java. The Toan Huat was the supercargo[9] of a Netherlands East Indies registered steamship. A lower court convicted him but the Council of Justice overturned the ruling on account of technicalities. The's case was one of the few that reached the courts. By the end of the nineteenth century, Singapore had long been playing a dominant role in the legal and illegal export of opium to islands in the Netherlands East Indies.[10]

Opium was brought to Singapore by ships from India and China. In some instances, the opium was not carried ashore but remained in transit. In the spirit of free trade, such opium in transit was not discouraged and it eventually found its way to the different parts of the Indonesian archipelago. It was the aim of Dutch policy to control the sale and consumption of opium, it being a drug that could be either useful or harmful, while at the same time yielding a tax revenue that formed the cornerstone of colonial finances. Since the 1860s, the preferred method was to auction the right to sell opium within a prescribed territory (called a farm) to the highest bidder. As it turned out, the highest bidders were usually Chinese. It was envisaged that through the Chinese, the Dutch could bar all illegal sales of opium while at the same time achieving their goals of revenue collection and control of consumption. The system had its defects. Most importantly for this study, it encouraged smuggling of opium from Singapore, where prices were usually lower, to the farm territories of the Netherlands East Indies where prices were fixed and usually higher. If smuggling were left unchecked, the profitability of the opium farms would be undermined and decrease the income of the colonial coffers.

The opium reached the Indonesian islands in various ways. The's case is one of many. Opium was also sold legally to Bali, then consisting of several independent states before the Dutch finally established their ascendancy by 1908. From Bali, the drug was smuggled to the north coast ports of Java for distribution to opium dens in the interior. Most of the smugglers were Chinese who could call upon the services of relatives in Singapore as a source

---

[9]   A supercargo was the representative on the ship of the ship owners and consignors. This representative was not responsible for the ship's navigation. That was the task of the captain. He attended only to the business side of the voyage.

[10]   For details on the opium connection between the Netherlands East Indies and Singapore, see Rush 1990:68-9, 80, 167-73, 226-31.

for opium. The Dutch colonial government was even compelled to operate a spy network in Singapore to alert the Batavia authorities about likely shipments.

The above-mentioned case illustrates some characteristic features of the Singapore opium connection. Its proximity made Singapore the ideal centre for obtaining opium for further distribution. For The, the Singapore-Bawean route was not particularly long or difficult. Many ordinary Bawean had made the crossing in more rickety vessels without accident.[11] The geographically dispersed locations of the Indonesian islands and their variety of political structures during most of the nineteenth century meant that each independent state was encouraged to promote international trade and international contacts to balance Dutch encroachments. It must not be forgotten that Dutch control over the Indonesian archipelago outside Java was not firmly established till the early decades of the twentieth century, and until that time, many quasi-independent states existed. Once on the high seas, the crew of a ship faced the risk of being searched by Dutch patrol boats, although this measure was illegal, strictly speaking, since the Dutch were acting outside their three-mile territorial limit. In any case, the number of patrol boats that the Dutch could deploy was limited, and the expanse of water to be patrolled was immense. Above all, opium was an ideal smuggling commodity, since the drug could be packed in small quantities, hidden away in the most unlikely places on a ship or attached to the human body, and still be sold at an attractive price.

For well over half a century till 1910, Singapore remained an important source of legal and illegal opium. If there were pressures to end this role, it was because humanitarian arguments were raised against the use of opium. Otherwise, opium contributed too much revenue to colonial coffers, both in the Netherlands East Indies and in British colonies, to be banned altogether.

Singapore, a base for diplomats and individual sympathizers

It must be remembered that in the nineteenth century, Singapore was surrounded by quasi-independent states governed by rulers who sought every opportunity to assert their freedom – freedom to trade and freedom to govern as they pleased. The second half of the nineteenth century was a time when Dutch colonial forces attempted to assert their authority in the Indonesian archipelago, especially those parts near Singapore. Dutch interests began to extend beyond Java because of a new emphasis on the exploitation of planta-

---

11 There are accounts of Singapore-Bawean crossings in the oral history collections of the Singapore National Archives. See bibliography.

tion crops and minerals. Indonesian rulers also fought among themselves for supremacy over each other. The natural reaction of some of these rulers was to seek the assistance of friends in Singapore and to cultivate the support of the British colonial government there.

Buleleng

In 1848, the Balinese ruler of Buleleng looked to Singapore for weapons to fight the encroaching Dutch forces.[12] This was a futile act of defiance and Bali succumbed to Dutch expansion. Under Dutch rule, and with the development of transport and port infrastructure, Bali saw an increase of trade with Singapore. In fact, Bali became the eastern extension of Singapore's entrepot.

Siak

Another ruler who tried to gain support from Singapore was Sultan Ismail of Siak (Reid 1969:25-6). In 1856, the sultan appealed to the governor of Singapore, E.A. Blundell, to resist Acehnese attempts at subjugating all the indigenous rulers on the eastern coast of Sumatra. The sultan also faced challenges from his own brother-in-law. Governor Blundell did not respond and Sultan Ismail then contacted one Adam Wilson, chief clerk in a Singapore trading firm, to support his struggle against threats to the Siak throne late in 1867. It was not unusual for indigenous leaders to seek the assistance of commercial contacts, especially if there had been prior business relations. Wilson organized a military force to demonstrate support for the Sultan of Siak against his opponents. When Governor Blundell heard of this, he advised Wilson against interference. Interference, of course, violated the terms of the earlier treaty of 1824 when Britain allowed the Netherlands a free hand to establish colonial authority south of Singapore. By this time, it was clear to the Sultan of Siak that no help was forthcoming from Singapore, and he appealed to the Dutch instead to assist him against his enemies. When a Dutch representative reached Siak, Wilson's support for the Sultan disintegrated. Interestingly, Wilson also subsequently tried to establish his firm's influence on Bengkalis island (near Siak), but he was chased away by the Dutch, causing him to be indignant since he could produce a document proving his firm owned a concession on the island.

Generally, private initiatives by individuals from Singapore were frowned upon. The governor of Singapore, supported by most British merchants, preferred a Dutch presence to check the anarchy and disorder in places like

---

[12] On Bali's contacts with Singapore, see Schulte Nordholt 1996:96-7, 160-9.

Siak. In the eyes of officialdom in Singapore, Wilson was little more than an adventurer with nuisance value, especially after it was learnt that the Dutch had no plans to discriminate against British merchants in the event of taking over control of Siak.

However, to assuage any remaining fears of Singapore merchants regarding the extension of Dutch influence on Sumatra's eastern coast, Governor O. Cavenagh (1859-1867) sent a gunboat (the *Pluto*) to visit Asahan, Deli, Langkat, and Serdang in an attempt to fly the flag.

Aceh

The Singapore connection became more important when the Dutch expanded into Aceh (Reid 1969:98-103, 134-49, 161, 208-10). In 1871, a treaty between Britain and the Netherlands gave the latter freedom of action to extend their influence into northern Sumatra where Aceh was located. From that year, Singapore became a focus of diplomatic activity as the Acehnese tried to win friends and influence friendly states to come to their aid. In 1872, Sultan Mahmud of Aceh sent his Shahbandar, Tibang, to Penang and Singapore to appeal for British support. Tibang was also given appropriate letters authorizing him to conclude treaties with foreign powers. In Singapore, many Western powers had established consulates. Although the number of Acehnese residents in Singapore was small and there was little trade between Singapore and Aceh itself, Singapore was still an important connection for the Acehnese. Apart from the diplomatic consulates, there was an important Arab population living there and the community was a good channel of communication with Muslim supporters in Turkey. Singapore was also an important transit point for pilgrims to Mecca and therefore it was an important target for propaganda work to cultivate support for the Acehnese, who were also Muslims.

Shahbandar Tibang met the American consul, who had grandiose but purely personal views on how the United States could help the Acehnese. There were also reports from Singapore that the Italians were interested in helping. Although nothing of substance emerged from these contacts, they presented the Dutch with a justification for going to war with the Acehnese for fear of foreign intervention if Aceh was not brought under their control. In 1873, a Dutch ship bombarded Aceh's shore.

War with Aceh raised the issue of Singapore's response. One prominent Arab leader in Singapore was Syed Alsagoff, who raised funds to help the Acehnese cause. Javanese businessmen in Singapore could be relied upon to act as propagandists and messengers. But would the governor permit the flow of arms to Aceh? Would the Straits Settlements government allow Dutch forces to purchase supplies in Penang? Underlying both questions was the issue of profit, for there was money to be made from selling weapons and general provisions. Meanwhile, to apply a stranglehold on the Acehnese, the Dutch imposed a blockade on the coasts of North Sumatra. This measure, of course, did not endear the Dutch to the Europeans and Chinese merchants in Singapore, and the general tenor there was one of support for the Acehnese. Many Europeans were also prepared to act as intermediaries to help the Acehnese. Many were little better than adventurers. Edouard Roura was one of these. He was a sailor and trader from Marseilles, who brought an Acehnese envoy to Singapore in 1874 to negotiate a settlement. At the official level, the principal Acehnese envoy – Abd ar-Rahman az Zahir – met Governor Andrew Clarke with the help of the Maharajah of Johore and sought his intervention to end the conflict with the Dutch. Clarke had just concluded an agreement (1874) with the ruler of Perak to end the civil war there. Fresh from this major success, he was prepared to act as mediator, but the Netherlands government balked at any third party interference in what it considered to be a strictly Dutch problem. Public opinion in the Netherlands would also settle for nothing less than forcing the Acehnese to surrender. War between Aceh and the Dutch forces resumed in 1875 and lasted intermittently for another thirty years.

The methods used by the Dutch to pacify Aceh anticipated those to be employed from 1947 onwards. The broad strategy was to impose a blockade on Aceh. In 1880, a shipping regulation was passed limiting the overseas trade of Aceh to four or five ports under Dutch control. There were howls of protest from the merchants in Penang. Some of them had made cash advances for exports worth over $100,000 to Acehnese traders in the ports that were closed. In 1882, the shipping regulation was modified to allow vessels to proceed anywhere on the north coast of Sumatra provided they cleared inspection at one of the Dutch-controlled ports.

Lombok

Similar, if less fierce, resistance took place on Lombok island, east of Bali. To counter the aggressive designs of the Dutch, the Raja of Lombok sent an emissary – Hadji Abdulrachman – to Singapore in 1892 with a large sum of money to solicit assistance (Van der Kraan 1980:40-52). The Dutch consul in Singapore reported that Hadji Abdulrachman bought two steamships, engaged English sailors, and visited a lawyer. When one of the steamships sailed into Lombok from Singapore, the Dutch detained the vessel. This unsuccessful attempt to seek external assistance did not discourage the Raja of Lombok from trying again. He retained the services of a lawyer in Singapore, someone by the name of J.C. Mitchell, to petition the Straits Settlements government (in 1892) for help to stop the Dutch from applying coercive measures. This came to nothing and Mitchell even tried, unsuccessfully, to seek an audience with the Dutch governor-general in Batavia to remonstrate on behalf of his client.

Failing to find a legal remedy, the Raja of Lombok then recruited an agent based in Singapore, this time a Russian adventurer by the name of W.P. Malygin. In 1893, Malygin tried to smuggle war materials into Lombok for the raja. Back in Singapore in 1894, Malygin bought a Chinese junk, loaded it with weapons, ammunition, and explosives, and set sail for Lombok in April of that year. The sea journey turned out to be a disaster. The ship was mistakenly steered to Dutch-controlled Bali, and the cargo was seized. Malygin managed to escape to Lombok.

With the benefit of hindsight, these can be seen as the last gasps of freedom expressed by the Raja of Lombok. The days of independence were numbered. The end came in 1894. Significantly, for this study, Singapore was the place where diplomatic, legal, military, and unofficial support could be cultivated, solicited, and obtained. With Lombok under Dutch control, the Singapore connection assumed a different form. Henceforth Singapore became the trade centre for Lombok's exports and imports, somewhat similar to the case in Bali. In fact, Singapore became Lombok's import lifeline, and the dependence was so great that the newly established Dutch administration was led to issue an ordinance in 1895 to levy duties on goods from Singapore.

Conclusion

It is not clear who first used the phrase 'the Singapore connection' to describe the contacts between Singapore and Indonesia during the period of the Indonesian revolution. It could have been the republican marine corps stationed at Tegal. During the period 1945-1946, the navy's position in Tegal was already sufficiently established to develop a network to import military requirements, or contraband, from Singapore (*Memoar pejuang* 1992:145-6).

Given the existence of the Singapore connection, was there a high level of knowledge within the Singapore community about the Indonesian archipelago? This is difficult to assess. Within the boundaries of contacts, there must have been a degree of professional knowledge that enabled the trader or lawyer to carry out his business efficiently such that counterparts in the Indonesian archipelago appreciated their services. However, beyond this limited niche, it cannot be confidently asserted that there was considerable expertise on the Indonesian archipelago within Singapore. Indeed, Western travellers were disappointed when they stopped over in Singapore on the way to Indonesia, hoping to gather some background information on their next destination.

One of these travellers was J.W.B. Money, a lawyer in the employ of the

British East India Company. In 1858, he toured some parts of Java, but before his arrival, he made some inquiries in Singapore about the Dutch colony. He found that the depth of knowledge in Singapore was rather shallow. This was how he described it:

> On our arrival at Singapore I renewed my inquiries but our countrymen there seemed hardly better acquainted with the state of Java. They told me that the Dutch Colonial Government was a secret, monopolizing, and tyrannical Government, of which little was known, except that it was said to be hated by its Indigenous subjects, who only wanted encouragement to throw off the Dutch yoke and to return to English rule.
>
> We arrived in Java, therefore, expecting to find an oppressed and poverty-stricken people, with general marks of misgovernment by the Europeans, and of discontent among the Natives. (Money 1985:4.)

Money probably encountered a paucity of information in Singapore because he was attempting to learn about Dutch Java, and not about 'the half-conquered dependencies which have most intercourse with Singapore' (Money 1985:39) of which there must have been greater familiarity.

The bulk of Money's account of Dutch rule in Java has since been discredited. However, his observation of the level of information in Singapore is interesting. It is valid to the extent that it reflected a mindset prevalent among colonial officials and British merchants convinced of the superiority of a free-trade system versus the closed monopoly that was attributed to the Dutch operating in the Indonesian archipelago. How the Dutch viewed the Netherlands East Indies was perplexing. In the West, the Dutch were champions of free trade, open seas, and republicanism. What changed them as they travelled beyond the Cape of Good Hope? Why did they become champions of monopoly? Why did the Dutch prefer controlled navigation and authoritarian government? This study will not explain the reasons for this transformation but certainly, restrictive practices continued to be very evident even in the later and difficult years after 1945.

Money's comment that there was little information available in Singapore is corroborated by another observation made in 1921, more than eighty years later. Lord Northcliffe, founder of the London *Daily Mail* and *Daily Mirror*, visited Singapore that year and echoed the same sentiments: 'In Singapore no one knows about any other place. We are trying to find out about Saigon (Indochina) and Batavia (Java). No one knows.' (*Traveller's Singapore* 1994: 194.)

CHAPTER II

Context of the Indonesian Revolution

To facilitate a better understanding of the materials that follow, it will be useful to explore the context in which the events of the Indonesian Revolution transpired before moving to the dynamics of the Singapore connection.

The history of the Indonesian Revolution has been the subject of many publications. Different authors frame their account of the revolution in different ways. Some representative views are given below:

> The mutual frustration of the *pemuda* (youth groups), who had revolutionary expectations but no revolutionary leadership, and the middle-class metropolitan intelligentsia, both collaborationist and underground, who were in a position to lead but totally inexperienced in doing so without external support, was to provide the leitmotif of the Indonesian Revolution. (Anderson 1972:109.)

Or, in the words of an Indonesian author in a recent publication, 'The most conspicuous characteristic of the Indonesian Revolution was the existence of dual leadership – the military and the political' (Salim Said 1991:5).

It is not the aim here to add yet another framework to the total number of ways to view this major event in Indonesian history.[1] The purpose here is merely to mention in chronological sequence the events that were significant for the Indonesians in Singapore and leave out the others that did not figure prominently in their horizon.

After the fall of Singapore in February 1942, Japanese military forces proceeded to drive the Dutch colonialists away from Indonesia, finally succeeding in March 1942. The only substantial opposition that the Japanese had to overcome was the resistance put up by the Netherlands navy. The so-called Battle of the Java Sea turned out to be the last-ditch stand of a colonial power against the invading Japanese. Although it failed to stem the tide, it did serve to bolster the pride of the Netherlands navy, which saw itself as the only military force to bear the brunt of the Japanese attack while the other services scrambled or retreated.

---

[1] For a collection of studies on how the revolution took different routes in the various regions of Indonesia, see Kahin 1985.

In Java and Sumatra, the Japanese sought to develop indigenous support against any prospective invasion by the Dutch and their allies. As part of this goal, the Japanese provided military training to large numbers of Indonesians. The trainees were organized into various paramilitary groups. It was these trainees who later formed the nucleus of the Indonesian army by seizing Japanese weapons in 1945 when the Japanese surrendered, and then forming themselves into autonomous groups not subject to centralized command. Military training was also accompanied by political indoctrination of the trainees such that Indonesian society in Java and Sumatra experienced considerable upheaval, with new elite groups emerging. At the same time, the war in the Pacific resulted in considerable hardship and deprivation. For example, labour supply and rice deliveries were high priorities in the Japanese war plans. Many Indonesians, especially those from Java, were forcibly recruited for labour gangs and sent north, via Singapore, to work in Burma and Siam[2] building railroads and so forth. Coupled with the complete stoppage of consumer imports, the conditions in Java and Sumatra were sufficiently unsettling to warrant a revolutionary upheaval. This was delayed till after the Japanese surrendered, when their tight control was finally lifted. Meanwhile, in Jakarta, pre-war nationalist leaders were co-opted into various political positions under the aegis of the Japanese and given the opportunity to exercise power and influence.

The Japanese surrender to the Western (Allied) powers was almost immediately followed by the Indonesian declaration of independence by Soekarno and Hatta on 17 August 1945. In Jakarta, this was supplemented by a series of hasty measures to develop the institutions of government. A constitution was adopted. Soekarno and Hatta were elected president and vice-president respectively by an existing committee that had been established by the Japanese to consider preparatory steps to take before setting up an independent Indonesian state. This committee transformed itself into the Komite Nasional Indonesia Pusat (KNIP, Central Indonesian National Committee), which functioned as the government of the newly proclaimed Republic of Indonesia. The entire archipelago was divided administratively into eight provinces, each headed by a governor.

These were some of the relevant events that took place in Jakarta, the national capital. In the regions outside of Jakarta, events took different turns. Depending on the configuration of power and resources, local leaders emerged to take initiative in government. In their respective ways, they interpreted the events in and directives from Jakarta, and then made the relevant

---

[2]   Siam was known as Thailand during the Second World War, and after the war as Siam. In 1949, the name reverted to Thailand again. Hence, Siam rather than Thailand is used throughout this study.

decisions for the regions under their control. Each region often went its own way, depending on the circumstances.

For the most part, there was a discontinuity between the centre and the periphery, and this was a logical consequence of the difficult communications, the lack of information, and the administrative divisions that were partly a legacy of the Japanese occupation. These all resulted in disparate developments. If there was any common experience during the days following the proclamation of independence, it was the existence of a vacuum of power that prevailed immediately after the Japanese surrendered and before the Allied (British, Dutch, and Australian) soldiers could return.

When the Allies finally landed in early October 1945, the soldiers consisted mainly of British-led Indian troops in Java, while Australian forces took charge in the eastern part of the archipelago. Sumatra was also placed under the jurisdiction of British-led troops, but lack of manpower prevented any major reoccupation from taking place. Even within Java, British officers did not attempt to extend their writ beyond the major urban areas except to visit prisoner-of-war camps located inland. The shortage of manpower and logistic support were, of course, difficult problems that restrained any attempt by the British to extend their authority. The Indian troops at their disposal, coming from a region – India – where independence was widely acclaimed, could not be relied upon to enforce the restoration of any semblance of order that approximated a return of colonial rule. The British officers also took their orders from Admiral Mountbatten, Supreme Commander of the Southeast Asia Command (SEAC) stationed in Singapore, a decidedly pro-decolonization official who made no attempt to hide his distaste for policies that would lead to the reimposition of colonial rule. In the Allied command structure, Dutch officials in Southeast Asia were required to take their orders also from Mountbatten. The latter also controlled the supply of ships transporting troops to Indonesia. For Mountbatten, the most important priority was repatriation of prisoners-of-war, and not the restoration of Dutch colonial rule in Indonesia. The Dutch themselves were almost totally dependent on the goodwill of their allies, because their home country was liberated rather late in the day and had other pressing priorities.

Under such circumstances, de facto control fell into the hands of pro-Republican forces. These forces, however, were by no means united in their views on how to deal with the Dutch, who were expected to return to Indonesia in larger numbers in due course to regain control of their pre-war investments if not to restore the pre-war situation. Yet the government led by Soekarno did not appear to possess the energy and drive to provide the requisite leadership. It seemed to be inert following the arrival of the first Allied soldiers. The prospects of further paralysis were also very great; Soekarno was a well-known collaborator during the Japanese occupation and the

Allies were not in a mood for dealing with collaborators. Yet urgent action was needed to give substance to the independence proclamation so that when the Dutch returned as expected, there would be a functioning authority capable of government in the eyes of the Allies and the rest of the world. The more militant groups also wanted to press ahead with direct confrontation against Dutch or Allied authority. These conditions all contributed to the feeling that Soekarno's government was immobilized by stagnation and the solution was to install a new and more responsive government.

This need was filled by the appointment of Soetan Sjahrir as prime minister on 14 November 1945. Sjahrir had the reputation of being a non-collaborator. During the Japanese occupation, he maintained his principle of not cooperating with the new rulers, just as he had refused to cooperate with the Dutch in the pre-war period. He was also young (in 1945, he was only 36), and youthfulness was an asset that made him more palatable to the more militant youths (or *pemuda*) who were then pushing for violent confrontation against the Dutch. As prime minister, Sjahrir also held the posts of foreign minister and interior minister, while his colleague, Amir Sjarifoeddin, became the minister in charge of information and people's security. Sjahrir's political convictions also made him acceptable to the Allied powers (and because of this, his eventual downfall came when he was seen as being too compliant). In a political pamphlet published on 10 November 1945, Sjahrir warned against allowing the Indonesian Revolution to end up as a racial struggle against whites. Indeed, he argued that since Indonesia lay within the sphere of influence of Anglo-Saxon capitalism, cooperation with foreign capital was necessary, and this included the ending of lawlessness and violent confrontations preached by the militant *pemuda*. Given that the Dutch had been the predominant foreign capitalists, it was inevitable that some kind of *modus vivendi* would have to be reached with them.

The Dutch, especially Lieutenant Governor-General H.J. van Mook, who was appointed as the official responsible for sorting out the confused state of affairs in Indonesia, were generally very positive towards Sjahrir's political statement. They felt that Sjahrir was very courageous to recognize the importance of the Dutch in Indonesia at a time when high nationalism was raging. Sjahrir himself contributed to the growing optimism that the Dutch had about him by stating shortly after his cabinet was formed that: 'The new government will be just as strongly nationalist as the old. But if we can find common ground between ourselves and the Dutch, in which we can mutually help solve the Indonesian problem, I shall encourage our getting together.' (Djajadiningrat 1958:44.)

There was therefore sufficient basis for the Dutch and the Republicans led by Sjahrir to begin negotiations. These started in Jakarta; then the talks moved to the Hoge Veluwe in the Netherlands before finally returning to

Indonesia, where a peace agreement was finally signed at the Linggajati resort in 1947. In between, various meetings also took place in Singapore to sort out other urgent details.[3]

Not every group in the Republic agreed with Sjahrir on how he should deal with the Dutch. Sjahrir's strategy was to negotiate, while those who opposed this coalesced around the counter-strategy of armed struggle, or *perjuangan*. These two strategies, of course, were not mutually exclusive but could in fact be complementary. Military pressure, applied at the right time and in right amounts, could be used to spur diplomacy; diplomacy itself could be an attractive alternative to military conflict. The leadership in Jakarta must have understood this symbiotic relationship between negotiations and *perjuangan*, but the correct balance between negotiations and armed struggle was difficult to determine. It varied with different groups, from person to person, and from locality to locality. In parts of Sumatra and the Riau archipelago, for example, the concern was not whether to negotiate with the Dutch, but fear that traditional rulers or pre-war beneficiaries of the Dutch colonial system (that is, Chinese and Eurasians) would continue to benefit from the post-1945 dispensation. In such cases, militant action was needed and took precedence over any plans to settle matters by negotiations or discussion. It must be noted, though, that there was an additional dimension in the regions outside Jakarta. There, revolution was not merely the overthrow of Dutch colonialism but also the restructuring of society. These were important differences, but since they concern the internal dynamics of revolution that affected Singapore only marginally, if at all, they will not be discussed here.

On the Dutch side, the leaders were also not agreed on common strategies. The target date of 30 November 1946, when the Southeast Asia Command would wind up its activities, hung like the sword of Damocles over the Dutch because by that time, Dutch military forces would have to be in place to replace the British-led troops. This meant the Dutch would need an estimated 75,000 soldiers to keep the peace in Java and Sumatra, and another 5,000 to 8,000 men for the rest of the archipelago, called Borneo and the Great East by the Dutch. The magnitude of the exercise was daunting, and opinion was divided over whether to establish Dutch control over Java and Sumatra or to concentrate first on Borneo and the Great East. Van Mook chose the latter, but this alienated his military colleagues who preferred what came to be known as the 'Java-first policy'.

Van Mook's decision accorded with the preferences of the British in Singapore. The British were concerned that the ongoing negotiations with

---

[3] Many of the details in the subsequent paragraphs, unless indicated otherwise, are taken from Yong 1982.

Sjahrir had not borne much fruit by December 1945. This they attributed partly to the undisciplined Dutch soldiers who had landed in Java and Sumatra as part of a forward command and then took part in rampages leading to violence. The problem was, of course, much more complicated than that. Many Republican supporters themselves were organized in gangs that were not amenable to central control or indeed any control. By late December 1945, the security situation in Jakarta had deteriorated to such an extent that Republican leaders no longer felt safe from the threatening situation caused by head-on clashes between the two opposing sides. The Republic was forced to shift its capital from Jakarta to Yogyakarta in Central Java, where there was no Dutch presence, making it unlikely that the unsettling clashes occurring in Jakarta would be repeated there.

As far as the British were concerned, the cause of the deteriorating security could be traced to the lack of discipline among Dutch soldiers, and this in turn was due to the inadequate training and officer control of the rank and file. The British thought the Dutch command, organizational, and administrative infrastructure was simply lacking or at least weak. There was no organization higher than a battalion. There were no companies trained in port operations. And it was not likely that the training situation for the Dutch would show any significant improvements before June or July 1946.

The Borneo-and-the-Great-East-first policy had one major impact on the Indonesian Revolution in Singapore. If Dutch soldiers were not ready for landing in Java and Sumatra, there was nothing to prevent the Netherlands navy from imposing a blockade to control the high seas. Such a measure would seriously impair the efforts of the far-flung Republican-controlled territories to contact one another. It would also undermine any efforts to establish international links. Thus, while negotiations took place between the Republic and the Dutch, the Netherlands navy began to tighten its control over coastal and sea traffic.

A peace agreement between the Dutch and the Republic was therefore critically urgent in order that all outstanding differences could be ironed out before the deadline of 30 November 1946, when the British buffer between the Republic and the Dutch would be removed and a bloodbath was very possible. Both Van Mook and Sjahrir feared the consequences if there was no peace agreement by then.

In the nick of time, Sjahrir and Van Mook signed the Linggajati Agreement on 15 November 1946, although the terms had yet to be ratified by their respective governments and this did not happen till the following year, on 25 March 1947. The important articles of agreement that had a bearing on the Indonesian Revolution in Singapore can be summarized as follows.

The Netherlands government recognized the Republic as the de facto authority in Java and Sumatra (Article I).

The Netherlands and Republican governments agreed to cooperate toward the formation of a sovereign democratic federal state called the United States of Indonesia (USI), which would consist of three states, namely the Republic, Borneo, and the Great East. The USI would then co-exist as an equal sovereign in a Netherlands–Indonesia union (Articles II, IV and VI).

The Republic would recognize all claims by foreign nationals for the restitution and maintenance of their rights and properties within areas controlled by the Republic. This was the famous Article XIV, which was used by the Dutch to claim that the goods on their estates should be returned to them.

Pending the formation of the USI and the projected Netherlands–Indonesia Union, the Netherlands would take the necessary legal measures to provide for the new constitutional and international framework (Article XV).

Many of the provisions were vaguely worded, but the essence of the negotiations was speed. The controversial and contentious issues were either left unmentioned or ignored. The chief of these was the issue of sovereignty, and this issue had a bearing on the Republic as well as on developments in Singapore.

The Republic simply took the view that the Linggajati Agreement conferred sovereignty on the Republic, since its de facto status in Java and Sumatra was recognized. The Dutch were less than forthcoming on this issue. Van Mook later declared that the Republic had not been recognized as sovereign at Linggajati. Indeed, it would be the United States of Indonesia (USI) that would be sovereign. But until this entity was formed, the extremely vague Article XV would be in force, namely, the Netherlands Indies government at Batavia would be transformed to meet the new conditions, and until this was accomplished, sovereignty would reside there.

The Republican leaders thought otherwise. Based on the assumption that the Republic was already sovereign, they felt justified in launching diplomatic activities abroad in Singapore and elsewhere. In the Republican view, the agreement also sanctioned efforts to lift the virtual blockade that the Dutch navy had imposed on the waters surrounding Republican territory. This was how the Republic interpreted the important Articles I and XV. This interpretation justified the Republican activities in Singapore.

Article XIV was vital for the economic recovery of Indonesia but was difficult to implement. The Republic was prepared to recognize the claims of all non-Indonesians to their goods in Republican-controlled territories, but it also demanded compensation for its role as guardian of those goods left on the estates at the time when the Japanese came. For the produce of the estates extracted during the occupation period, one part would be given to the investors as compensation for the use of their production facilities, while the investors had to pay compensation to the Republic for the protection of the goods produced. The same guidelines would apply to the goods produced after 17 August 1945. The Dutch rejected these arguments, asserting that Article XIV did not empower the Republic to attach any conditions to its implementation. The estate goods produced before, during, and after the occupation should be restored to the rightful owners without conditions, since the investors would have returned to their estates if not for the fact that the Republic had prevented them from doing so. The Dutch arguments were somewhat thrown into confusion because Van Mook himself did not identify fully with the investors' demand to reclaim their properties. He thought the investors could not count on the government to intervene in every conflict of interest. Instead, the investors should learn to adapt themselves to the new post-war situation, whatever that meant. Coming from someone as high-ranking as Van Mook, the investors were left extremely dissatisfied. Meanwhile, everybody knew that there was significant movement of goods across the waters to Singapore. Nothing could be done to stop that as long as the two sides were locked in dispute save for the measures taken by the Dutch navy.

The impasse that greeted the signing of the Linggajati Agreement was not a situation that the Dutch could tolerate. While the Republic could have allowed the situation to continue without too much sacrifice on their part, the situation was draining the resources of the Dutch tremendously. Food stocks for the Dutch were also getting low. Meanwhile, as more and more Dutch troops arrived, the financial burden of supporting them became heavier. Militant Republican *pemuda* who had opposed the negotiations all along were not disposed to implement the provisions of the Linggajati Agreement at all. In June 1947, Sjahrir resigned his prime ministerial position in the face of considerable opposition to the agreement he had negotiated with the Dutch. This resignation ended all hopes of any peaceful resolution of differences with the Republic, as the Dutch had always considered Sjahrir one of the most reasonable and acceptable Indonesian leaders.

On 21 July 1947, Van Mook launched what the Dutch called a Police Action. In this study, this event will be identified as the First Military Action. It was a 'first' because there was a second one later in December 1948. It was a military exercise, notwithstanding the Dutch claims that the operations were an internal police matter to handle unrest. The Republicans accused the Dutch of mounting an act of aggression pure and simple. The tactical aim of the military action was two-fold: to destroy the Republic's armed forces and to capture the estate products in Republican-controlled territories. The first aim was not achieved because the Republican soldiers refused to meet the Dutch army head-on and instead melted into the jungles to conduct guerrilla warfare. There were some successes registered for the second aim. Dutch military units fanned out from their positions in urban locations and increased their areas of control in parts of West, East, and Central Java. In Sumatra, units moved out from Medan to capture control of important plantations around there. Near Palembang, the oilfields were brought under Dutch control. Limited areas were captured in the Padang region. The Republican opposition responded by applying a scorched-earth policy, but this seemed to be directed more at buildings and installations than at the estate goods that played such a major role in the trade with Singapore. The military action ended when the United Nations Security Council ordered a ceasefire that came into force on 4 August 1947.

The subsequent months were a combination of frenzied activities and signs of drift. The military action provided an opportunity for those Indonesians who were opposed to the Republic or who wanted to restore their traditional positions of authority to emerge into the open and begin organizing states that would enjoy equal status with the Republic. Van Mook welcomed this development, and many Dutch officials connived at the formation of what came to be known as federal states. Attention was focused on major federal states like those in West Java and the Great East. In respect of the Indonesian Revolution in Singapore, two developments attracted major attention. The first was not new. It concerned the treatment meted out to the Chinese residents in Indonesia, but especially those in Sumatra with whom the Singapore Chinese were linked, either as relatives or as business associates. The Indonesian proclamation of independence presented a major dilemma to the Chinese. Many of the Chinese were neither Indonesian nor Netherlands citizens; they were uncertain how they should ally themselves. If they followed past experience, they would have thrown their lot in with the Dutch because during colonial rule, their businesses and livelihood had benefited considerably. However, if the future belonged to the independent Republic, then it seemed sensible to cut their moorings with the past and shift their loyalties.

From 1945 onwards, the situation seemed fluid enough to make it difficult for them to decide. On the one hand, some Indonesians showed a xenophobic attitude. On the other hand, there was the possibility of a Dutch military action that would restore some semblance of colonial authority. Thus many sat on the fence. As a result, clashes between Indonesians and Chinese took place, for example in Medan and Pematang Siantar in Sumatra as early as September 1945. The Chinese were left without any protection. News of their plight filtered into Singapore, probably leaving the impression that the Dutch were unable to provide security and the territories in Sumatra were unsafe for their compatriots and relatives. The second development was the attempt in the Riau islands off Singapore to restore the old sultanate (abolished in 1911); this will be discussed in greater detail in a subsequent chapter.

Meanwhile, negotiations took place between the Dutch and the Republic on board the American ship, the *USS Renville*, to bring the hostilities to an end. Like the previous negotiations, these were slow, uneventful, and even discouraging. This time, the United Nations was involved in the peace process. The details of the Renville discussions need not be discussed here. When they ended in January 1948, there was little change in the determination of the Republic to continue its international relations posture in Singapore and elsewhere.

This is not to say that it was business as usual for the Republic. The First Military Action had left the Republic in a stranglehold. Cut up into bits and pieces of varying size and strength, the Republic was in dire straits. Economically it was hardly viable. The food-producing areas had fallen under Dutch control. The main harbours on the north coast of Java and some of the more active ones in Sumatra were no longer freely available for the Republic to use.

The agreement hammered out on the *Renville* contributed little to the alleviation of these difficulties. It provided for the withdrawal of 35,000 Republican combatants, who were evacuated in February 1948 from Dutch-held areas. These taxed the resources of the remaining Republican-held territories. Prisoners held by both sides were released. In all other respects, there was little improvement over the hostilities that were generated. Both sides seemed to be eyeing each other with reserve and suspicion as if expecting the Renville discussions to be merely a lull in the storm yet to come. The Renville Agreement had promised 'fair representation' of the Republic in the proposed USI, but this was very vague since it was not known how the Republic would be fairly represented before it was clear how many states there would be in the USI. Meanwhile, the situation encouraged groups (including those in the Riau archipelago) that were more lukewarm towards the Republic to emerge to stake their claims of statehood within the proposed USI. On its part, the Republic wanted to retain its international contacts. These were its attributes of de facto sovereignty during the interim period before the USI was formed. There were also disagreements over the powers of the proposed Netherlands–Indonesia Union.

A second clash seemed imminent because the Dutch, including Van Mook, were beginning to feel that the Renville discussions were leading to a blind alley. The Republic attempted to break free from the stranglehold that the Dutch continued to apply. This led the Republic to adopt such unconventional measures as the smuggling of opium to Singapore for sale in order to raise revenues to finance its diplomatic service and administration. The desperate situation also encouraged communist sympathizers in the Republic to launch the abortive 18 September 1948 PKI-Musso coup at Madiun in an attempt to topple the Republican government. This coup attempt came at a time when an emergency had been proclaimed by the British in Singapore and Malaya in June 1948 to fight the communists there. Acting on the assumption that these debilitating circumstances would weaken Republican resistance, the Netherlands government launched the Second Military Action on 18 December 1948 by attacking Yogyakarta, capturing the entire top leadership of the Republic (including Soekarno and Hatta) and sending them into exile on Bangka island.

The military action was a miscalculation. Far from driving the Republic to its knees, it unleashed widespread resistance. The Republic resorted to guerrilla warfare. Major federal-state governments resigned in protest. The United Nations stepped in again to call for a ceasefire on 28 January 1949 and the release of political prisoners, including Soekarno and Hatta. The Republic refused to enter into any negotiations with the Dutch until those leaders were released. This did not happen till after May 1949, upon which both sides met at the Round Table Conference in The Hague on 23 August 1949 to discuss once again all the unresolved issues that had not been addressed conclusively since the Linggadjati Agreement of 1947. This time, with the weight of world opinion on its side, the Republic was able to obtain an agreement that was more to its liking. A federal state, the USI, was formed in which the Republic became a constituent part. On 27 December 1949, the Netherlands transferred sovereignty to the USI and Soekarno, its first president, entered the palace in Jakarta where former Dutch governors-general used to live.

Reading the accounts of the struggle in Indonesia, one can be forgiven for drawing the conclusion that the Indonesian Republic would inevitably win. In the post-Second World War (or post-war) world, colonialism represented by the Dutch was making a last-ditch stand against the tide of nationalism. Nationalism was the new wave of the future. How else could events turn out? However, this would be an ahistorical perspective to adopt.

The participants in that struggle did not view the eventual outcome as a sure thing. In the heat of contest, struggle, and confrontation, the Indonesian Republicans were hardly confident that victory was inevitable. Republican leaders gave confident assurances to supporters, but such assurances appeared to be mere rhetoric in the face of reality – the reality of two armed clashes against advancing Dutch forces, not to mention many other minor skirmishes. As for the Dutch, the outcome was also not certain. Uncertainty was the order of the day. Given this scenario, what must have been uppermost in the minds of the Indonesian Republican supporters in Singapore as they pondered their future? How far could they cultivate the support of the British? How should they finance their struggle? By legal trade, smuggling, or a combination of methods? What would be the proportionate importance of each of these methods? To what extent could the Indonesian Republicans rely on the Chinese traders of Singapore?

Meanwhile, the Chinese traders were calculating their own risks. Too much open support for the Republican cause would alienate the Dutch. Too much reliance on the Dutch could render them suspect in the eyes of the Republic. Most Chinese traders chose to sit on the fence. Yet fence sitting is an art, not an exact science. A wrong move could jeopardize their very delicate balance. Backing the wrong horse could result in serious financial losses, both immediately and in the future. For example, to help the Republic, the Chinese considered a boycott of trade with the Dutch, but this strategy might prove to be mistaken.

Even the Indonesian or Malay communities in Singapore could not be relied upon to give continuous support to the Republican cause. It was not a foregone conclusion that the Malay population of Singapore would give unstinting support to the Indonesian cause despite sharing blood and religious ties with their compatriots across the waters. Their support had to be courted. Indonesians living in Singapore were also divided in their loyalties to the Republican cause and their individual interests.

Neither were the colonial authorities (both British and Dutch) safe from the twists and turns of developments during the years of conflict. The British were confronted with a choice between the two disputants, their erstwhile Dutch allies and the cause of the Indonesian nationalists. An error of judgement, such as favouring one over the other, could lead to difficult problems in the long term. Finally, the Dutch authorities in Singapore found themselves operating in a difficult environment. They did not wield decision-making powers in what was a British colony. At the same time, they had to defend the interests of colonial investors and the colonial authorities in Batavia. This very act of defence was pursued with different rigour at different times. Their judgements were important when deciding how the complaints of the Chinese traders had to be accommodated, and how to implement the tough measures to discourage smuggling and illegal trade on the high seas.

In short, for all the parties concerned, there was no uninterrupted success story. Everybody was engaged in an experiment based on trial and error. Through the labyrinth of struggle, chance events also occurred to complicate matters. Readers looking for rational explanations to understand the Singapore connection in the Indonesian Revolution will be disappointed.

CHAPTER III

Constituents of the Singapore connection

For Indonesians, the gateway in Singapore was Clifford Pier, the entry point where people from Indonesia landed and completed their immigration formalities. On a typical day, Clifford Pier bustled with activity. It was crammed full of goods and personal belongings carried by individuals, scattered all over the floor awaiting collection. A day at Clifford Pier in 1946 was no different. A barrier prevented unauthorized access to and from the boats anchored off Clifford Pier. There was only a single official in blue uniform standing guard. A fat woman was passing through the barrier, carrying a chicken in a basket. The official poked her in the ribs, looking (he would no doubt say) for concealed bottles of *samsu* (illicit liquor), but actually for some fun. She grinned and he grinned, and she moved through the barrier. Such a scene could be true of the periods before or after the war – but with one major difference. Before the war, Singapore belonged to the Indies and looked out on the Indies through Clifford Pier. Clifford Pier was Singapore's window on the Indies. After the war, Singapore was beset by internal problems – hunger, rehabilitation, crime, and so on. But to pass through that barrier on Clifford Pier was to leave all that behind. The Indies – and the world – was again open. In this sense, Clifford Pier was part of Indonesia although Singapore was then a British city. It lay outside the incomprehensible political barriers. The sea at Clifford Pier was not a barrier but a link, where people could come and go freely. Clifford Pier lay outside the idea of colonial possessions. It had nothing to do with British flags or Dutch flags or Indonesian flags or Chinese flags. Clifford Pier had no colour on the map. Singapore – and not only Clifford Pier – served as the gateway, the transit point, for many people from Indonesia to stay or to move elsewhere. Indonesians did not necessarily regard Singapore as a British colonial territory, even though they themselves resided in a different political entity controlled by the Dutch. Singapore was a staging point. It was a *merantau* destination, which can be translated roughly as a place away from home where someone tries to make a fortune. If travellers from Indonesia had not entered Singapore by Clifford Pier, they would have found another way via Pasir Panjang or Beach Road. Clifford Pier was only a symbol.

The Indonesians in Singapore

During the Japanese occupation, Singapore's role as a major transit point did not change. There was considerable movement of labour recruits from the Indonesian archipelago to other parts of Southeast Asia, particularly to the labour camps near the Siamese-Burmese border. When the Japanese surrendered, many were stranded there, and their numbers gradually increased as other Indonesians were sent to Singapore to await repatriation.

In the immediate post-war world, Singapore was a kind of El Dorado, a haven for Indonesians across the waters. It offered something for everyone and its attractions were not merely those related to the pursuit of nationalist aims. Indonesian businessmen came because of the commercial possibilities. Youths who had a bit more money to spend viewed Singapore as an entertainment complex. Criminals thought they could exploit Singapore's opportunities by terrorism. Smugglers found Singapore a haven. Government and semi-government agencies despatched their representatives to Singapore. They came with impressive-sounding missions to accomplish, for example weapons acquisition (*mencari senjata*) or investigations (*penyelidikan*) of this or that.

Estimates of the number of Indonesians resident in Singapore in 1945 vary. According to Captain D. Gerritsen, a Dutch official working in Singapore, there were 5,000 Javanese labourers in Singapore alone.[1] This figure appears small compared to one given by the Refugees and Displaced Persons branch of the British Military Administration. It gave an estimate of 20,000 Javanese labourers brought to Singapore as forced labourers. At war's end, only 8,000 of these were rounded up and taken to a transit camp in Waterloo Street, where the sick were separated from the healthy. The sick, about 1,000 of them, were then sent on to a camp in Nee Soon village which had been turned into a hospital. Those who were healthier were accommodated in camps in Geylang Serai and Henderson Road. They were employed to wash, sweep, and clean, or they were drafted for guard duty. Allowances included small amounts of pocket money. Later, clothes were also given.[2]

These measures were not enough to keep the Javanese off the streets, however. A year later, a large number of Javanese were still seen wandering around Singapore with no homes and no means of subsistence. An estimated number of over one thousand Javanese in Singapore had no regular employment. They turned to crime.[3] They ate from rubbish dumps and they were

---

[1] 'A little bit of Holland in Singapore; By a Special Correspondent', *Straits Times*, 6-10-1945, p. 2.
[2] '8000 Homeless Javanese given shelter', *Straits Times*, 8-10-1945, p. 2.
[3] Directie Verre Oosten 450, 'Police plan arrest of loitering Javanese', *Sin Chew Jit Poh*, 19-9-1947.

the beggars who gathered at the Sultan mosque every Friday.[4] (The Sultan mosque, located in the Arab quarter, was an important centre of worship for all Muslims.) There were a few reports that these Indonesian ex-*romusha* (labourers recruited by the Japanese) had been repatriated from Singapore. One account indicated that 900 Indonesians had returned home.[5]

For the Indonesians who remained behind, Singapore was an unsafe place to live. Crime was rampant. Housing conditions were crowded. Many Indonesians who entered Singapore were illegal residents. Singapore was dangerous. There were relics of explosives, left behind by the retreating Japanese soldiers. Weapons had fallen into the wrong hands and violence was a way of life. Indonesians who unknowingly handled items like detonators were often accidentally killed. Sjahroedin, the journalist responsible for the establishment of the Antara news agency in Singapore, was killed in an accident like this.[6] Sjahroedin's accidental death illustrates the difficulties of Indonesians residing in Singapore. Like Sjahroedin, many did not possess proper documents granting them the right of residence in Singapore. Ironically, Sjahroedin was luckier than most. Illegal residents who were injured could not expect treatment from hospitals, and were usually left to die. They were then buried in unmarked graves (*Samad Ismail* 1987:3). Sjahroedin was quietly buried for fear of attracting the attention of the Criminal Investigation Department in Singapore (*Memoar pejuang* 1992:41-2).

Yet Singapore was like heaven when compared to Jakarta. In Jakarta, even Prime Minister Sjahrir was not safe. He was subject to assassination attempts (*Memoar pejuang* 1992:25). The situation became so untenable that the government was forced to move from Jakarta to Yogyakarta in 1946. Singapore seemed different. A young reporter of 22 years, Anwar A. Moe'in, left a description of Singapore (circa 1946) in which he wrote:

> For us young people, who came from a country experiencing a revolution, Singapore was a kind of heaven. Just imagine. In a city that was still under a war administration, there was no sound of gunfire. We felt secure. The harbour was busy. The shops were full of attractive goods, and at night, the flickering lights were impressive. (*Memoar pejuang* 1992:54.)

Based on the extensive documentation available, Singapore from 1945 through 1947 was actually a confusing world of divided loyalties and differing affiliations. Despite the proclamation of independence and despite the existence of what might be termed mainstream nationalism of the Republican variety, the Indonesians in Singapore owed allegiance to no single leader, association, or

---

[4] 'Home for vagrants planned in Singapore', *Straits Times*, 8-2-1947, p. 5.
[5] '900 Indonesians return home', *Straits Times*, 19-6-1946, p. 5.
[6] Mochtar Lubis 1977, see dedications page by author.

strategy. No doubt there were many who were inclined to sympathize with the ongoing struggle against the Dutch attempts to re-establish colonial rule. But there were also groups of Indonesians in Singapore who were employed by the Dutch, and they stood on the side of their employers. Many worked as sailors on Dutch ships and sailing was an important source of livelihood for them. Conflicting loyalties led to at least one fistfight that broke out at Clifford Pier in 1946 between Indonesians working on Indonesian and Chinese ships against those working on Dutch vessels. Animosity continued to simmer and there were further quarrels between the two groups on the street and at bus stops. There was another major fight at the 'Happy World', an important entertainment centre in the eastern part of Singapore often frequented by Indonesians and Malays. Weapons used included bottles and sticks. The fight continued in the nearby Geylang Serai district the following day. This time, the violence engulfed the adjoining Wilhelmina Camp, where Dutch soldiers were billeted. (Wilhelmina Camp was established on 19 August 1945, together with the neighbouring Juliana Camp that was reserved for civilians. The camps bordered on Tanjong Katong, Geylang, and Haig Roads – all in the vicinity of Geylang Serai.[7]) There were three Dutch casualties. Before the Dutch soldiers could retaliate, the British military police arrived in time to make some arrests. Such were the emotions prevailing in Singapore among Indonesians on both sides of the fence.

The Indonesian organizations

The first attempt to channel these emotions for the cause of the Indonesian Republic was made only after an interlude of 65 days following the proclamation of independence. This delayed reaction was not unique to Singapore. All over the Indonesian archipelago, news of the proclamation led to substantive actions only after some passage of time.

The PKBI

On 20 October 1945, a group of Indonesian residents in Singapore assembled and formed an association called the Persatoean Kaoem Boeroeh Indonesia (PKBI), referred to in official Dutch documents as the Indonesian Labour Party. It might appear strange that the new organization did not even coin a name that evoked sentiments of nationalism or unity. However, as a strategic move, the formation of a labour organization like the PKBI seemed to be the most logical step to take. The proclamation of independence had highlighted

---

[7] 'A little bit of Holland in Singapore; By a Special Correspondent', *Straits Times*, 6-10-1945, p. 2.

a consciousness of rights and interests of Indonesians. In Singapore, most Indonesians were workers of various types. Many had been transported by the Japanese en route to Burma or Siam for forced labour but, upon repatriation, were now stranded in Singapore either because they lacked money to make the journey home or because they were prevented from going because of the breakdown of transport networks. Labourers formed the most fruitful group for the PKBI to organize, and in fact, one of the principal achievements of the PKBI later was the repatriation of ex-forced labourers (*Rahsia perdjuangan* 1948:27-8). In that sense, the PKBI has been described as an organization with social goals in addition to its national aspirations (Nasution 1978a:316).

The list of founding members did not read like a 'Who's Who' of Indonesia or Singapore. Those who participated at the meeting of 20 October were S.L. Tobing, Herman Simandjoentak, Abdoel Ahmad, Aminoellah, and Noerdin. There was also a representative, Abdul Gani, from the General Labour Union (GLU) – a radical political federation of labour groups in Singapore. Tobing was elected president of the executive board on 1 November 1945.

There is little information on Tobing. Tobing himself was a Christian, born in Sumatra but having come to Singapore from Java.[8] At best, Tobing was a shadowy figure. Dutch intelligence reports, usually very comprehensive and substantial, were rather reticent when it came to providing biographical details on Tobing. One report submitted in December 1946 by the Dutch army commander, S.H. Spoor, to the lieutenant governor-general, described Tobing as an appointee of the Republican Ministry of Defence. The minister, at that time Amir Sjarifoeddin, wanted to nominate someone to represent his ministry in Singapore, most likely for the clandestine purchase of weapons and to serve as the contact person for the Republican army units that were established in Malaya. (The intention was to relocate these units in Sumatra or elsewhere.) Tobing was this representative. The fact that he was an ex-soldier (Mestika Zed 1991:313) already conveniently stationed in Singapore was a factor in favour of his appointment. Dutch intelligence accused Tobing of dealing in arms, plotting to overthrow Dutch authority, recruiting army volunteers for Sumatra, and so on. He maintained regular contacts with the Republican army and Republican leaders. He was also suspected of alliances with local gangsters.[9]

As a labour movement, the PKBI affiliated itself with the mainstream labour organization in Singapore, the GLU. In terms of ideology, the PKBI initially seemed to be infected by the pro-left and anti-colonial rhetoric of the labour (GLU) movement in Singapore. As early as October 1945, the GLU led

---

[8] Eerste periodiek verslag van de NEFIS, afgesloten per ultimo december 1945, *Officiële bescheiden*, II:584.
[9] *Officiële bescheiden*, VI:608-9.

a strike of workers on the docks to protest against loading ammunition on Dutch ships sailing to Indonesia. The presence of Abdul Gani at the founding meeting of the PKBI ensured that the left was not ignored and, in fact, on 7 November 1945, the PKBI celebrated the anniversary of the Russian revolution. However, its leader, Tobing, began to display his nationalist credentials as soon as it became apparent that the GLU was more pro-active on behalf of its Chinese and Indian members. Continued affiliation would only sacrifice the interests of the Indonesians.

The decision whether to cut links with the GLU provided the occasion for a split within the PKBI. Two groups within the PKBI formed. Tobing led one group, and his supporters were mainly Batak like himself. The other group consisted of people from Minangkabau and they coalesced around Ahmad Taharoeddin, himself a Minang. Ahmad Taharoeddin was a member of the Hodobu (a Japanese anti-West propaganda unit in Singapore) during the occupation. Tobing's group began to distance itself from the GLU, and they proceeded to establish a new PKBI, with headquarters at 20 Baghdad Street. The Minangs, led by Ahmad Taharoeddin, seized the opportunity to form the Persatoean Kaoem Boeroeh Indonesia Melayu, or Perkabim. Ostensibly, the Perkabim did not oppose continued affiliation with the GLU, but it appears that the split between the two groups led by Tobing and Ahmad Taharoeddin respectively were also caused by ethnic differences between the Bataks and the Minangs (Mestika Zed 1991:313).

The new PKBI under Tobing made its first public appearance on 14 November 1945 when a procession was held and its headquarters were bedecked with flags. The organization claimed one thousand members, many originally from Java.[10] A high profile together with large numbers was a symbol of organizational strength, and in the early months after the Japanese surrender, symbols spoke louder than words. Tobing was also a clever manipulator. By establishing his headquarters in Baghdad Street, he was attempting to revive a link with the cultural and historical heartland of the Malay community in Singapore. Baghdad Street was smack in the middle of the Kampong Glam district where the last sultan of the Johor-Riau empire lived out his days. In 1945, the palace and mosque were still intact. To the Malays of Singapore, Kampong Glam evoked memories of past

---

[10] Eerste periodiek verslag van de NEFIS, afgesloten per ultimo december 1945, *Officiële bescheiden*, II:584. Membership lists are notoriously unreliable for any organization during this period. And itinerant organizations were not unwilling to stoop to low tactics to boost membership. Thus the PKBI would declare a person to be a 'member' of its organization even though that was not true. This resulted in police investigations, and invariably the 'member' concerned became so annoyed with the authorities that he could be more easily approached by the PKBI. (See RI 551, Tweewekelijksche berichtgeving der Residentie Riouw over de periode 16 t/m 31-7-1946, By J. van Waardenburg, Resident, Tandjong Pinang, 6-8-1946.)

III Constituents of the Singapore connection

grandeur when the Johor-Riau empire was one of the last strongholds of resistance to Dutch colonialism. In the post-war world of confusing developments, leadership of the Malays, Indonesians, and related peoples was a role that Kampong Glam could be expected to provide. In the years to come, Kampong Glam continued to play this role. (In 1948, for example, there was a report that when a meeting was organized to protest against the bad treatment of Malays in the four southern states of Siam, the venue was appropriately Kampong Glam.)[11]

Any competitor for influence among the Malays would find it important to drive out the PKBI from the heartland of Malay history and culture. The dissenting wing of the original PKBI represented in the Perkabim attempted to do this by trying to deprive the new PKBI of funds so that it would be difficult to maintain its headquarters and other activities. On 4 January 1946, three officials from the Perkabim tried to get the new PKBI to surrender its treasury, but their PKBI counterparts of course refused. Again, on 15 January 1946, more Perkabim officials came on the same mission, this time with GLU representatives. On 21 January 1946, the Perkabim even sent its solicitors to request the account books of the new PKBI (*Rahsia perdjuangan* 1948:18). Financial viability was, of course, most important and it was therefore not surprising that the Perkabim should set its eyes on what little the PKBI had. On its own, the Perkabim depended on the fees collected for the issue of passes for members who wanted to visit Sumatra. These cost $4.50 each.[12]

On the whole, Perkabim did not present a major threat to the new PKBI. The former fell foul of the British authorities. A later president, S.M. Zainoen, was even evicted in July 1946 for being a troublemaker.[13] A new president was appointed in October 1946. This was a 47-year-old Indonesian resident of Malaya called Hoessein. He hailed from Sumatra, and his previous occupations included sailing and a stint as a bus conductor in the Singapore Traction Company.[14] These credentials suggested that the people who led Perkabim had little or no strong links with mainstream nationalism in the Republic of Indonesia, having left their home country for long periods.

It was Hassan, the Republican governor of Sumatra, who tried to reconcile the different Indonesian groups. On 19 October 1946, he sent Tahir

---

11   'Colony meeting accuses Siam', *Straits Times*, 8-3-1948, p. 1. For an article on how the Malays regarded Kampong Glam, see 'Kampong Glam and Java', *Straits Times*, 4-9-1946, p. 4.
12   RI 551, Tweewekelijksche berichtgeving der Residentie Riouw over de periode 1 t/m 16-8-1946, By J. van Waardenburg, Resident.
13   RI 551, Tweewekelijksche berichtgeving der Residentie Riouw over de periode 1 t/m 15-7-1946, By J. van Waardenburg, Resident, Tandjong Pinang, 23-7-1946.
14   RI 551, Tweewekelijksche berichtgeving der Residentie Riouw over de periode 15 t/m 31-10-1946, By L.B. van Straten, Assistent-Resident I, Singapore, 31-10-1946.

Karim Loebis[15] to Singapore to settle the differences between the Perkabim and the PKBI by creating a new organization with a new name. The Hiwarni (Himpoenan Warga Negara Repoeblik Indonesia) was founded sometime between 15 and 30 November 1946. Tobing opposed these efforts.[16] Apparently, it was Governor Hassan's intention to make this new organization the official representative of Indonesians in Singapore and Malaya.[17] Details on the Hiwarni are not available, but after its formation, the founder pledged to cooperate with the British and, if necessary, the Dutch, to take action against Indonesians who were guilty of misdemeanours. Its attention would be focused on protecting the good name of the Republic, but first it had to work towards recognition by the Republic itself.[18] There was no evidence that this recognition was ever obtained, and by February 1947, a Dutch report noted that the Hiwarni showed no more signs of life after its establishment.[19]

Within three months after the new PKBI separated itself from the GLU, it plunged into a frenzy of activities. These included scouring for weapons. Circulars were issued to promote the spirit of struggle and to spread propaganda. Indonesians who were sick were given assistance. The children of those arrested by the Dutch police in Batavia were provided with support. Campaigns were directed to free those PKBI members who had been arrested by the Dutch for spreading propaganda in Dutch camps. In general, all efforts were directed at promoting the independence of the Republic (*Rahsia perdjuangan* 1948:19). Tobing held mass meetings, reportedly attended by thousands, at the 'Great World' and 'Happy World' entertainment complexes. At the meetings, propaganda – pieces of white paper with red lettering containing anti-Dutch sentiments – was disseminated. The meetings were often followed by processions. Members of the new PKBI were issued with a red-and-white membership card and a red-and-white insignia bearing the letters 'RI'. Tobing himself planned to fly the red-and-white Indonesian flag every Friday.[20]

---

[15] AS2, 596, 31-10-1949. Loebis was a 31-year-old youth from Medan who studied in Jakarta before the war and then worked in Medan as a teacher and journalist.
[16] RI 551, Tweewekelijksche berichtgeving der Residentie Riouw over de periode 15 t/m 31-10-1946, By L.B. van Straten, Assistent-Resident I, Singapore, 31-10-1946; Tweewekelijksche berichtgeving der Residentie Riouw over de periode 15 t/m 30-11-1946, By J.B. van Schendel, Assistent-Resident, Tandjong Pinang, 10-12-1946.
[17] *Officiële bescheiden*, VI:456. According to Mestika Zed, it was Governor A.K. Gani of South Sumatra (as opposed to Governor Hassan of the entire Sumatra) who sent Loebis (in August 1946) to work towards reconciliation. See Mestika Zed 1991:314.
[18] *Officiële bescheiden*, VII:198.
[19] *Officiële bescheiden*, VII:609.
[20] RI 551, Tweewekelijksche berichtgeving, Residentie Riouw tot 15-1-1946.

The PKBI-PI

The intense pace and range of activities organized by the new PKBI indicates that it had moved beyond the confines of labour unionism. The next logical step was to change its name to reflect its wider interests, and this was formally completed on 1 February 1947 when the new PKBI changed its name to Persatoean Indonesia (PI) (*Rahsia perdjuangan* 1948:18). This marked its transformation into a political party.[21] (Henceforth, reference to the new PKBI or PI in the following chapters will be denoted by the name PKBI-PI.)

The adoption of a new name was not just an exercise in cosmetic surgery. It brought into the open a major image problem that confronted the party. The PKBI-PI's sudden appearance on the scene in Singapore – almost like a bright shooting star in the heavens – invited speculation about its origins. According to one of the major rumours that were circulating, the PKBI-PI leaders were lackeys of the Dutch.[22] They were accused of having been induced by the former colonialists to sow division and confusion among the Indonesians resident in Singapore. The change of name, adopting the word 'Indonesia', was designed to emphasize the nationalist credentials of the PKBI-PI.

Switching to a new name was not a particularly difficult exercise. As the first organization of its kind to appear in Singapore, the field was wide open with no competitors. The PKBI-PI could therefore label itself in any way it liked. Taking advantage of this situation, it assumed for itself the monopoly associated with an all-encompassing name like Persatoean Indonesia.

An abrupt dismissal of the importance attached to a mere name would also miss another major point. By 1946, there were indications – and the PKBI-PI leaders must have been aware of these – that rival groups with influence within the resident Indonesian community in Singapore were beginning to compete for recognition of their standing by the newly proclaimed Republic of Indonesia (*Indonesian intentions* 1964:4) or its constituent parts. Such recognition was important because of the political and economic opportunities that would also follow.

The political assets of a name change are mentioned above. The economic advantages to be gained also provided major stakes. The PKBI-PI leaders – who were mainly Bataks – controlled the trade with Sumatra. This was due in no small part to the generosity of the then Republican governor of South Sumatra, A.K. Gani, who was also a Sumatran. He also made grants avail-

---

[21] *Officiële bescheiden*, VII:609.
[22] RI 551, Tweewekelijksche berichtgeving der Residentie Riouw over de periode 16 t/m 31-8-1946, By J. van Waardenburg, Resident, Tandjong Pinang, 10-9-1946; RI 551, Tweewekelijksche berichtgeving der Residentie Riouw over de periode 16 t/m 30-9-1946, By P.A. van der Poel, Commissaris van Politie I, 1-10-1946.

able for the PKBI-PI from the coffers of the trading firm Namsoco.[23] (Further details on the Namsoco are given below in this chapter.) However, it was the business connections that gave the PKBI-PI some sense of financial security. Thus, for example, rubber and gambir from Sumatra were sold by the PKBI-PI in Singapore with a levy of 2% commission. Travellers from Singapore wanting to visit Sumatra for purposes of trade were also required to possess a pass issued by the PKBI-PI to avoid being branded as a Dutch agent.[24] A similar arrangement was made between the PKBI-PI and the Indonesian Resident of Riau that all agricultural products must be sold in Singapore only through its auspices.[25]

Other miscellaneous Indonesian groups

Such profitable arrangements could not but attract others to set up shop in Singapore, each appealing to their own groups of constituents but all hoping to have a piece of the cake. Most of these established their headquarters in the Geylang Serai area that had become a nest of anti-Dutch and even anti-British activities. Their names indicate a whole range of sectional interests. They are Muslim Welfare Association, Peheman, Api, Koempoelan Kampong Geylang Serai, Geylang Serai Club, Kemadjoean Pemoeda Aman. The governor of South Sumatra, A.K. Gani, also sponsored the Badan Kebadjikan Indonesia (BKI) in July 1946 to represent Sumatran Republican interests in Singapore. Groups formed and reinvented themselves. As late as 1947, a new group, the Kesatoean Pemoeda Indonesia (Indonesian Youth Association), sprang up as a result of a merger of four Indonesian underground movements operating in Singapore. These four movements were the Koempoelan Pemoeda Indonesia (Indonesia Youth Group), the Badan Pemberontak Kalimantan (Kalimantan Revolutionary Movement), the Badan Pemberontak Indonesia Blakang Mati (the Indonesian Revolutionary Movement of Blakang Mati), and the Roekoen Agawi Santoso (Disciples of Agawi Santoso) (*Indonesian intentions* 1964:7). Other Indonesian groups in Singapore were a mixture of or even part of other organizations in Malaya, for example Gerakan Angkatan Muda, the Republican Party, the Palang Merah Indonesia, and the Indonesian Tourist Pilgrim Association (Mestika Zed 1991:313). Their existence resembled the *bersiap* period of the Indonesian revolution in Java, during which many organizations flowered in a wave of agitation and enthusiasm. Some of these groups embraced mainstream programmes associated with the political

[23] PG 168, CGDN, No. 202-48, Singapore, Report by J.W.J. de Haas, 6-12-1948.
[24] RI 551, Tweewekelijksche berichtgeving, Residentie Riouw tot 15-1-1946.
[25] RI 551, Tweewekelijksche berichtgeving, Residentie Riouw van 16 t/m 31-1-1946, Singapore, Report by G. van Brakel, 8-2-1946.

developments in Malaya. Others were probably mere gangs in conflict with each other and thriving on extortion.[26] In September 1947, the president of Kesatoean Pemoeda Indonesia was arrested, together with three other members, for possession of arms (*Indonesian intentions* 1964:7). There was even one organization, Sarikat Rahasia Tanah Air or SERTA, which enshrined the use of violence in its constitution. SERTA was founded on 15 August 1947 in Singapore. It had plans to establish branches in Malaya and the territories occupied by the Dutch. Its goals included the infiltration of enemy organizations in enemy-occupied territories, the perpetration of sabotage, the propagation of rumours. Netherlands consulate officials were not unduly perturbed. A consulate official, the secretary for Special Services (S. van Hulst), commented that the SERTA was no more than a boy-scout organization and nothing much could be expected from it. However, he recommended that the information about SERTA be forwarded to the British authorities.[27]

Reports filed in later years made mention of the rise of other organizations that were formed on ethnic lines. Indonesians of Minangkabau origin, of whom there were many in Singapore, also tried to establish a nationalist organization for their ethnic group. The proposed name of their new organization was Soesoenan Pemoeda Indonesia, and it claimed that it could send eighty volunteers to fight the Dutch in Sumatra if financial support was available.[28] Another group of young Minangs who were small businessmen established an association called Persatoean Anak Kapaoe. The association had trade links with Rengat, Pakan Baru, and Bukit Tinggi.[29]

The Bataks also established their own organization, called Sahata (or unity). The aim: to provide assistance to all Bataks in difficulty.[30] There seemed to be rivalry between the Bataks and the Minangs, with the Bataks ousting the Minangs in February 1947 from positions of prominence. This did not contribute to cooperation between the two groups in politics and trade.[31]

Indonesia Office (Indoff)

Of all the organizations that were established in Singapore, special mention must be made of the Indonesia Office, or Indoff for short. It was Indoff that could justly claim legitimacy conferred upon it by the Republic of Indonesia's

---

[26] PG 173, Rapport van den Inlichtingendienst der Algemeene Politie (Singapore), No. 529, Singapore, By S. van Hulst, 30-8-1947.
[27] PG 170(II), 2-10-17, Letter from S. van Hulst, to the Attorney-General, 3-5-1948.
[28] PG 558, CGDN, No. 24-49, Singapore, By P.A. van der Poel, 3-2-1949.
[29] PG 558, CGDN, No. 55-49, Singapore, By P.A. van der Poel, 19-3-1949.
[30] PG 558, CGDN, No. 24-49, Singapore, By P.A. van der Poel, 3-2-1949.
[31] *Officiële bescheiden*, VII:609.

Ministry of Foreign Affairs, and this status qualified it as an official organization in contrast to the likes of the PKBI-PI.

As an official representation of sorts, the chronological history of Indoff parallels developments at the national and even international level. A convenient starting point to launch a discussion of Indoff, beginning with its birth, is therefore the Linggajati Agreement, signed on 15 November 1946 but only officially ratified on 25 March 1947.

This agreement, concluded between the Netherlands and the Republic of Indonesia, and brokered by the British, paved the way for Soetan Sjahrir, the Republican prime minister and foreign minister (November 1945-June 1947), to mount a diplomatic offensive for international recognition of the Republic of Indonesia.

One tangible measure was the establishment of diplomatic missions in a number of strategic capitals. These included Singapore, Bangkok, Rangoon, Delhi, Karachi, Cairo, Canberra, London, and Washington. A permanent delegation was also sent to the United Nations in New York. Like all diplomatic missions the world over, the principal duties of the Republic's representatives abroad were the presentation of Republican views abroad and the garnering of material and financial support for the government back home in Indonesia.

The choice of Singapore

Singapore was one of the most important and choicest locations. Explanations for this are not hard to find. Its close proximity to Indonesia immediately qualified it as a forward base. Its port infrastructure, well known to Indonesian businesses long before the war broke out, was important in helping the Republic restore trade links and supply routes. In particular, the Chinese business network could be relied upon to transship commodities especially from Sumatra, whose territory was still free of Dutch control at the time the Linggajati Agreement was signed. Since the end of the war, other very important factors had also emerged to qualify Singapore as a vital location for a Republican diplomatic mission. The use of Singapore as a navy and army depot by the Japanese during the war gave the impression that there were lots of weapons stored in arms caches awaiting disposal. If only part of that could be siphoned off for military use by the Republic! Equally important, Singapore was host to many British officials who were partial to the Republic, for example, Admiral Mountbatten. The British government in London was also pro-Republic. Whitehall had not been impressed by what it viewed as the tardy process of decolonization pursued by the Dutch. As a result, there was potentially a very tolerant environment in Singapore whereby the activities of a Republican diplomatic mission would be viewed with indulgence.³²

Early steps leading to the establishment of Indoff

During the very early period soon after the proclamation of independence, rumours circulated in Singapore that the interests of the Republic in that city would be represented by appointing a senior resident in Singapore, such as Abdul Samad, as consul of the Republic. Samad, the first Malay to become a doctor in Singapore, had established contacts with the Chinese there whose business relations with the political leaders in Java were deemed to be important.³³ The choice of Samad was therefore appropriate, as it was expected that the Chinese would play a major role in business linkages with the Republic. Samad also had Indonesian parents.

There are various references tucked away in the primary sources relating to the initiatives taken to establish an official presence in Singapore.

Soekarno is reported to have appointed one Oemar Selamat as the principal representative of the Republic in Singapore. Oemar Selamat was involved in trying to establish communication links between Yogyakarta and Singapore, succeeding in the process to charter a plane to fly to Yogyakarta. Sometime in March and April 1947, he made a major transaction to bring a shipload of goods, probably of a military nature, from China to Java. Oemar Selamat's activities, however, were short-lived as the Dutch intensified their surveillance of the Indonesian islands.³⁴ Little more was heard of him and it can be presumed that this attempt by Soekarno to appoint a representative – probably his representative – was little more than a commercial-military transaction that fizzled out.

A Malaysian White Paper, written during the period of Indonesian Confrontation (1963-1966), suggested various antecedents that led to the evolution of Indoff in its final form. It noted that one Suryono Daroesman attempted to set up a provisional Indonesian 'Republic' office in Singapore in September 1946 (*Indonesian intentions* 1964:5). Although Daroesman was indeed closely associated with Indoff that was eventually set up in Singapore, this single-line reference in the White Paper is uncorroborated by other data.

The White Paper also listed, as another antecedent, the attempt by the

---

³² Suryono Darusman made these same points in an unpublished typescript entitled 'Singapore and the Indonesian Revolution 1945-1950'. I am indebted to Darusman, who served in the Indonesia Office during its early years, for making this typescript available to me. Later, he published his oral history version. See Darusman 1992. See also *Officiële bescheiden*, VI:456.
³³ *Officiële bescheiden*, VI:456.
³⁴ *Officiële bescheiden*, VIII:471.

Republican governor of Sumatra, Hassan, to appoint his own representative to act on behalf of Republican interests originating from Sumatra in Singapore. This was Tahir Karim Loebis, who arrived in Singapore in the company of four colleagues. They established the Kantor Perhoeboengan Propensi (literally, Provincial Liaison Office). According to the Malaysian White Paper, the office – located at Change Alley in the heart of the commercial district of Singapore – was a cover operation for propaganda and espionage activities (*Indonesian intentions* 1964:5). After Loebis's departure for Java, Hassan's next representative was Djohan Meoeraksa, who was given the mandate to represent Sumatra's economic affairs in Singapore.[35] However, at best, Governor Hassan's representatives could be described as holding briefs for provincial, as opposed to Indonesia-wide, interests.

Oetoyo Ramelan and the early representatives of the Republic

One other reference in the Malaysian White Paper bears further scrutiny, because its general thrust meshes comfortably with the data in other sources. According to this line of explanation, various Sumatra-led groups in Singapore were disputing among themselves. This inspired Prime Minister and Foreign Minister Sjahrir, himself a Sumatran of Minangkabau origin, to send his Javanese secretary-general in the Foreign Ministry, Oetoyo Ramelan, to establish a single representative office. This was Indoff in Singapore. According to the White Paper, Oetoyo was entrusted with the duty to curb the activities of unwanted trading corporations that all aspired to act as the official Republican representative and to coordinate the activities of all Indoff branches in Malaya (*Indonesian intentions* 1964:5).

It should be noted at this point that Oetoyo was by no means the first official from a central government source to arrive in Singapore. The central government of the Republic of Indonesia was itself not a monolithic entity. It consisted of many agencies, each operating independently of the others.

One of the first known representatives of the Republicans in Singapore was not Oetoyo, but Oetomo from the Ministry of Information. The British needed an Indonesian who could explain British policies and actions to the Indonesians in their own language. In early 1946, Oetomo was seconded to the British Far Eastern Broadcasting Service (FEBS), an organization that was originally set up during the Japanese occupation to broadcast to enemy-occupied territories in Asia. After the Japanese surrendered, the FEBS was transferred to Singapore. At first, it worked with the South East Asia Command (SEAC). Later, it was placed under the management of

---

[35] *Officiële bescheiden*, VIII:471.

the British Foreign Office. The FEBS[36] organized a branch known as the Indonesian Information Service, or Indonesian Malay Service as it was also known. Oetomo was chosen because he met the criteria of Lord Killearn (a British diplomat and special commissioner for Southeast Asia), who thought it prudent to find a person who was not too well known so as not to attract attention.[37] According to a Dutch report, the number of Indonesian officials seconded by the Republican Ministry of Information to the British-controlled Far Eastern Broadcasting Service in Singapore actually numbered three (that is, not just Oetomo alone).[38] To allay any suspicions of the Dutch, the British explained that this appointment was not a pro-Republican move but merely to facilitate the explanation of Allied policies to the Indonesians in their own language. In short, the seconded officials did not enjoy editorial powers concerning the news items to be broadcast to an Indonesian-speaking audience.[39] Oetomo was placed in charge of the Indonesian Malay Service within the British media organization.[40] He was given considerable latitude in making broadcasts. His appointment continued until 1 May 1946, when the Indonesian Malay Service was dissolved. Oetomo then started the Indonesian Information Service under the orders of his Minister, Mohamed Natsir.[41] The Dutch suspected that this Indonesian Information Service was receiving help from the British for some time after its inception. It was reported that the English press attaché in Jakarta undertook to facilitate the postal communications of the information service via the British diplomatic mail system. In British eyes, the information service was little different from a consular representation that would, quite naturally, serve a major role in the dissemination of information. Also, it was Lord Killearn's intention that a Republican information service could later be upgraded to a consular representation.[42]

Another Republican agency that was operating in Singapore before the establishment of Indoff was the Indonesian National Press Agency, or

[36] The British Far Eastern Broadcasting Service (Singapore) ceased to exist when it was taken over by the British Broadcasting Service in June 1947. See 'The B.B.C. in Malaya', *Straits Times*, 16-6-1947, p. 4.
[37] PG 304, Letter 809A, from S. van Hulst, Secretaris voor Speciale Diensten, to Procureur Generaal, 26-6-1948; PG 861, Tweewekelijksche berichtgeving der Residentie Riouw over de periode 15 t/m 28-4-1947, p. 5, By P.A. van der Poel, Commissaris van Politie I.
[38] *Officiële bescheiden*, IV:271, 279.
[39] *Officiële bescheiden*, IV:406.
[40] PG 171, Letter from M.W. van 't Hef (Procureur-Generaal bij het Hooggerechtshof van Ned. Indië) to Hoofd van de Regerings Voorlichtings Dienst at Batavia, dated 4-12-1947.
[41] PG 173, Rapport van den Inlichtingendienst der Algemeene Politie Riouw (RIAPR), No. 382, Singapore, By S. van Hulst, 25-4-1947.
[42] PG 304, Letter 809A, from S. van Hulst, Secretaris voor Speciale Diensten, to Procureur-Generaal, 26-6-1948; PG 861, Tweewekelijksche berichtgeving der Residentie Riouw over de periode 15 t/m 28-4-1947, p. 5, By P.A. van der Poel, Commissaris van Politie I.

Antara. Antara began its work in Singapore in February 1946. Its office was located on the top floor of a three-storey building on Raffles Place, an important commercial area fronting the harbour.[43] Antara faced serious difficulties in its operations. It did not receive subsidies from the Republic and hence, faced funding problems (*Memoar pejuang* 1992:68-9). It was also not recognized by the authorities in Singapore as the official Republican press agency.[44] Therefore, by early 1946, the Republic had two semi-official agencies operating in Singapore, the Antara and another through Oetomo.

The establishment and development of Antara in Singapore merits a study of its own. The founder was Sjahroedin, who was editor of Domei, the Japanese news agency during the Japanese occupation in Indonesia. Sjahroedin was sent to Singapore to establish an agency that would provide news services to break the Dutch or Allied monopoly on news about Indonesia.[45]

It was against this complex background that Indoff made its appearance in Singapore. What remained unclear was the relationship between Oetoyo and the press officials who had arrived in Singapore earlier. Oetoyo, after all, was an appointee of the Minister of Foreign Affairs, but Oetomo was an appointee of Minister Natsir. Both are known to have guarded their own turf jealously.[46] Oetomo and Oetoyo worked from different locations, the former at Cecil Street and the latter at Raffles Place.[47] There were disagreements over the payment of rental monies.[48] In order to resolve the disagreements between Oetomo and Oetoyo, it was agreed to refer to Yogyakarta for further instructions, and until then, the information service would remain independent.[49] By May 1947, Oetomo felt that enough was enough. Fed up with the politics, he applied for a visa to proceed to the Netherlands for studies.[50]

---

[43] Suryono Darusman, 'Singapore and the Indonesian Revolution, 1945-1950', unpublished manuscript.
[44] PG 173, Rapport van den Inlichtingendienst der Algemeene Politie Riouw (RIAPR), No. 392, Singapore, By S. van Hulst, 5-5-1947.
[45] *Memoar pejuang* 1992:45. The story of Antara's founding in Singapore is mentioned in Chapter II.
[46] PG 861, Tweewekelijksche berichtgeving der Algemeene Politie Riouw, Nederlandsch Consulaat-Generaal, Singapore, over de periode 13 t/m 26-5-1947, Rapport No. 422A, p. 6, Singapore, By S. van Hulst, Commissaris van Politie II, 26-5-1947.
[47] PG 173, Rapport van den Inlichtingendienst der Algemeene Politie Riouw (RIAPR), No. 395, Singapore, By P.A. van der Poel, 6-5-1947.
[48] Inventaris van de archieven van het Consulaat-Generaal te Singapore, 1945-54, Ministerie van Buitenlandse Zaken (MBZ) 220, Letter from S. van Hulst to Procureur-Generaal, No. 698A, 28-5-1948.
[49] PG 173, Rapport van den Inlichtingendienst der Algemeene Politie Riouw (RIAPR), No. 432, Singapore, By S. van Hulst, 4-6-1947.
[50] Inventaris van de archieven van het Consulaat-Generaal te Singapore, 1945-54, Ministerie van Buitenlandse Zaken (MBZ) 220, Letter from S. van Hulst to Procureur-Generaal, No. 698A, 28-5-1948.

Goals of Indoff

The goals of Indoff were fivefold:
- To develop a working relationship with the colony of Singapore as a result of the *de facto* recognition accorded to the Republic by the British government;
- To develop a network of communications with the international press in order to counter the pro-Dutch sentiments of Western newspapers;
- To coordinate the business and other operations of Indonesian representatives, using Singapore as a base;
- To provide guidance for Indonesians in Singapore and Malaya in order to mobilize support for the Republic;
- To be the sole representative of the Republic of Indonesia in Singapore for political, economic, and military matters. (*Memoar pejuang* 1992:89.)

These goals met the needs of the times. They emphasized the importance of people, money, material, mass media, and moral righteousness. Their attainment would effectively incorporate Singapore into the field of operations of the Indonesian nationalists. Success in Singapore would mean that the Dutch had failed to confine the revolutionary struggle. To leapfrog over the Dutch in Jakarta, a presence in Singapore was essential.

The establishment of the Singapore connection was never in doubt, but even so, practical considerations dominated. Strapped by funds, unsure of itself, and constrained by the need to tread prudently in British colonial territory, Indoff's opening was a low-key affair. There was no celebration or ceremony, no ribbon-cutting or traditional customs. Indoff simply glided into existence in October 1947 (*Memoar pejuang* 1992:51).

Bio-data of Indoff leaders

More attention can be paid to the leaders of Indoff and more details about them are now available. Oetoyo Ramelan was born on 31 October 1906[51] in Klaten, Central Java. The son of a *regent* (Javanese administrative title) in the Solo area, he attended primary school in Surakarta and then secondary school in Yogyakarta. Then, for two years, he was a law student in Batavia, after which he went to Leiden University and graduated with a master of law degree. He is often described as 'Dr Oetoyo' in the primary sources. It

---

[51] Another source indicates that Oetoyo was born in 1918 in Solo itself. See PG 304, 'Indonesian agencies in Malaya', Secret (109) in M.S. 815, Written by H.Q. Malayan Security Service, 23-6-1948. On Oetoyo's spouse and family, see *Straits Times*, 7-7-1948, pp. 1 and 5. A photograph of Oetoyo can be found in *Memoar pejuang* 1992:213. Other photographs of Oetoyo are reproduced in Darusman 1992. See pp. 49 and 52 (man in dark trousers wearing a dark tie).

was the British military administration in Jakarta that gave him the title of 'Dr'. This was probably a misunderstanding of the Dutch title 'doctorandus' or 'Drs' Oetoyo acquired upon graduating from Leiden University in law. Oetoyo continued to be popularly addressed as 'Dr Oetoyo' in Singapore circles (*Memoar pejuang* 1992:57). He also signed himself as 'Dr Oetoyo'.[52] But his colleagues addressed him as 'Mr Oetoyo'. Official Republican documents also refer to him as 'Mr Oetoyo'.[53] He was employed at the Ministry of Foreign Affairs, rising to the rank of secretary-general. He first came to Singapore in April 1947. On that occasion, the assignment, given to him by Prime Minister Sjahrir, was to report on Indonesian activities there. He visited Lord Killearn, whom he had met earlier in Jakarta, impressing upon him that what the Indonesians wanted was a trade representative in Singapore. They did not mind what formal status he would be granted or the title, or whether he had any title at all, 'as long as he was there'.[54] After returning to Indonesia to submit his report, he was sent back to Singapore in November 1947 by Sjahrir to represent Republican interests there. The office given to him was called 'Representative of the Government of Indonesia in Singapore'.[55] He admitted that he was a member of the Socialist Party (led by Sjahrir), which probably explains why the prime minister placed confidence in him.[56] His mission in Singapore was to reorganize Indonesian affairs there, especially trade and diplomatic matters. Although this task was particularly urgent, Oetoyo's appointment was also part of a package of measures to establish an Indonesian diplomatic presence in other countries, including Australia and Egypt.[57]

Colleagues of Oetoyo have described him as friendly, but always correct and disciplined. He possessed strong powers of persuasion. Like Prime Minister Sjahrir, he was a social democrat and was particularly suited to diplomatic work because he was careful with his words and actions. He spoke slowly and was not disposed to fiery speeches.[58]

[52] PG 181, Letter KLN/220/8 from Oetoyo to Dr Goh Kok Chuan, 8-12-1947.
[53] *Memoar pejuang* 1992:91-2, 107. However, one of Oetoyo's colleagues used the title 'Dr'. See Darusman 1992:40, 45. Mr, or Meester is the Dutch title for a law graduate.
[54] FO 810/5, No.876, Telegram from Killearn to Foreign Office, April 1947.
[55] PG 304, Letter from S. van Hulst to Procureur-Generaal, 12-7-1948. Another Dutch record provides a different account. Oetoyo was in charge of the postal communications service in Palembang. He was nominated by Governor A.K. Gani of South Sumatra to be *assistent-resident* in Jambi in September 1946, but he hardly spent any time in his new office before he was sent to Singapore. However, this version does not show how he was associated with the Ministry of Foreign Affairs. See *Officiële bescheiden*, VI:52-3.
[56] PG 304, Letter from S. van Hulst to Procureur-Generaal, 12-7-1948.
[57] 'Indonesians to make early trade moves', *Straits Times*, 27-3-1947, p. 1.
[58] *Memoar pejuang* 1992:58, 60, 92. For an account of Oetoyo's speech mannerisms, see Coast 1952:67.

III Constituents of the Singapore connection 43

When Oetoyo first landed in Singapore, Indoff employed only a skeleton staff. People with suitable qualifications were hard to recruit at such short notice. The pioneer group of staff was selected from the pool of Indonesians available in Singapore without too much regard for stringent qualifications. Knowing English helped (*Memoar pejuang* 1992:29, 57, 90-1). As time passed, other capable officials were added to the establishment.

Oetoyo's deputy was a lawyer called Zairin Zain. He hailed from Pariaman in West Sumatra (*Memoar pejuang* 1992:91, 93). Before arriving in Singapore, he had been working in London to promote the cause of the Republic.[59] Zain was distinguished by his devotion to the central goal of promoting national Republican interests as opposed to the needs of individuals. An organization like Indoff was often besieged by pleas for help of all kinds. Zain clarified his position on this matter very clearly in a letter to the Malay newspaper *Utusan Melayu*, dated 18 September 1948. In it, he explained that the daily life of the people was not a primary concern of Indoff. The organization existed to defend the national interests of the people. It had to be fair to all and therefore could not protect any one group (*Rahsia perdjuangan* 1948:126). However, given the state of conflict and confusion in the late 1940s, it would have been difficult for Zain to implement his ideas without encountering criticism. The best testimony to Zain's abilities comes from his erstwhile opponents, the Dutch themselves. When Zain was finally transferred to Cairo in 1949,[60] it was the Netherlands consulate-general who evaluated this transfer as a great loss for Indoff because of his competence and the extent to which the Indoff leadership depended on him. Indeed, the consul-general (A.M.L. Winkelman) knew Zain personally, and regarded him as having a quiet and peaceful demeanour. He embraced moderate ideas and was not anti-Dutch.[61] Winkelman thought that, compared to Zain, Oetoyo was a mere 'glamour boy', basking in the prestige generally enjoyed by foreign representatives.[62]

Dutch sources also suggest there was a rift between Zain and Oetoyo over the choice of strategies to defend Republican interests. While Oetoyo was eager to condone smuggling by individuals, Zain was more interested in organizing exports from Aceh (then not under Dutch control) to pay for goods that were needed by the people there.[63] However, this difference was not necessarily a rift, as these could also be concurrent strategies.

Another luminary in the Indoff leadership was Suryono Daroesman. Born

[59] For a description of Zain, see Coast 1952:15.
[60] PG 558, CGDN, No. 86-49, Singapore, Report by R.W. van Lier, 11-5-1949.
[61] Directie Verre Oosten 336, Letter from A.M.L. Winkelman (Consul-General Singapore) to Director of Directie Verre Oosten (T. Elink Schuurman), VIII-C-3, No. 26298/362.
[62] PG 558, CGDN, No. 91-49, Singapore, Report by P.A. van der Poel, 25-5-1949.
[63] Directie Verre Oosten 74, Consul-General A.M.L. Winkelman to Minister of Foreign Affairs, VIII-B-2a/22600/513, 26-9-1949.

in 1919 in West Sumatra, he was the most cosmopolitan of all. His father was a doctor from Java, his mother hailed from Jakarta. He grew up in West Java. In Singapore, he was placed in charge of public relations, a vaguely defined task that was a multi-function job to handle everybody who approached Indoff for any matter. Like Zain, he was faced with requests of all kinds, to which, invariably, his answer was 'no'. For this, Daroesman was accused of being a NICA (pro-Dutch) agent. Daroesman explained that caution was required because the Indonesians were operating in a British colony and there were spies around.[64]

For a time, Saroso Wirohardjo led Indoff's trade and finance department. He was born in Java in about 1914. He studied in Rotterdam and took a degree in economics. He arrived in Singapore in August 1947. Originally, he had been en route to Havana to attend a conference as representative of Indonesia. His mandate for that meeting came from President Soekarno and not from Sjahrir, who had left office by then. However, he stayed in Singapore to compile a report on economic affairs for Sjahrir's successor, Prime Minister Amir Sjarifoeddin, and remained there because he felt that Singapore was a more important centre for Indonesian activities.[65] Saroso's network of political affiliations did not correspond entirely with that of Oetoyo. While Oetoyo was a Ministry of Foreign Affairs appointee, Saroso was a career officer with the finance departments of the Republic of Indonesia government. The two held different views over the disposal of profits from trade.[66] Saroso viewed trade as a means to meet the Republic's internal needs, but Oetoyo was more concerned with funding the Republic's international interests. The differences were sufficiently serious to warrant the closure of the trade and finance department (about April 1948), and the transfer of its duties to Oetoyo. Saroso returned to Indonesia and became a roving ambassador as Indonesian trade commissioner for Southeast Asia.[67]

The dissemination of information by Indoff was the task of Taharoeddin Ahmad. His job was made difficult because Indonesians in Singapore demanded up-to-date news bulletins from Indoff, but for Taharoeddin Ahmad, access to accurate news was difficult at best. As a result, people were forced to listen to oral accounts from visitors who had just returned from Indonesia. Such news was disseminated at restaurants. Restaurant Kita was one such place. Located along busy North Bridge Road near the junction

[64] PG 558, CGDN, No. 7-49, Singapore, by J.W.J. de Haas, 11-1-1949.
[65] PG 304, 'Indonesian Agencies in Malaya', Secret (109) in M.S. 815. Written by H.Q. Malayan Security Service, 23-6-1948.
[66] Interview with Darusman in Jakarta, 20-3-1992.
[67] *Memoar pejuang* 1992:98-100. According to John Coast, Vice-President Hatta mandated him to mediate between Oetoyo and Saroso, but he only aroused the suspicion of both. See Coast 1952:163, 185.

with Arab Street and smack in the heart of the Malay quarters of Kampong Glam, it was a popular meeting place for Indonesians of many persuasions. This was the place where news about Indonesia circulated. Not all the news was accurate. Some was coloured and embellished, but most was accepted as true because there were witnesses who had just landed in Singapore from Indonesia.[68] Told as yarns over dinner to crowds gathered at Restaurant Kita for a meal, they were exciting distractions to the humdrum life in Singapore devoted to making ends meet.

Beneath this echelon of leaders in Indoff was a group of 'field officers', as they came to be known, or blockade-runners. These were the operations staff who navigated boats across the body of water separating Singapore and Indonesia, carrying goods of all kinds, conveying messages, intelligence, or escorting emissaries. They braved the dangers of sailing on rough seas, and they also risked their lives evading Dutch patrols and attacks. They were the unsung heroes of the Singapore connection. Their exploits are recorded for posterity in a joint publication (*Memoar pejuang* 1992, Chapters VI, X-XVII). The most famous of these 'field officers' was John Lie, about whom more will be said in a later chapter.

There were also blockade-runners who were not ethnic Indonesians. Republican sympathizers like the Englishman John Coast chartered aircraft to ferry people and materials between Singapore and parts of Sumatra and Java.[69] They were the counterparts of the field officers who sailed boats.

Anti-Republican organizations in Singapore

With such a spate of anti-Dutch activities, it would be useful to ask whether there were organizations operating in Singapore that were not supportive of the Republic. From the historical records, at least two such organizations can be identified. Neither lasted very long. The first was set up with Dutch support.

On 11 April 1948, the news broke that an Indonesian organization with pre-war roots, Hidoep Seresam, had been revived. Hidoep Seresam was founded in February 1940 and at one time even enjoyed the protection of the Dutch consulate-general. Its aims were cultural and social. It proposed to advance the educational level of Indonesians, promote Indonesian culture, and provide help to needy Indonesians. In its post-war reincarnation, the Hidoep Seresam was made up of Sumatrans who were fiercely anti-Indoff.[70] Almost

---

[68] PG 558, CGDN, No. 8-49, Singapore, By R.W. van Lier, 12-1-1949.
[69] On the attempts to break the air blockade, see Darusman 1992:21. (On p. 62, there is a picture of John Coast.) John Coast has published his own account; see Coast 1952, chapter VII.
[70] PG 168, CGDN, No. 94-48, Report by S. van Hulst, 10-4-1948.

immediately, it faced strong criticism from Indonesians themselves, who felt that the organization would further the existing divisions. Its founder, Hadji M. Ideries, was a fierce opponent of Oetoyo.[71] The local Malay/Indonesian population also seemed adept at identifying the *dalang* (puppeteer) working behind this organization and generally distanced themselves from it.

The second organization enjoyed a longer history. It was called Djawatan Kuasa Penghoeroes Rakyat Riouw, Riouw People's Committee, or Djawatan Kuasa for short. The organization did not owe its origins to the Dutch. It more closely resembled the ethnic Minangkabau or Batak organizations mentioned earlier. They all represented regional aspirations to promote their own interests except that the Djawatan was not pro-Republic. The aim of the Djawatan was to restore the Riau sultanate that had been abolished by the Dutch in 1911. After the abolition, its descendants and supporters dispersed, with many of them ending up in nearby Singapore. The confusing and turbulent times following the Japanese surrender presented a golden opportunity to enable supporters of the sultanate to regain past glories. Singapore was a suitable place to start activities of this nature because the island had once been part of the Riau sultanate and latent sympathy could still be exploited. Its proximity to the Riau islands would also enable Djawatan leaders to pay visits regularly and even relocate when the conditions were propitious.

The immediate factor responsible for the formation of Djawatan in Singapore was the news of the toppling of the indigenous rulers of East Sumatra, an event also known as the social revolution. On 15 April 1946, prominent leaders of the Riau community met under the chairmanship of Radja Hadji Abdoellah, a descendant of the royalty of the sultanate.[72] This Abdoellah was a shadowy figure. On the one hand, he was well known in Johore for his opposition to the Sultan of Johore, Sir Ibrahim. He thought that the seat of the Johore government in the former Johore Empire should be returned to Riau. On the other hand, he was portrayed by Dutch reports as a kind of double agent, allegedly working for the Johore branch of the Malayan security service.[73] Among the Indonesians in Singapore, he was nicknamed 'Sultan Lima Dollar' (the Five Dollar Sultan), because he offered $5 to each of his friends who supported him.[74]

In a Singapore where neither the Republicans nor the Dutch were the governing authority, Radja Abdoellah was free to press for the restoration of the sultanate, given, as he described, the ideal circumstances of Riau

[71] PG 168, CGDN, No. 98-48, report by S. van Hulst, 17-4-1948.
[72] RI 561, Nota G. Diest Lorgion, Commissaris van Politie eerste klasse, Batavia, 31-3-1947.
[73] RI 552, Tweewekelijksche berichtgeving van de Residentie Riouw over de periode 15 t/m 30-9-1947, By J. van Waardenburg, Resident, Tandjong Pinang, 13-10-1947.
[74] RI 551, Tweewekelijksche berichtgeving der Residentie Riouw over de periode 1 t/m 15-5-1946, By J. van Waardenburg, Resident, Singapore 17-5-1946.

during the earlier golden years of the sultanate. Support for Abdoellah was unanimous and Djawatan was formed with Abdoellah as chairman. Other members included his son-in-law and an immigration officer. Inexplicably, a pretender was not identified at that time.[75] Thus Djawatan represented another group of Indonesians in Singapore with identifiably separate interests, and it remained active until there was no hope of reviving the former sultanate.

The trade organizations

A network of trade had existed between Singapore and the Indonesian islands since time immemorial. This trade was not disrupted by the political boundary drawn between Singapore and Indonesia by the colonial authorities. After the Japanese occupation, the trade network quickly revived and had resumed its pre-war status by 1945-1946. Barter was the mode of this trade. Transactions took place quite independently of banks and other financial institutions. This was a perfectly acceptable system of trade because barter was simple and time-honoured. In the Indonesia-Singapore context, it simply referred to an operation in which small wooden boats called *tongkang* (barges), carrying a range of agricultural products, arrived in Singapore from Java, Sumatra, or elsewhere, usually without proper customs clearance. Their task was simple: sell the goods and return with all the essentials required by Indonesians, including military hardware.

When the barter system was restored to its pre-war prominence, its first concern, not surprisingly, was the acquisition of weapons. This was an almost inevitable development since all commercial dealings between Indonesia and Singapore before August 1946 were controlled by agencies of the Indonesian navy and army. Weapons being difficult to acquire, Indonesian defence personnel were sent as barter traders to Singapore to look for weapons. This overriding concern led to unhealthy attitudes that could be expressed as follows: 'We don't care about prices, as long as we can get weapons'. Since weapons could only be obtained at great risk, suppliers could quote prices arbitrarily high. The barter traders were also amateurs at their job – people who came to Singapore with 'a clear conscience and a real fighting spirit' but little experience in trade; or they were adventurers and black market operatives. The result was confusion and disorder in the commercial relations between Singapore and Indonesia, with the name of the Republic tarnished and blemished. Their counterparts, on the other hand, were firms established in Singapore who were far more experienced and professional. They could

[75] RI 561, Nota G. Diest Lorgion, Commissaris van Politie eerste klasse, 31-3-1947, Batavia.

quote prices at will.[76]

This unbalanced trade relationship is best seen from the figures that were made available after a study commissioned by the Republican government. During the three months of October, November, and December 1946, it was estimated that imports into Singapore from Riau, Bali-Lombok, Bangka-Billiton, Borneo-Celebes-Maluku, Java, Sumatra, and other islands was $25 million per month or about one-quarter of the total value of imported goods. Of the $25 million, Java and Sumatra combined contributed about $18 million ($3 million from Java and $15 million from Sumatra). Using this as a yardstick, it was estimated that for the eighteen months that the Republican government had existed, a total of $324 million ($18 million per month times 18 months) worth of goods had arrived in Singapore, or $54 million from Java and $270 million from Sumatra. The question to be answered was the extent of returns that Indonesia obtained from this outflow. Since there was neither proper customs accounting nor statistics at the Java-Sumatra end, it was not possible to provide a clear-cut answer. Moreover, some of the goods landed in Singapore were exchanged for weapons. The only estimate of returns that could be obtained was based on the prices of various articles (like textiles, soap, toothpaste, and toothbrushes) that ended up in Java and these were found to be five or even ten times higher than prices prevailing in Singapore. An estimate would place a return of only $10 million in exchange for the $54 million worth of goods from Java landed in Singapore each month. No estimate was possible for Sumatra, but it would not be surprising if there were also similar 'losses'.[77] These losses had to be written off as 'bad debts'.[78]

A semblance of order was required in order that benefits for the Republic could be maximized. The individual barter traders and their patrons soon realized the importance of getting organized so as to deal more effectively with traders at the Singapore end. Also, as the Dutch filed more and more protests with the British to deny business opportunities to Republican traders, there was a greater urgency to respond by establishing organizations that could promote profitable barter and at the same time camouflage the more shady-side businesses.

By the last quarter of 1946, several organizations were formed to act more

---

[76] AS 2/1072, Report of the 'Bank Negara Indonesia' on the Singapore journey from 31-3-1947 up to 10-4-1947, By President Director Bank Negara Indonesia, R.M. Margono Djojohadi-koesoemo, Batavia, 15-4-1947.

[77] AS 2/1072, Report of the 'Bank Negara Indonesia' on the Singapore journey from 31-3-1947 up to 10-4-1947, By President Director Bank Negara Indonesia, R.M. Margono Djojohadi-koesoemo, Batavia, 15-4-1947.

[78] AS 2/1072, Report of the 'Bank Negara Indonesia' on the Singapore journey from 31-3-1947 up to 10-4-1947, By President Director Bank Negara Indonesia, R.M. Margono Djojohadi-koesoemo, Batavia, 15-4-1947.

or less as trade or official representatives of the various Republican government agencies. The most prominent of these was Namsoco, representing A.K. Gani. The founder of Namsoco was a fugitive businessman from Yogyakarta, called T. Oesman bin Abdoellah Rahman. He enjoyed the support of Gani, who was Minister of Economic Affairs in the Sjahrir cabinet in 1946. It was Gani's job to exchange Indonesian commodities for essentials. Apart from sending individuals to execute this task, Gani decided in October 1946 to establish an import-export authority in Singapore. This was Namsoco, with headquarters in Palembang, which was the biggest and most important Republican port in Sumatra. Namsoco turned out to be a giant of sorts. Apart from trade, it also became a communications centre and an organization in charge of various activities, including the payment of stipends to students studying overseas. It also bankrolled the propaganda issued by the PKBI and Antara, and was given the authority to approve the programmes before making disbursements. It also provided assistance to Indonesians who wanted to return to Indonesia, but this support was available only for journeys to Palembang at the furthest.[79]

The other organizations included one called Indonesia Import and Export located at 80 Robinson Road (representing the trade branch of the Republican government's Department of Welfare). Its principal trading area was concentrated on Java, but there was another organization with a similar sounding name, the Indonesia Importing and Exporting Company, focusing on the trade with Sumatra (*Indonesian intentions* 1964:4). There was also Oesaha Baroe (representing the Ministry of Defence), and Noesantara Agency representing the Republican government in Sumatra. Noesantara's founder was Tahir Karim Loebis from Padang. Within a month of Loebis's arrival in Singapore, he was able to set up his trading agency. Its trading activities, however, were only a front. It maintained extensive contacts with Indonesian associations established outside of Indonesia as well as political leaders in Malaya.

Of the trade organizations, Namsoco had the best track record, but none of them, including Namsoco, had a surplus balance to the credit of the Republic of Indonesia; on the contrary, all of them suffered from deficit balances.[80]

There was also an Atjeh Trading Corporation (ATC), founded by A.K. Gani in 1946 to provide financial support to the army. In 1947, the ATC

---

[79] *Rahsia perdjuangan* 1948:151-3. For a brief mention of Namsoco, see *Officiële bescheiden*, VII: 185. Gani's role in Namsoco and other business dealings deserves separate treatment. A locally trained doctor, he played a pivotal role in the central government of the Republic and wielded considerable influence over the trade between Sumatra and Singapore. For details, see Twang 1998:140-1.
[80] AS 2/1072, Report of the 'Bank Negara Indonesia' on the Singapore journey from 31-3-1947 up to 10-4-1947, By President Director Bank Negara Indonesia, R.M. Margono Djojohadikoesoemo, Batavia, 15-4-1947.

switched its attention to economic matters and remained from 1948 the trade arm of the government in Aceh. Its office was located at 133 Chulia Street in Singapore.[81] Its relations with Indoff were poor because Indoff had once seized some tons of goods belonging to the ATC,[82] an incident on which details are not available. The ATC then concentrated its attention on Penang where many of its trade activities were found anyway.[83]

From January 1948, the ATC became a part of the Sumatra Banking and Trading Corporation (SBTC).[84] The SBTC was established in Singapore in April 1947, with Marah Taharuddin as manager, upon the urging of the Republican authorities in Bukit Tinggi (*Rahsia perdjuangan* 1948:155-6). The SBTC was a sister company of the BTC (founded in Jakarta in December 1946, see below). The SBTC's founder was Vice-President Hatta. Its primary task was to facilitate the export of products from Sumatra (Sutter 1959, II:548).

The BTC was the brainchild of another famous Sumatran leader. Sumitro Djojohadikoesoemo, who in his capacity as president of the Perseroean Bank dan Perniagaan, or Banking and Trading Corporation, Limited, arrived in Singapore on 30 May 1947 to assess the feasibility of establishing a branch bank.[85] Sumitro had always felt that top priority should be given to the establishment of an export and import bank. In Jakarta, this plan materialized on 31 December 1946 when the Banking and Trading Corporation (BTC) was established and he became its president (Sutter 1959, II:443-4). But the plans for the BTC branch in Singapore were short-lived because the BTC headquarters in Jakarta became moribund after the first Dutch military action, when it lost its administrative offices and valuable cargo (Sutter 1959, II:548). There was another organization also called the Banking and Trading Corporation (but this time with headquarters in Yogyakarta) established by Saroso, Sjahroedin, A.P. Lim, and Machsus. (The first three constituted a triumvirate in Indoff's trade and finance department) (*Memoar pejuang* 1992: 107). This BTC imposed a seven per cent levy on all goods entering Singapore from the Republic. It also acted as a bank to enable Indonesians to cash their cheques. However, the outflow of funds exceeded its income and BTC Yogya became financially unstable. Another blow to BTC Yogya came when it tried to bail out an ailing company, Durham Traders. This group's founder was the former prime minister, Sjahrir, and was established in 1947. Its principal aim was to establish a shipping system for transportation links with the Republic.

---

[81] PG 168, CGDN, No. 176-48, Singapore, Report by S. van Hulst, 18-10-1948.
[82] PG 556, CGDN, No. 131-49, Singapore, Report by P.A. van der Poel, 24-9-1949.
[83] For a list of Acehnese trade organizations in Penang, see PG 168, CGDN, No. 66-48, Singapore, Report by S. van Hulst, 13-3-1948.
[84] PG 170(II), Penang kantoor van Mr Oetoyo, unsigned, undated.
[85] PG 173, Rapport van den Inlichtingendienst der Algemeene Politie Riouw (RIAPR), No. 437, Singapore, By S. van Hulst, 7-6-1947.

As a first step, two ships were purchased but the income generated from the vessels was insufficient. BTC Yogya intervened to help and the new responsibility added to its difficulties (*Rahsia perdjuangan* 1948:153-5).

There were also two other specifically Batak-based organizations that were engaged in sending goods to Sumatra: E. Tambunan and Company and Sjarikat Dagang Tapanoeli. The goods sent from Singapore by these two firms were reputed to be usually cheaper than similar goods sent by Indoff (*Rahsia perdjuangan* 1948:156).

The organizations represented a major contribution to the attempts to break free of trading restrictions reimposed by the Dutch after the Japanese surrendered, and this in itself was an act of economic diplomacy and defiance. Of course these trade organizations were also operating on a small scale compared to the Chinese business houses established in Singapore. Also, many of them were ephemeral in staying power. However, collectively, as a group – and there is no way to prove this point statistically – their manifold activities raised the profile of the Republic of Indonesia in Singapore as a new entity struggling to establish a lifeline of its own.

The Chinese in Singapore

The Chinese traders

There were many Chinese traders operating between Singapore and the Indonesian islands of Java and Sumatra.[86] These worked individually on a small scale, or were employed by Chinese firms. Many were already established traders operating in Singapore from pre-war days. They were also joined by Chinese businessmen from Indonesia who had fled because of the insecurity following the Japanese occupation, or because they were often forced to make compulsory donations to the Republican cause.

Within Singapore, the largest organization representing their collective interests was the Singapore Overseas Chinese Importers and Exporters Association (SOCIEA), founded in January 1946.[87] Its membership included approximately sixty per cent of the importers and exporters doing business in Singapore. They had established an excellent barter trade system before the Japanese occupation and they were able to restore barter links very smoothly after that. Exports from Singapore included goods like salted

---

[86] In this study, the term 'Chinese' is used without distinguishing the various groups within that community. In fact, there were important differences in terms of dialects, and whether they were recent immigrants or long-time residents. These differences have been explored in other publications, and will not be discussed here because this study is not focused on the Chinese. See Twang 1998:178-81; Darusman 1992:10-1.

[87] For an account of the early history of SOCIEA, see Twang 1998:206-7.

fish, gambier, cloves, salt, vegetables and fruits from China. In return, the Singapore traders took sugar, rubber, and other plantation products from the Indonesian islands.

The smugglers

There were two main categories of smugglers defined according to whether the goods handled were contraband or non-contraband. Contraband included weapons and opium while non-contraband goods included estate products that were sometimes sold in exchange for contraband. Smuggling will be discussed in a subsequent chapter.

The Malays in Singapore

Usually, the first contact that Indonesians had when they landed in Singapore was the opportunity to meet up with Malays in one capacity or the other. Immigration and customs officials were invariably Malays. Even when the Indonesians had their first brush with the law, the rank and file of the police force in Singapore consisted largely of Malays. Although many of them were not personally involved in Indonesian affairs and many might not have had family ties in Java and Sumatra, there were still feelings of brotherhood. Such intangible bonds were translated in practical ways that directly benefited the Indonesian cause.

When Indonesians arrived in Singapore without proper papers, which was often the case in 1945 and 1946, it was not unusual for immigration officers to adopt a benign and accommodating attitude.[88] It was as if these officers were 'suddenly struck by temporary blindness, when Indonesians were carrying out their patriotic duties in contravention of local laws'.[89] Oetoyo himself was the beneficiary of the pro-Indonesia outlook among many of the Malays in Singapore. The lower echelon of the immigration service in Singapore was the preserve of Malays, and that made movement in and out of Singapore easier. Thus Oetoyo could travel to Bangkok without valid Singapore papers and, what was more surprising, return to Singapore without any hassle.[90] Generally, the existence of a sympathetic Malay population meant that Indonesians who got into trouble with the authorities could easily disappear into the local population in Geylang Serai or some other area of

---

[88] Suryono Darusman, 'Singapore and the Indonesian Revolution 1945-1950', typescript.
[89] Photocopied newspaper cuttings made available by Suryono Darusman.
[90] PG 304, Letter from S. van Hulst to Procureur-Generaal, 12-7-1948.

Malay settlement and merge with other faceless individuals.

Within the Malay community in Singapore, many were generally supportive of the Republic's struggle for independence. Within this community, the Indonesians who had settled in Singapore for a considerable period were an important group. They regarded Singapore as their home even though they continued to show interest in events taking place in Indonesia. Among these were Javanese and Bawean (immigrants from the island of Bawean off Madura). Many were supporters of the Republic's struggle against the Dutch. They were not necessarily direct participants in Indonesian revolutionary activities in Singapore. However, they were affected by the vicissitudes of Dutch-Indonesian relations and their varying responses formed the staple of much of the local news in Singapore.

The 1947 census of Singapore showed that Javanese and Bawean were the two largest immigrant communities from Indonesia, counting 24,715 and 15,434 respectively. The Javanese were the oldest Indonesian migrants to Singapore, most having come as labourers or pilgrims. Adaptable to Malay society in Singapore, the Javanese continued to maintain links with their homeland, perhaps even planning to return after amassing enough funds. Many Bawean were recent immigrants. Especially between 1947 and 1948, they arrived in Singapore driven by dire economic conditions with memories fresh from the unrest in Indonesia. By then, so many men had forsaken Bawean for Singapore that the former island was nicknamed 'island of women'. A ditty sung by the Bawean showed their preference for migration to Singapore:

> Kalau mau makan enak2 pergi Java
> Kalau mau dikubur ke Malaya; tetapi
> Kalau mau cari wang dan pakaian ke Singapura[91]
>
> If you want to eat well, go to Java
> If you want to be buried, go to Malaya; but
> If you want money and clothing, go to Singapore

Unlike the Javanese who integrated with the local Malay population, the Bawean maintained a separate existence in their *pondok* (communal accommodation). The Bawean also formed an association, Persatuan Bawean Association (PBA), after the end of Japanese occupation of Singapore. In 1947, the name was changed to Persatuan Bawean Singapura (PBS), showing the identification of the Bawean with their new homeland. This move had an impact on the degree of support the Bawean could mobilize for the

---

[91] Vredenbregt 1964:120-1, 128; See also Abdullah bin Malim Baginda 1967 and the oral history interviews with Haji Badron bin Sainullah (reel 46), Haji Mohamad Sadli bin Mohamad (reel 13), Singapore: National Archives, Oral History Centre.

Indonesian revolution. Although originally from Indonesia, younger Bawean began to question the need to fight for Republican interests that were not directly concerned with their welfare in Singapore. Thus, support from Indonesian communities in Singapore was not automatic.

Malay leaders partial to the Republic

The person regarded as the leader who could mobilize the support of the Malay community was A. Samad Ismail. He was an influential journalist working on the *Utusan Melayu* newspaper, the mouthpiece of the Malays in Singapore and Malaya. A. Samad Ismail's parents were Javanese but he identified with the Malay community into which he had settled. He admired the Indonesian revolution although he did not support the revolutionary overthrow of colonialism. Consequently, he came to know many of the Republic's leaders, like Sjahrir, Adam Malik, and even Soekarno. His relationship with these Indonesian leaders was not confined to the official level. They became his personal friends. Many years later, during the 1950s, President Soekarno interrupted himself in a speech at the Indonesian embassy in Singapore and asked, 'Is Bung [brother] Samad here?' Just as suddenly, he continued, 'Never mind, give him my regards'(Samad Ismail 1987:53). A. Samad Ismail was also involved in smuggling intelligence, arms, and foodstuffs to Indonesia. It was therefore not surprising that A. Samad Ismail's *Utusan* office was almost a compulsory stopping place for the Republic's leaders and emissaries.

A Malay community leader was Abdul Samad, a medical practitioner who helped Indonesians to procure weapons for their cause. Other leaders included Sa'adon bin Jubir, member of the Singapore legislative council and chairman of a local Malay political party, the Kesatuan Melayu or Malay Union. Another was Gaus Mahyudin. Gaus, a doctor and formerly from Minangkabau, was a fiery and fierce supporter of the Republic. The Aljunied family, of Arab descent with deep roots in Singapore society, was another important source of support for the Republic. Other leaders who made contributions to the Republican cause were Zubir Said (a prominent promoter of Indonesian art in Singapore during the 1940s) and Mochtar Effendi.[92]

British colonial officials in Singapore

Under the influence of Lord Louis Mountbatten, the commander of SEAC, the British officials in Singapore, as a group, generally supported the nationalist ideals of the Republic. This pro-Indonesia sentiment continued through

---

[92] *Memoar pejuang*, 1992:29, 94-5; See also Darusman 1992:25, 56, note 5.

III Constituents of the Singapore connection

the tenure of Lord Killearn and lasted till about 1948. That year, with the departure of Lord Killearn and the onset of the communist revolt, political activities in Singapore experienced major restrictions and pro-Indonesia feelings were significantly absent among British colonial officials.

Apart from their favouring of the anti-colonialist stand of the Indonesian Republic, there was another matter about the Dutch that needled the British. At the end of the Japanese occupation, Malaya and Singapore were heavily dependent on rice imports to feed their population. This dire circumstance was worsened by conditions in Java, where the fighting between the Dutch and the Republic had rendered rice production all but impossible. Before the Japanese occupation, the regions of East and West Java had formerly contributed an export surplus of 450,000 tons of rice. However, this surplus had turned into a deficit, with the ravages of fighting. At the best of times, the intricate irrigation systems that supported the rice surplus required the skills of Dutch engineers. Now Java – especially the parts controlled by the Dutch – had to compete for rice imports from the remaining rice-exporting regions of Southeast Asia, namely, Siam and Burma. For minimum needs, it was estimated that the Indonesian population required an infusion of 280,000 tons annually.[93] It all meant that there was less rice available to meet the needs of British-controlled Malaya and Singapore. In March 1946, the British government appointed a senior diplomat to sort out the difficulties of rice distribution in Southeast Asia. Lord Killearn assumed the office of Special Commissioner for Southeast Asia.

Upon arrival, Lord Killearn had to tackle many non-political problems left by the Japanese occupation. At that time, there was no sign of regional cooperation to solve the rice shortage problem. There was near-famine in most areas. There was disease and malnutrition even in the rice-producing areas. There was near-paralysis of non-military communication links. With the dissolution of the earlier Southeast Asia Command under Lord Mountbatten, Lord Killearn no longer enjoyed the military muscle to enforce his will. He had to depend on diplomacy alone. He could advise, he could plan, he could suggest, and he could persuade. But he could never command. Very early on, he learned that success could only come if politics were avoided like the plague. He also understood very clearly that Singapore played a central role in the developments occurring in Indonesia and elsewhere. At a press conference at the end of his tour of duty, he said: 'One only has to look at a map to see that the countries of South-East Asia form a chain, and that Malaya and Singapore are in a central point of that chain'.[94]

In public, he tried to be neutral between the Dutch and the Republic,

[93] 'Rice behind the lines', *Straits Times*, 9-1-1948, p. 4.
[94] 'Killearn on two years' work; Departing for England today', *Straits Times*, 27-5-1948, p. 7.

but there were times when he showed his inclination to help the Republic. Despite the dire need for rice within Indonesia, he allowed the Republic to negotiate for the export of 100,000 tons of Indonesian rice to India.[95] In this case, the Republic was driven to employ 'rice diplomacy' to break out of the encirclement imposed by the Dutch, and also to thank India for its support. As for the Dutch, Killearn confided privately in his diary that he never trusted M.F. Vigeveno, the Netherlands consul-general in Singapore (1946-1947). He called Vigeveno 'a snake in the grass'.[96] A newspaper published in The Hague, *Het Dagblad*, collected information on a number of instances of Lord Killearn's partiality to the Republican leaders. It noted that Sjahrir stayed fourteen days in Lord Killearn's residence, and when he travelled to Australia, a British diplomat accompanied him. Lord Killearn was alleged to have told Republican leaders that the Netherlands government consisted of weaklings and the Netherlands was in dire financial straits. He advised the Republican leaders to refuse Dutch demands. At the Singapore naval base, boats capable of speeds faster than Dutch patrol boats were sold to Chinese traders who were engaged in smuggling. The newspaper also accused Dutch officials in Jakarta of possessing documents that could compromise Killearn but did not release them for fear of embarrassing him. (Later, P.J. Koets, a leading Dutch civil servant in Jakarta, stated in an interview in the Netherlands that the allegations of *Het Dagblad* were 'pure nonsense'.[97])

Oetoyo's relations with Killearn got off to a bumpy start. As far as can be ascertained, one of the early meetings Lord Killearn had with Oetoyo was held in Jakarta in August 1946. There, at a meeting together with Republican ministers Natsir and Salim, Killearn described all three men as follows: 'It is a curious type, very small, and not physically particularly impressive, but there is a sort of tough look about them, and they struck me as full of suspicion'.[98] At subsequent meetings in September, also in Jakarta, Killearn noted that Oetoyo 'asked many intelligent questions'.[99]

Through Lord Killearn, virtual recognition was extended to the Indoff representative, Oetoyo, as the Republican consul. Killearn held many private meetings with him and maintained continuous contact, inviting him for dinner when entertaining passing Republican dignitaries, like former prime minister Sjahrir.[100] Also, it was through Killearn as intermediary that Oetoyo

---

[95] 'Dutch attack on Killearn', *Straits Times*, 1-3-1947, p. 5.
[96] Killearn Diary 1947, p. 118.
[97] The *Het Dagblad* allegations (of 27-12-1947) are found in appendices enclosed in Directie Verre Oosten 320.
[98] Killearn Diary 1946, Vol. 2, p. 224-5.
[99] Killearn Diary 1946, Vol. 2, p. 261.
[100] Killearn Diary 1948, p. 37.

met the governor of Singapore.[101] However, Killearn's personal support for Indoff was not to be confused with the official position of the British government in Singapore. The governor of Singapore only met Oetoyo unwillingly. When Killearn left Singapore in 1948 and his pro-Republic staff was transferred, the attitude of the British agencies towards the Republic cooled and the Republican authorities missed him.[102]

When the communist challenge to British rule in Malaya and Singapore led to the proclamation of the Emergency in 1948, its restrictive regulations applied to all, including the Indonesian organizations in Singapore. Political expression was severely limited, as indeed were all forms of political activities, not to mention trade in weapons. This explained the mute response from both Indoff and the PI towards the December 1948 Second Military Action against the Republican government in the archipelago. The Indonesian community in Singapore complained, quite unjustifiably, that their representatives did little to undertake initiatives or organize public protest meetings to discuss retaliatory measures.[103] The Netherlands consulate in Singapore was able to report that nowhere in Singapore were there significant cases of protest or sabotage against the Dutch. This was quite unlike the response to the First Military Action, when there were public expressions like boycotts, intimidation and harassment of servants and chauffeurs who continued to work for the Dutch, and stoning of Dutch residences.[104] Indeed, there were reports of discussions among Indonesians in December 1948 on measures to be taken against the Dutch. These included sabotaging KLM planes or the Shell oil station on nearby Pulau Sambu, but in the end, little action was taken.[105] There was also no mention of events in Indonesia during speeches held at a mass rally at the Singapore Jalan Besar Stadium on the occasion of the Prophet's birthday the following January 1949, even though speakers included pro-Indonesia leaders.[106]

---

[101] PG 861, Tweewekelijksche berichtgeving der Algemeene Politie Riouw, Nederlandsch Consulaat-Generaal, Singapore, over de periode 13 t/m 26-5-1947, Rapport No. 422A, p. 6, Singapore, By S. van Hulst, Commissaris van Politie II, 26-5-1947.
[102] Inventaris van de archieven van het Consulaat-Generaal te Singapore, 1945-54, Ministerie van Buitenlandse Zaken (MBZ) 220, S. van Hulst (Secretarie voor Speciale Diensten) to Procureur-Generaal bij het Hooggerechtshof van Nederlands Indie, 26-6-1948.
[103] PG 168, CGDN, No. 215-48, Singapore, Report by R.W. van Lier; 30-12-1948; PG 558, CGDN, No. 4-49, Singapore, By S. van Hulst, 6-1-1949; PG 558, CGDN, No.10-49, Singapore, By R.W. van Lier, 12-1-1949; PG 558, CGDN, No. 32-49, Singapore, By P.A. van der Poel, 15-2-1949.
[104] PG 168, CGDN, No. 213-48, Singapore, Report by R.W. van Lier, 28-12-1948.
[105] PG 558, CGDN, No. 4-49, Singapore, By S. van Hulst, 6-1-1949.
[106] PG 558, CGDN, No.10-49, Singapore, By R.W. van Lier, 12-1-1949.

The Dutch in Singapore

After the Japanese occupation, Singapore was the staging point for Dutch troops on the way to Indonesia. In 1945, there were an estimated five hundred soldiers undergoing military training for service. (Some of these soldiers were ex-POWs, and in October it was reported that a first group of patrols was ready for assignment on Karimun island in Riau.[107]) Together with their families, and other civilian support staff (for the Dutch merchant navy), the Dutch lived in two camps in the Katong district in the eastern part of Singapore. To make living more pleasant, the Dutch had organized their own newspaper, news service, a radio station, postal unit, and even entertainment outlets like cinemas and an orchestra.[108] The Dutch continued to live in camps through 1947[109] and there was always a Dutch military presence in Singapore, at least till the end of 1948.

Individual Dutch soldiers were marked men while staying in Singapore. Living among hostile Indonesians, they were often the target of assaults. Dutch soldiers who left the safety of their camp to visit friends or cinemas risked being stabbed to death or waylaid. The motives may have been politics or simply robbery.[110]

For official matters, the liaison body was the Netherlands consulate. In Singapore, a consul looked after the interests of the Netherlands. He was the heir to an illustrious history beginning from the middle of the nineteenth century. The first consul was W.H. Read,[111] an active and ardent supporter of the cause of colonial expansion. In 1945, the consul in Singapore could do no less than defend Dutch interests with similar vigour. With the end of the Japanese occupation, the consulate resumed its former roles. An additional duty was to prevent the trade in estate products that were exported without permission to Singapore from Western-owned enterprises. This duty complemented the NEI agencies in Jakarta (for example the commission for tracing Netherlands Indies

[107] '5000 ex-pows ready for orders for Java', *Straits Times*, 17-10-1945, p. 3.
[108] 'A little bit of Holland in Singapore', by a Special Correspondent, *Sunday Times* (Singapore), 6-10-1945, p. 2.
[109] 'Singapore Dutch fete birth of new princess', *Straits Times*, 20-2-1947, p. 7; 'Dutch soldier freed on murder charge', *Straits Times*, 20-9-1947, p. 7.
[110] 'Dutchman found murdered', *Straits Times*, 4-7-1946, p. 5.
[111] Read was consul from 1857 to 1871 and consul-general from 1871 to 1884. He published his memoirs as *Play and politics; Recollections of Malaya by an old resident* in 1901. Read dedicated his book to Governor Andrew Clarke, whose 'prescient and decisive policy' to intervene in the affairs of the Malay states made possible development and prosperity. In the memoirs, Read claims (pp. 25-9, 43) that he was responsible for providing the 'key' that enabled Clarke to intervene. He also accompanied Clarke to Pahang to settle a civil war, leading finally to the appointment of a British Resident. As consul, Read accompanied the King of Siam (Chulalongkorn) on a visit to Batavia. While holding office in Singapore, he played an active role in maintaining law and order (by restraining drunken seamen and Chinese secret societies).

property, or COMIE, and the NIGIEO, an export-import agency) responsible for ensuring that estate produce was not stolen and illegally sold.

To Indonesians, the consulate was the symbol of the Dutch factor in the conflict with the Republic. Any shortcomings or wrongdoings were ascribed to the consulate. The local Malay community was not slow to place blame on the consulate when trouble brewed. It was accused of tardiness in issuing visas to travellers from Singapore who wished to visit Indonesia for reunions with families that were separated. Sometimes the delays lasted three to four months. To applicants, a visit to the consulate was not pleasant and could even be demeaning. They were reminded of their experience with the colonial behaviour of pre-war Dutch bureaucrats.[112]

Among the staff of the consulate was a network of local spies who supplied information on all kinds of details. Much of this information was captured in regular reports compiled by the consulate and currently deposited in the Netherlands archives. Because its reliability and accuracy varied, the information was usually graded into various categories. It is not impossible that the consulate was able to infiltrate Indoff, considering that some of the information is so private and personal.[113]

As a defender and promoter of Dutch interests, the consulate served a useful function. Its consuls were indefatigable workers who applied themselves diligently to their job of enforcing trade regulations. However, the consulate was weaker in projecting the public relations side of the Netherlands. Although the main strategy advanced by the Netherlands to resolve the dispute with the Republic was the formation of a federal state of Indonesia, there was little or no advertisement in Singapore about the federal states that formed from 1948 onwards. Minor brochures were distributed, but there was never a significant public relations blitz. A suggestion was even made to buy up shares of *Utusan Melayu* and influence public opinion through that established newspaper. To this, a prominent Indonesian adviser of Van Mook, Abdoelkadir Widjojoatmodjo, made the sharp comment that it would be difficult to supervise newspaper content in Singapore if 'there was no competent person' there.[114] The consul in Singapore (J.B. Haverkorn van Rijsewijk) thought the plan to buy shares in *Utusan Melayu* was 'naive'.

---

[112] Directie Verre Oosten 568, Report by R. Moehtadi and R. Djajadikoesoema on mission (24-6-1948 to 5-7-1948) to Singapore and Kuala Lumpur to assess opinion about Indonesian federalism, 8-7-1948. (Moehtadi worked at the general secretariat in Jakarta while Djajadikoesoema was deputy resident in Banten.) The Chinese who applied for visas at the consulate confirmed the complaints of the Malays.
[113] The consulate was even able to produce a table containing the salaries of individual staffers at Indoff, beginning with Oetoyo down to the lowly clerks.
[114] Directie Verre Oosten 568, Letter quoting Abdoelkadir, 11-8-1948. See also other letters in same file.

Everybody would know, and the newspaper would lose its credibility. Better to send Indonesian federal leaders to Singapore and Malaya and show that there were alternative voices other than those of the Republic. He also suggested that *Utusan* editors be invited to tour Indonesia.[115]

Effects of Dutch colonial policy in Singapore

It was the duty of the consulate to defend Netherlands colonial policy. In this respect, two major challenges presented themselves in the form of the First Military Action and the Second Military Action. These events had repercussions on the Dutch community in Singapore, although the effects were not as serious as previously expected.

The First Military Action (July 1947)

The Dutch launched a military offensive to achieve two tactical aims, namely, to destroy the largest part of the Republic's armed forces and to capture the export products that had been bottled up in Republican-held territories waiting to be smuggled to Singapore. To achieve these aims, military units fanned out to attack various parts of Java, and northeast and southern Sumatra.

Reactions in Singapore

Immediately, the military action aroused anti-Dutch feelings in Singapore. The reporting in local newspapers (both the English-language *Straits Times* and the Malay daily, *Utusan Melayu*) aroused people's nationalist emotions. The military action thus galvanized the Indonesians living in Singapore. Almost spontaneously, two hundred Indonesians working for the Dutch went on strike at Wilhelmina Camp. Elsewhere, after two days of dispute, Indonesian labourers, cooks, messengers, and drivers employed by the Dutch stopped work. At at least twenty Dutch firms doing business in Singapore, Indonesian clerks, manual workers, and drivers threatened to go on strike.[116] At the Sultan Mosque in Kampong Glam, there was a protest meeting sponsored by the chief *kathi* and other prominent Malay leaders of Singapore.[117] Three thousand Muslims passed a resolution condemning the 'unprovoked aggression'. This meeting at the Sultan Mosque could have

---

[115] Directie Verre Oosten 568, Letter No. IX-A 22611/313 from J.B. Haverkorn van Rijsewijk (Consul Singapore) to T. Elink Schuurman (Chief, Directie Verre Oosten), 29-9-1948.
[116] 'Indonesian strike in Singapore', *Straits Times*, 1-8-1947, p. 6.
[117] 'Big Muslim protest meeting on Java War', *Straits Times*, 1-8-1947, p. 6.

developed into a *jihad* (holy war), as there were calls for a ceasefire before the conflict became 'a volcanic issue for the Muslim world'.[118] Indonesian dockyard workers refused to serve two Dutch ships – the *Kota Gede* and the *Rondo* – that were berthed alongside the Singapore wharves. A few hours later, the Singapore Harbour Board Labour Union decided to participate and impose a complete boycott on the handling of goods on Dutch vessels on their way to Netherlands East Indies ports.[119] (However, this boycott was ineffective, as Chinese and Indian labourers took over and the Dutch ships left Singapore with cargoes.[120]) Servants and chauffeurs working for the Dutch were intimidated into joining in protest action; Dutch residences were stoned.[121] A young Singapore woman, Lucy Lee, left her job with Lloyd's Insurance to offer her services to the International Red Cross for work in Indonesia.[122] Left-wing organizations in Singapore and Malaya cooperated with various Indonesian groups to recruit volunteers to fight the Dutch, provide humanitarian relief, and boycott Dutch shipping. It was decided to appeal to Western powers to intervene. Since the Dutch were supplied by American weapons and trained in Singapore, there was an excellent opportunity to criticize the Malayan government for condoning Dutch actions.[123] Surprisingly, the consulate was not itself the target of much opposition.[124]

Even the British authorities were appalled at the Dutch military action. They showed their disapproval by closing British military clubs and PX stores to Dutch military personnel, but declined to adopt more punitive measures like refusing landing rights to the Dutch airline, the KLM, as suggested by friends of the Republic in India.[125] British Foreign Secretary E. Bevin announced that supplies of materials from Singapore and British territories in Asia were suspended, and all training facilities for the Dutch were off-limits. The Dutch must have anticipated such measures because their military strength in Singapore was already scaled down considerably. Even as Bevin made his announcement, three hundred remaining Dutch troops left Singapore for Java. Only fifty Dutch soldiers were retained for military

---

[118] '"Indies war" volcanic issue, say Muslims', *Straits Times*, 2-8-1947, p. 7.
[119] 'Singapore dockers boycott Dutch vessels', *Straits Times*, 13-8-1947, p. 1.
[120] 'Labourers won't load Java-bound vessels', *Straits Times*, 6-8-1947, p. 5.
[121] PG 168, CGDN, No. 213-48, Singapore, Report by R.W. van Lier, 28-12-1948.
[122] 'Big Muslim protest meeting on Java war', *Straits Times*, 1-8-1947, p. 6.
[123] 'Singapore support for Indonesians', *Straits Times*, 28-7-1947, p. 5.
[124] Inventaris van de archieven van het Consulaat-Generaal te Singapore, 1945-54, Ministerie van Buitenlandse Zaken (MBZ) 450, Letter ('Singapore sinds de actie op Java en Sumatra') from A.M.L. Winkelman (Consul-General Singapore) to Minister of Foreign Affairs, No.16066/209, 2-8-1947.
[125] PG 169(I), Halfmaandelijksche Berichtgeving van den vertegenwoordiger der Algemeene Politie van Nederlandsch-Indie te Singapore over de periode van 1-8-1947 t/m 17-8-1947, No. 518A, Singapore 19-8-1947, by S. van Hulst, Commissaris van Politie II.

liaison work, war crimes investigations, and routine guard duty of Dutch stores. However, the shipment of Dutch-owned, British-made munitions of war continued because they had been purchased at war's end by the Dutch from Allied supply dumps in India and other parts of Asia, and stored in Singapore awaiting transshipment.[126]

More effective trade controls

The major impact of the July 1947 military action was a more effective enforcement of the trade blockade. At a very local level, even innocuous products like wood, previously shipped from the coast of Sumatra to Singapore, ceased almost immediately in August 1947. In Karimun (Riau islands), fishing was severely affected because fishermen needed ice to store their catch and they bought the ice off boats from Singapore. Such contacts were immediately cut off by news of the fighting.[127] At a more general level, the extensive array of regulations governing the import of goods instituted during the military action continued unchanged. Military-related supplies were of course prohibited, but permits were also needed for other items like machinery, instruments, steel in various forms, steel and copper wire, steel and iron pipes, oxygen, sulphur, asphalt, alcohol, vehicles, aircraft, railway material, telegraph, radio-telegraph, and telephone material, fuels and lubricants, and uniforms. Permits were also required for a whole range of exports (Yong 1982:176-7). This was all extremely disruptive and the efforts to surmount the difficulties faced by Indonesians and Chinese in Singapore will be described in later chapters. The blockade was so effective that even a mercy flight from Singapore to the encircled Republic was shot down. This led to another protest meeting at the Istana Kampong Glam. There, left-wing politicians denounced the Dutch action and praised the Indonesian struggle in the framework of the Asian struggle for self-determination.[128] Within Singapore, one rubber-processing factory shut down and thirteen others found there was little work to do as supplies of indigenous rubber were disrupted.[129] The Lieutenant Governor-General in Batavia, Van Mook, instructed his officials to stand firm. They should not be swayed by threats of a boycott led by Chinese traders in Singapore. In his view, the military action would lead to the reopening of ports. The Chinese

---

[126] 'Singapore ban on war goods to Indonesia', *Straits Times*, 31-7-1947, p. 1; 'Army club ban on Dutch', *Straits Times*, 8-8-1947, p. 1.
[127] RI 552, Tweewekelijksche berichtgeving van de Residentie Riouw over de periode 1 t/m 15-8-1947, By J. van Waardenburg, Resident, Tandjong Pinang, 28-8-1947.
[128] 'Indonesia aid gathering', *Straits Times*, 4-8-1947, p. 3.
[129] '7000 may lose jobs in Singapore because of Java war; First rubber factory shut; By Tribune staff reporter', *Malaya Tribune*, 26-8-1947, p. 1.

would benefit and they would have fewer reasons to support the Republic, but ports should not be reopened in response to threats of boycott because it would give an impression of weakness.[130]

The Second Military Action (December 1948)

Meanwhile, negotiations were being conducted to translate a Security Council ceasefire of 4 August 1947 into something more permanent. Held on board the *USS Renville* anchored off Batavia, the discussions finally resulted in the so-called Renville Agreement of 17-19 January 1948, which envisaged the formation of a federal United States of Indonesia (USI) with the Republic as one of its constituent members. The details need not be discussed in this context, except to note that for the interim period, the Republic understood that it could continue its foreign diplomatic activities. That meant business as usual for Indoff and other Indonesian groups operating in Singapore. The Renville Agreement also expressed the hope that trade links between Dutch and Republican-controlled areas could be established, but this was not accomplished. All in all, the agreement achieved little. The period of drift that followed taxed sorely what was left of Dutch patience, and on 18 December 1948, another military action – the second one – was launched, this time resulting in the arrest of the principal Republican leaders. Access to ports like Bagansiapiapi, Bengkalis, and Rengat-Tembilahan was denied, where previously there had been a lively barter trade with Singapore (Nasution 1991c:261). The various Indonesian army units retreated into the countryside to wage guerrilla warfare. All that was left of the Republic was its fighting army, an emergency government that was proclaimed in Sumatra, and, what is most important for this study, the foreign-based Indonesian organizations of which those in Singapore had crucial roles to play.

Reactions in Singapore

But, unlike the situation after the July 1947 military action, the Indonesians in Singapore were now filled with shock and bewilderment at the news of the events that were taking place back home. To begin with, the arrest of the principal Republican leaders, including Soekarno and Hatta, was rather difficult to understand for people in Singapore without access to news. The Republican capital, Yogyakarta, seemed to have fallen into Dutch hands. The Indoff spokesman, Soepardjo, denied that Yogyakarta had fallen when Indonesians flocked to Indoff for news. He admitted that near the city there

---

[130] Directie Verre Oosten 336, Memorandum from Lieutenant Governor-General (Batavia) to Chief, Directie Verre Oosten, 21-8-1947.

was heavy fighting, but Republican army units were on the brink of retaking Maguwo airport, Yogyakarta's only link with the outside world. In other places, Dutch troops were on the run now that the Indonesian forces had time to counterattack. To everyone, Soepardjo urged: 'Continue the struggle for the country. Don't give up; ultimately victory will be achieved. Do not believe Dutch propaganda.'[131] But apart from encouraging words, there was no repeat of the direct actions like demonstrations and protests and sabotage that had taken place after the July 1947 military operations. The state of emergency proclaimed by the British in Singapore earlier in June 1948 would have ruled out such expressions of political sentiments. On those occasions that might have provided a platform for expressions of anti-Dutch sentiments, there were only mild references to Indonesia, for example those made by speakers at the memorial service on 25 December 1948 for Mohamad Ali Jinnah, the founder of Pakistan. On another occasion, at a mass meeting in Jalan Besar Stadium, a speech in Arabic was delivered by Said Abdullah bin Yahya in which Muslims were called to take strong measures to support the Republic. Another speaker, Ahmad Ibrahim, the president of the Young Muslim Association, was more moderate. He described the Indonesia question as one of the difficulties facing Muslim countries.[132] Stronger, but still verbal, denunciations of the Dutch, accusing them of 'wholesale torture, murder, and butchery of defenceless civilians including women and children', invited unwelcome attention. The Dutch drew the attention of the Special Branch of the police force to such language, and the Special Branch agreed to take the necessary action[133] to prevent passions from being incited. There was some loose talk among the Chinese to boycott Dutch ships, but support for a boycott was lukewarm. According to a coolie subcontractor at the Singapore Harbour Board, workers did not even dare to use the word 'boycott' for fear that they would be arrested under the emergency regulations.[134]

The Dutch were delighted at the relatively mild response to the 1948 operations. It exceeded their wildest expectations. Even in Malaya, adverse reactions were low-key in tone. Except for the Malay left wing, which roundly condemned the Dutch military operations, the more moderate UMNO (the dominant Malay party) did not criticize the Dutch openly. In Penang, the representative of India called for joint sanctions against the Dutch throughout Southeast Asia, but his remarks were scarcely reported in the press. The Chinese press was relatively calm. Its concern was limited to

[131] PG 168, CGDN, No. 209-48, Singapore, Report by R.W. van Lier, 22-12-1948.
[132] PG 168, CGDN, No. 213-48, Singapore, Report by R.W. van Lier, 28-12-1948.
[133] PG 304, Letter from A.M.L. Winkelman, Consul General, to T. Elink Schuurman, Chef Directie Verre Oosten van het Ministerie van Buitenlandse Zaken, Batavia, No. VIII-B-2a, No.2894/28, 8-2-1949.
[134] PG 558, CGDN, No.24-49, Singapore, By P.A. van der Poel, 3-2-1949.

the immediate future of trade with Sumatra. The Dutch were confident that the influential Chinese leaders would pass a favourable verdict on the Dutch actions should the prospects of trade improve as a result of the 1948 military actions. As for the Singapore British authorities, especially the department of economic affairs, economic sanctions were frowned upon. Generally, the Dutch got the impression that the general public in Singapore and Malaya could countenance the military actions if they served to advance trade with Sumatra. Also, the state of emergency in Singapore and Malaya ensured that protest strikes, especially at the harbour, would be most unlikely,[135] a far cry from what had happened at the docks in July-August 1947.

With this rather lengthy description of the constituent groups operating in Singapore completed, it is time to advance to a discussion of the competition among these groups as they engaged the Indonesian revolution from their respective perspectives.

[135] *Officiële bescheiden*, XVI: 443-4.

CHAPTER IV

Competition between Indonesians in Singapore

Far from cooperating with one another, the multitude of political, trading, and smuggling groups remained an uncoordinated mass of diverse organizations, each seemingly bent on the pursuit of its own goals. The stakes were high. The security and the interests of the newly independent Republic were paramount. However, in the cut and thrust of disputes and acrimonious arguments among the Indonesians in Singapore, it was difficult to deny that the competing groups were also concerned about the immeasurable benefits of being recognized as the most representative of Republican interests in Singapore. Cooperation often seemed to be forgotten as the various Indonesian organizations in Singapore vied with each other for control of one or other of the lucrative areas of business, both legal and illegal, between Indonesia and Singapore.

Political leadership

In the context of Singapore, it was important for an organization claiming to represent the Indonesian community to maintain a high profile. Operating in a foreign country without the accoutrements of an armed force or the assistance of the mass media meant that a prominent posture had to be adopted in order to draw the loyalties and political recognition of the local Indonesian population. At the same time, a high profile with a large following would attract the attention of Republican authorities scattered all over the archipelago (especially those in Sumatra) and assure continuous supplies of raw materials to provide the wherewithal to advance the cause of the Republic.

The PKBI-PI and Indoff exemplified this tendency to compete with one another, often to the point of cut-throat rivalry. The political leadership claimed by Indoff was not uncontested even though it was an arm of the Ministry of Foreign Affairs that, in turn, was an agency of the central government. The Republic of Indonesia during the period 1945-1949 was often a hydra-headed animal, each part with a mind and a method all its own.

The PKBI-PI was totally against Indoff. Before Indoff appeared on the scene, all the signs indicated that the PKBI was recognized as the representative of Indonesians in Singapore whenever there was mention of Republican agencies abroad. Tobing felt that he had led his organization in the frontline defending the Republic in Singapore and deserved that status. The PKBI-PI, he maintained, was the pioneer of all Indonesian organizations in Malaya. The organization had many accomplishments to its name and had accumulated much respect for the Republic. Considerable propaganda work had been carried out to publicize the Indonesian cause overseas, including Russia. The organization had even urged the British government to repatriate Dutch troops from Singapore and close the Dutch camps. It also sent photographs of examples of Dutch cruelty in Indonesia to Russia, and the Russian delegates at the United Nations used these photographs to condemn the Dutch. When the situation in Indonesia became even more critical, the PKBI-PI contacted left-wing leaders in England who were prepared to send a commission to Indonesia to undertake an on-the-spot inspection. Letters to that effect were received by the PKBI-PI. Tobing claimed that when these documents were shown to Oetoyo, the latter refused them point-blank, saying that they were of no value. It was from experiences such as these that Tobing ceased to trust Oetoyo.[1]

The ill feelings between Oetoyo and Tobing were intensified by the fact that Tobing was never taken seriously by Oetoyo and his colleagues. To them, Tobing had only 'nuisance value'.[2] It was therefore important to both the PKBI-PI and Indoff to monopolize the symbolic expressions of Republicanness.

Independence Day celebrations

One of these symbols was readily found in the annual celebrations to commemorate the 17 August 1945 declaration of independence. Seemingly petty matters like who should organize the event, where it should be held, or what people should attend such a function all suddenly assumed an importance quite beyond normal expectations.

The 1946 celebrations were quiet and tame, leading to little contention or rivalry. Indoff had not yet been founded. The field was wide open for interested parties to profess their allegiance to the Republic in any way they pleased. A committee was set up. It had ambitious plans. Attempts were made to hire

[1] PG 304, No. 276/G/III, Letter from S. van Hulst, Secretaris voor Speciale Diensten, to Procureur-Generaal, 4-11-1948.
[2] Interview with Darusman in Jakarta, 20-3-1992.

IV Competition between Indonesians in Singapore

Victoria Memorial Hall and invite foreign diplomats, including the Dutch consul. These plans did not materialize and the 1946 celebrations were held on a more modest scale. The city itself was not bedecked with the Republican red-and-white flag.[3] The celebrations began with a meeting in the morning presided by Bizar Ahmad, the president of Perkabim. A few others also attended. There was a delegate called Badoet Soepardjo. Then there was Mahjudin, who was the father of the local Malay leader Gaus. Mohd Samin Chaidir was a representative from the Riau islands. Abd Ghany represented the Ali Jinnah South Indian Muslim League. A representative called Sjafei came from Borneo, and there was one other person called Bachtiar Effendi. The presence of diverse individuals suggests that the dividing lines between the various groups that had sprouted in Singapore were not yet distinct. Attendance at the evening reception held at the Istana (former palace of the old Johore sultans from the pre-British era) in Kampong Glam was good. One of the committee organizers, Rashid Manggis, gave a speech describing the oppression of the Dutch. Representatives of non-Indonesian organizations that were sympathetic to the Republican cause also attended the reception. Considering the wide cross-section of people and groups represented at the celebrations, it was quite an achievement. One of those present was Taharoeddin Ahmad, who later joined Indoff to work with Oetoyo. He submitted a proposal that the organizing committee should be transformed into a political organization called the Komite Indonesia Merdeka. This was not accepted, apparently because Taharoeddin's overbearing attitude alienated many supporters.[4]

What was significant about the 1946 celebrations? Based on contemporary reports, the general impression was that the celebrations were a makeshift affair, as different groups coalesced to organize an event. At the time, it was little more than that. There has been some attempt to impute significance to the choice of the Istana at Kampong Glam to hold part of the celebrations. According to this interpretation,[5] the Istana at Kampong Glam was a historic spot in the Malaysian world. There, under the minarets of the nearby Sultan mosque and in the shadow of the old palace of the ancient Riau Sultanate, the echoes of the old Malay Empire of Johore could be heard again. Such an interpretation would imply there were attempts to use the Republic to restore the old Johore Empire. However, in 1946, it was more likely that the celebration was cobbled together merely to commemorate the Republic's declaration of independence and the Istana offered a central venue.

---

3 RI 551, Tweewekelijksche berichtgeving der Residentie Riouw over de periode 16 t/m 31-7-1946, By J. van Waardenburg, Resident, Tandjong Pinang, 6-8-1946.
4 RI 551, Tweewekelijksche berichtgeving der Residentie Riouw over de periode 16 t/m 31-8-1946, By J. van Waardenburg, Resident, Tandjong Pinang 10-9-1946. For a brief description of the 1946 celebrations, see also Nasution 1977:486.
5 'Kampong Glam and Java', *Straits Times*, 4-9-1946, p. 4.

By the time of the 1947 celebrations, Indoff had come to adopt a high-profile posture in Singapore. The occasion started with a mass meeting at the Kampong Glam palace. Six hundred people attended. The proceedings began with a military drill by members of the various organizations instrumental in the revolutionary struggle in Indonesia. Next, the Indonesian flag was raised and those present sang the national anthem. There were prayers for the fallen and for those still fighting in the Indonesian army. The declaration of independence of 17 August was then read, followed by speeches. These were sufficiently belligerent. The chairman for the occasion was Gaus, a Malay leader who was prominent in the local community in Singapore. Undoubtedly, he was chosen to encourage the Malay community to identify with the Indonesian struggle. The venue of the celebrations was also chosen to achieve maximum impact. Gaus rallied the crowd by saying: 'Ours is a life-and-death struggle. We must not only drive the Dutch from Indonesia but also expel them from the whole of Asia. Indonesians must participate actively in this struggle and talk less.' Oetoyo, who represented Indoff, called upon every Indonesian living outside Indonesia to be loyal to the Republican government. Reiterating that the struggle for independence began with the youth movement, he called upon the youths that were present to be prepared to give their lives if necessary to the cause of the Indonesian flag.[6] The language used by the speakers was strong, but when the fire and brimstone had subsided, the meeting ended with a whimper. Gaus presented a set of resolutions that Oetoyo promised to forward to the Indonesian government.[7] The proceedings ended on an amiable note with a tea party held at Kita Restaurant opposite the mosque.[8] There were no indications that the PKBI-PI attended the celebrations or organized their own separate activities.

The 1948 celebrations were held at Oetoyo's house (5 Elliot Road in Siglap district in the eastern part of Singapore) and this clearly made it impossible for PKBI-PI members to attend (*Rahsia perdjuangan* 1948:120). By that year, rivalry between the PKBI-PI and Indoff had taken a turn for the worse, and there was no putting aside differences to celebrate a common cause. The Indoff-sponsored celebrations featured a flag-raising ceremony, the singing of the national anthem, and the reading of the declaration of independence. These were all major icons of the revolution. These were followed by a moment's silence in remembrance of the fallen. On that day, 17 August 1948, all Indonesian households also flew the Republican flag (Nasution 1991a:

---

[6] PG 173, Rapport van den Inlichtingendienst der Algemeene Politie (Singapore), No. 519GE, Singapore, By S. van Hulst, 20-8-1947.
[7] PG 173, Rapport van den Inlichtingendienst der Algemeene Politie (Singapore), No. 519GE, Singapore, By S. van Hulst, 20-8-1947.
[8] PG 170(I), Letter 715/4/xvii, dated 3-9-1947, from A. Wahab of 511-J, Kampong Batak, Jalan Eunos, Singapore, to M. Ali, Overseas Association of Indonesians and Malayans.

586). The festivities at Oetoyo's house attracted some two to three thousand participants, some arriving twelve hours before the festivities began. However, as PKBI-PI sources were quick to point out, British and American representatives were conspicuously absent (*Rahsia perdjuangan* 1948:134). By August 1948, relations between Indoff and the Singapore authorities had experienced a downturn. This differed starkly from the previous year, 1947, when Lord Killearn had extended a warm welcome to Sjahrir when he passed through Singapore; the British in Singapore also applied many restrictions to curb the privileges of Dutch military officers after the Dutch Military Action in Java of July 1947. Such was not the case any more in 1948. The Dutch security organization, Netherlands Forces Intelligence Service (NEFIS), had begun exchanging information with the Malayan Security Service on communists, nationalists, smugglers, and journalists operating through Singapore.[9] Republican passports issued by Indoff were no longer recognized. British colonial authorities were also increasingly concerned about the effects of the continuing conflict in Indonesia on the Malays in the peninsula. All of this influenced the decision of British officials to downplay their connections with Indoff activities, and diplomatic representatives from other nations including the United States followed suit (*Rahsia perdjuangan* 1948:135-6). Apart from these diplomatic problems, those attending must have been greatly satisfied because they were treated to Indonesian dances, stage plays, cocktails, and a buffet dinner.[10]

The 1949 celebrations were also held at Oetoyo's house. A cocktail party was held but there was considerable disagreement whether the Indonesian community in Singapore or Indoff should take charge and who should provide the funds. These were important matters by 1949. As will be shown, Indoff had been reduced to dire straits by then, strangled by the Dutch economic blockade of Republican territories and faced with an increasingly unfriendly British host in Singapore. The fact that the fortunes of the PKBI-PI and other Indonesian organizations in Singapore were not better was poor comfort to Indoff. They made little difference to the practical difficulties that Indoff faced in trying to project its image as the representative of Republican interests in Singapore.[11]

---

9   A state of emergency had been proclaimed in the Federation of Malaya in June 1948 to curb communist activities, and in Singapore police maintained a very high state of vigilance. In fact, twenty Indonesians – believed to be communists – were arrested on the eve of the third anniversary of the Indonesian Republic. Those arrested would be banished. 'Indonesian Reds held', *Straits Times*, 18-8-1948, p. 5.
10   'Indonesians mark anniversary today', *Straits Times*, 17-8-1948, p. 7.
11   PG 556, CGDN, No. 111-49, Singapore, Report by P.A. van der Poel, 15-7-1949; PG 556, CGDN, No. 113-49, Singapore, Report by P.A. van der Poel, 22-7-1949; PG 556, CGDN, No. 116-49, Singapore, Report by P.A. van der by Poel, 2-8-1949; PG 556; CGDN, No. 117-49, Singapore, Report by P.A. van der Poel, 6-8-1949.

As agent provocateur

Although the symbols and trappings of office were important, Indonesian organizations operating in Singapore were also expected to prove by their actions that they were working in the interests of the Republic. Since the Republic was struggling for its existence in fighting the Dutch, one important field of endeavour would be propaganda and infiltration in areas where Dutch influence was relatively strong. Such activities could not easily be carried out by organizations like Indoff that purported to be an official diplomatic representation. But there were no restrictions on the PKBI-PI and this advantage was quickly exploited.

Before July 1947 (when Dutch military actions circumscribed its activities), the PKBI-PI, or PKBI as it was then known, was able to launch propaganda forays into the Riau islands. This place was probably chosen because it was the closest to Singapore where the Dutch had managed to establish some sort of presence, and because communication by sea with those islands was relatively easy. At Tanjung Uban in the Riau islands, the PKBI-PI tried to do some propaganda work for the Republic. It met with little support from the local Riau population but managed to touch a sympathetic chord among the Javanese and Bataks living there. One Javanese by the name of Seno even spread the news that a Republican army unit was preparing to launch an attack on the Riau islands in October or November 1946. When arrested, he confessed that his information and propaganda materials came from the PKBI-PI.[12] The PKBI-PI in fact toyed with the idea of organizing an attack on the Riau islands. As part of this plan, it was intended to send agents from Singapore to Tanjung Pinang, Dabo, and Tanjung Balai. This infiltration would be coordinated with an attack by the Republican army from Sumatra. The plans remained plans. The PKBI-PI did not embark on any action of substance, as the leaders realized that such actions would surely offend the British.[13] However, in the course of 1946, the PKBI-PI was reported to have recruited and sent around two hundred youths to various parts of Sumatra for service in the Republican army. Most of the recruits ended up in Selat Panjang, and others at Pakan Baru, Tembilahan, Jambi, Palembang, and Medan. These youths had previous experience serving in paramilitary groups during the Japanese occupation.[14]

In Singapore itself, the PKBI-PI leader, Tobing, tried to start a printing

---

[12] RI 551, Tweewekelijksche berichtgeving der Residentie Riouw over de periode 16 t/m 31-8-1946, By J. van Waardenburg, Resident, Tandjong Pinang, 10-9-1946.
[13] RI 551, Tweewekelijksche berichtgeving der Residentie Riouw over de periode 15 t/m 31-10-1946, By L.B. van Straten, Assistent-Resident I, Singapore, 31-10-1946.
[14] RI 551, Tweewekelijksche berichtgeving der Residentie Riouw over de periode 1 t/m 15-12-1946, By J. van Waardenburg, Resident at Tandjong Pinang, 27-12-1946.

IV Competition between Indonesians in Singapore 73

house for a daily paper called *De Jure*. Appropriately, a *'de jure'* status was the legal title of recognition sought by the Republic.[15] This he hoped to do with funds from the sale of goods brought over from Palembang. He also had plans to establish an organization of volunteers called the Barisan Istimewa (Special Forces) to fight against the enemies of the Republic in Malaya and Singapore, and as a step in that direction he decided to start a scout movement.[16] Dutch intelligence in Singapore associated the activities of the PKBI-PI with those of the so-called 'extremist' elements who were mainly identified as Batak in ethnic origin, as was Tobing, the leader of the PKBI-PI. Houses in Kampong Glam and Lorong 17 (Geylang), both Malay precincts, were well-known recruitment centres. There was even a secret society called the Gadjah Hitam (Black Elephant) that threatened retaliation against the Perkabim and others of Minangkabau origin if they continued their anti-PKBI-PI agitation.[17]

Although these activities may have been conducted in secret, they raised the stakes for leadership of the Indonesian community in Singapore and gave the PKBI-PI the opportunity to be confirmed as the vanguard of the revolutionary struggle there. Although the substantive results of these actions may be called into dispute (since some of the figures quoted above may be erroneous or exaggerated), the point is that recruitment to advance the Republican cause was an ongoing activity in Singapore and the PKBI-PI was deeply involved.[18]

The champion of welfare

One reason for the establishment of Indonesian organizations in Singapore was to give assistance to compatriots in need. The nature of these needs took many forms, but not surprisingly, those in need, especially those who had

---

[15] RI 551, Tweewekelijksche berichtgeving der Residentie Riouw over de periode 16 t/m 30-9-1946, By P.A. van der Poel, Commissaris van Politie I on 1-10-1946.
[16] RI 551, Tweewekelijksche berichtgeving der Residentie Riouw over de periode 1 t/m 15-10-1946, Singapore, 16-10-1946.
[17] RI 551, Tweewekelijksche berichtgeving der Residentie Riouw over de periode 1 t/m 15-7-1946, By J. van Waardenburg, Resident at Tandjong Pinang, 23-7-1946.
[18] It should be noted that the TRI (Tentera Repoeblik Indonesia) also attempted direct recruitment in Singapore. A First Lieutenant Hoetabarat, from the TRI at Pakan Baru, arrived in Singapore in October 1946 and canvassed for volunteers. Application forms were not openly distributed but particulars of candidates were recorded. There was no specific place that was used as a recruitment centre but it was known that a tailor shop in Bussorah Street in Kampong Glam served this purpose. A total of 68 applicants responded. See RI 551, Tweewekelijksche berichtgeving der Residentie Riouw over de periode 15 t/m 31-10-1946, By L.B. van Straten, Assistent-Resident I, Singapore 31-10-1946.

just arrived, tended to seek assistance from those who preceded them. In Singapore, there were Indonesians who were indigent; there were also individuals representing various Indonesian regional authorities who thought help should be available from Indonesian organizations.

As an organization representing a central government agency, Indoff had its fair share of supplicants knocking at its doors for help. A typical instance was on 25 March 1948 when two Bataks (Simorangkir and Sitoemorang) visited Oetoyo at his residence and demanded $10,000 for the 'struggle outside the Republic'. There was a fierce exchange of words and the Bataks eventually left empty-handed, but not before giving Oetoyo a warning that he had to produce the money in four days. The next day, on 26 March, it was reported that Daroesman called on Tobing to mediate but Tobing refused. The matter would have been left on the shelf if not for the fact that some days later, Oetoyo received a package through the post from an unknown sender containing a portion of human waste.[19] Oetoyo also had to attend to requests for loans from Sumatran leaders. There seemed to be the impression that Indoff was a golden goose and that it would be in a position to help indigent Indonesian leaders. The *wedana* of Indragiri Hilir in Sumatra wrote to Oetoyo asking for a loan of $12,000, not realizing that Indoff did not have such funds.[20]

To the ordinary Indonesian in Singapore, it was assumed that providing assistance was a principal activity of any government representation like Indoff, and it was in this area that Oetoyo appears to have fallen far short of the ideal. The local Indonesian community, instead of finding Indoff a source of help, came to regard Indoff only as a place to obtain permits and passports. According to the PKBI-PI, indigent and destitute Indonesians were neglected by Indoff and had to suffer the indignity of being caught by the Singapore police before being sent to a prison in Outram Road for further processing. Oetoyo, however, reported to Hatta, the Republic's vice-president, that all Indonesian vagrants were either repatriated or had found employment (*Rahsia perdjuangan* 1948:111-3). As for passports, it was not long before the British authorities in Singapore decided to withdraw recognition of those documents issued by Indoff that were previously valid for entry into Singapore (*Rahsia perdjuangan* 1948:115-7). As a result, of course, there was a lot of inconvenience. Residents of Bawean who used to come to Singapore to trade or to visit their relatives now could not land (*Rahsia perdjuangan* 1948: 119). The PKBI-PI expected Indoff to 'do something' and was naturally disappointed when nothing could be done. In contrast, as noted by the PKBI-PI,

---

[19] PG 168, CGDN, No. 85-48, Singapore, Report by S. van Hulst, 5-4-1948.
[20] PG 304, Letter from Dr R. Oetoyo, 3-C, Raffles Place Singapore, to Jamal Lako Soetan, *wedana* Indragiri Hilir, Tembilahan, 11-12-1947.

IV Competition between Indonesians in Singapore

there were other leaders in Singapore that did try to resolve the issue. These included Sjarifoeddin Adam, the chairman of the Malay Seamen's Union in Singapore, who wrote to Malay and English newspapers to plead the case for those who had come from afar but could not land in Singapore. Sa'adon bin Haji Zubir, a Singapore Legislative Council member, and Thaha Kalu, chairman of the Malay Nationalist Party in Singapore, also tried to resolve the passport issue (*Rahsia perdjuangan* 1948:119).

In one of the few encounters between Oetoyo and the Indonesian public in Singapore that are on record, Oetoyo's caution and guarded reluctance to commit Indoff to some degree of charity work became very evident. At a meeting on 3 April 1947, convened especially to enable Oetoyo to meet Indonesians in Singapore as well as to provide an opportunity for local Indonesians to ask questions of the Republican representative, Oetoyo cut a poor figure because his answers were very vague. The dialogue session included questions and answers such as the following.

Q: What is the difference in status between Indonesians in the Republic and those living outside [Republican territories]?
A: No difference, except that those living outside the Republic are more free to conduct trade.
Q: Will Borneo be incorporated in the Republic?
A: That is still being considered.
Q: Are the Baweans within the jurisdiction of the Republic?
A: I believe so.
Q: What about establishing an Indonesian consulate or something similar in order to serve local Indonesians?
A: This is being considered.
Q: Will Riau and Banka be incorporated in the Republic?
A: This is still being discussed.[21]

The weak PR image led to the feeling that nothing much could be expected of Indoff. Gaus, the Indonesian leader resident in Singapore, decided to form another organization that attempted to compensate for the shortcomings of Indoff. He called it Panitia Penolong Kemerdekaan Indonesia, or Committee of Supporters of Indonesian Independence. According to Gaus, the organization would also provide an alternative for those Indonesians who advocated more extremist actions than what the existing organizations were prepared to tolerate. If not for the Committee, Gaus argued, the excesses of extremists would not be controlled and would lead to a clampdown by British authorities. The programme of the Committee would include sending resolutions to friendly foreign governments, holding mass meetings, and collecting

---

[21] PG 173, Rapport van den Inlichtingendienst der Algemeene Politie Riouw (RIAPR), No. 364, Singapore, By S. van Hulst, 8-4-1947.

medicine for the Republican population.²² If Gaus thought he was going to be more effective than Indoff, he was in for a disappointment. His attempts to organize a mass meeting came to nothing when the British colonial secretary denied his request for a permit submitted on 20 January 1949.²³ The Committee was also never successful in its application for registration, and in the end, Gaus advised his supporters to abandon the organization.²⁴

The ability or willingness of Indoff to dole out support of any kind must be weighed in conjunction with its mandate. What kind of function was it supposed to exercise? When it was first founded, Indoff could have been conceived as a general political representative and mouthpiece of the Republic in Singapore, but as circumstances changed, it became necessary to review its priorities. Later, when British authorities suspected Indoff of engaging in clandestine activities like opium smuggling or when the control of weapons became urgent because of the proclamation of a state of emergency in Malaya in 1948, Indoff was required to review its role in Singapore. Some indication of the changes forced upon Indoff is the revelation given by Oetoyo himself after a visit to Yogyakarta in 1948 that Indoff should refocus its role to give priority to its economic interests.²⁵ The Indonesians in Singapore were therefore not at all satisfied with Indoff since they could not expect counsel or support from the organization.

A pan-Indonesia organization

Reports of the outbreak of the revolution in the various parts of the Indonesian archipelago invariably assumed an ethnic dimension. This is quite understandable in view of the fact that particular ethnic groups tended to dominate the leadership of various regions. Ethnicity was also an important issue for the Indonesian groups operating in Singapore, but there, the approaches to this issue were twofold.

On the one hand, there were organizations like Indoff that wanted to project a pan-Indonesia image and could not afford to run the risk of exclusively serving the interests of any one ethnic group. Thus the ethnic issue was far from the minds of Indoff leaders.²⁶ Indeed, the leadership of Indoff was made up of people of diverse ethnic groups. Oetoyo was Javanese but

---

[22] PG 558, CGDN, No. 14-49, Singapore, By S. van Hulst, 17-1-1949.
[23] PG 558, CGDN, No. 24-49, Singapore, By P.A. van der Poel, 3-2-1949.
[24] PG 558, CGDN, No. 40-49, Singapore, By P.A. van der Poel, 25-2-1949.
[25] PG 304, Letter 157/H/I, from S. van Hulst, Secretaris voor Speciale Diensten, to the Procureur-Generaal, 20-10-1948.
[26] In the interview of 20-3-1992, Darusman denied that ethnicity was of any concern in Indoff. He did not think it was important even among the Indonesians in Singapore.

his wife was Dutch. Daroesman's father was West Javanese but he was born in West Sumatra and later married a woman from South Borneo. He grew up in various parts of Indonesia. Given the mixed composition of its leadership, it was therefore not in Indoff's interests to stress the ethnic dimension.

On the other hand, most of the other Indonesian organizations in Singapore were quite dissimilar because they were often unashamedly identified with particular ethnic groups. In the Singapore context, especially by mid-September 1947, with the Dutch blockade of the Java coast, the Sumatrans had come to play a dominant role among the Indonesians in Singapore. Of the Sumatrans, the most important were the Minangs and the Bataks. Between these two groups, there seemed to be some rivalry. Reports about these Indonesian ethnic groups in Singapore did not agree on which group was more influential. The Acehnese were more active in Penang. With links between Singapore and Java cut off or severely impeded, the logical alternative was to use the Sumatra-Singapore connections, and this inevitably advanced the importance of the Sumatran ethnic groups.[27]

The PKBI-PI was quick to exploit the issue of ethnicity. Itself a predominantly Sumatran (Batak) organization, it accused Indoff of being a Javanese outfit and could not understand how its ethnic bias could be tolerated. It was conceded that there were a couple of Minangs in Indoff but most were Javanese. Oetoyo himself was accused of having described the Minangs as 'not sincere' and the Tapanuli as 'too stubborn'.[28] Tobing was not alone in pointing an accusing finger at Indoff. Ethnic bias was a *cause celebre* that easily aroused indignation or anger. The Bawean people, an important Indonesian business community in Singapore, also decided that their own federation, Persatuan Bawean Singapore, should not have anything more to do with Oetoyo.[29]

International recognition

Recognition by the world of the standing of an organization based in Singapore was a prize well worth working towards. If the PKBI-PI wanted to acquire the status of being the representative Indonesian organization in Singapore, it was necessary to advertise its name to foreign countries. Thus it made active forays into the world of diplomacy.

It did this by writing letters to many world leaders to explain the

---

[27] RI 552, Tweewekelijksche berichtgeving van de Residentie Riouw over de periode 1 t/m 15 Sept., By J. van Waardenburg, Resident, Tandjong Pinang, 29-9-1947. See also *Officiële bescheiden*, VII: 609.
[28] PG 304, No. 276/G/III, Letter from S. van Hulst, Secretaris voor Speciale Diensten, to Procureur-Generaal, 4-11-1948.
[29] PG 558, CGDN, No. 6-49, Singapore, R.W. van Lier, 7-1-1949.

Republican cause. Usually, complaints about Dutch abuses were listed, and there was satisfaction when notes of acknowledgement were received (*Rahsia perdjuangan* 1948:60-7). Hence telegrams were sent to foreign powers with which there had been no previous links. If an answer or even an acknowledgement was received, political mileage was gained[30] and much made of. The PKBI-PI executive was so carried away by the attention it thought world leaders were giving to Indonesia that even a standard acquisition request from the library of the University of California (Berkeley) for copies of its publication was displayed as evidence of its international renown (*Rahsia perdjuangan* 1948:69). But there was probably little substance in its efforts and few results to show, so that as far as using Singapore as a base to make international contacts, the achievements of the PKBI-PI were probably hollow.

For Indoff, international recognition was not a difficult problem at first. The British welcomed its presence. Generally, many countries in the world were sympathetic towards the Republican cause and since Indoff was a central government agency, at least tacit recognition was forthcoming. The international stature of Indoff was considerably enhanced when Republican leaders stayed in Singapore on their way to international meetings. Such visits provided photo opportunities to show Indoff as visibly identified as a legitimate organization within the Republican struggle. In April 1947, Prime Minister Sjahrir arrived in Singapore at the inconvenient time of 03.25 hours on his way to India, but was nevertheless welcomed by twenty Indonesian and Malay residents with cries of 'merdeka'. On his return journey, thousands of Indonesians and Malays flocked to the airport. One report gives a figure of thirty thousand people who declared a holiday from work to welcome Sjahrir.[31] Although there were no press reports on the role played by Oetoyo in the welcoming reception, a speech by Gaus expressing the importance of Malay-Indonesian cooperation[32] was a common refrain repeated by Oetoyo in his speeches elsewhere.

Other Republican leaders who passed through Singapore included Hadji Agoes Salim, who was returning to Batavia from the United Nations Assembly at Geneva.[33] A.K. Gani, in his capacity as Republican deputy prime minister, passed through on his way to Havana to attend a conference on international trade.[34] Even after Sjahrir resigned as prime minister, he con-

---

[30] RI 551, Tweewekelijksche berichtgeving der Residentie Riouw over de periode 16 t/m 31-7-1946, By J. van Waardenburg, Resident, Tandjong Pinang, 6-8-1946.
[31] 'Big Singapore welcome for Dr Sutan Sharir; Premier gives 3-min press conference; By Tribune staff reporter', *Malaya Tribune*, 10-4-1947, p. 5.
[32] 'Sjahrir passes through Singapore', *Straits Times*, 1-4-1947, p. 1; 'Singapore welcomes Shahrir; Premier tells of Indonesia's aims', *Straits Times*, 10-4-1947, p. 1.
[33] 'Indonesian minister in Singapore', *Straits Times*, 21-10-1947, p. 1.
[34] 'Indonesian Vice-Premier in Singapore', *Straits Times*, 11-11-1947, p. 3; 'Indonesian Vice-Premier in Singapore; "Republic needs foreign capital"', *Straits Times*, 12-11-1947, p. 4.

IV Competition between Indonesians in Singapore

tinued to visit Singapore on his way to United Nations discussions (as in July and December 1947). There was always a lot of publicity from photograph sessions and news conferences. Furthermore, it was newsworthy that he was invited by Lord Killearn to stay at the latter's residence at Bukit Serene in Johore Bahru.[35] Generally, Indoff was actively involved in preparations to assist passing delegations (*Memoar pejuang* 1992:23-5).

During the dark days of 1949, the PKBI-PI held a meeting to debate Tobing's idea of promoting the struggle for Indonesian's independence beyond Singapore to those countries that were favourably disposed towards the Republic. Tobing proposed to make a tour, ending up in the United States.[36] But these attempts to gain international recognition took place in the abstract. Letters written, letters received, and visits reflected the status desired. All organizations in Singapore could aspire to this kind of status, but the litmus test lay in the extent to which the documents issued by these organizations carried any authority and influence in international transactions. The most critical of these documents were the passports that were actually issued by at least three different groups within Singapore between 1945 and 1947. The state of affairs was rather messy. Although there was widespread acceptance in Singapore of the idea that Dutch passports should be rejected, it was not clear which office should be the authority to issue the Republic of Indonesia passport. In 1946, both the PKBI and Perkabim issued passports on their own authority. In the Republican territories, some areas (for example Pakan Baru) accepted the PKBI passports, while others (for example Tanjung Balai) recognized the Perkabim documents. The confusion deepened when the Dutch declared that neither the PKBI nor the Perkabim passports were recognized in Tanjung Pinang, Rengat, and several other places (Nasution 1977:313). Up till 1947, the passports issued by the PKBI-PI still enjoyed *de facto* recognition (Nasution 1978b:436).

The stakes were high for all the Indonesian groups in Singapore. Those stakes were also sufficiently numerous and varied that there was room for one Indonesian group to excel in some, leaving others to fill the gaps. It was not a world of monopoly in Singapore, although the game plan for each player was to work towards one. The following chapters explore the strategies used in this contest of high stakes.

---

[35] 'Shahrir arrives in Singapore', *Straits Times*, 3-12-1947, p. 1.
[36] PG 558, CGDN, No. 83-49, Singapore, Report by P.A. van der Poel, 4-5-1949.

CHAPTER V
Contest for influence

Given the multitude of persons and organizations in Singapore all claiming to act on behalf of the Republic, it is only to be expected that the range of methods used to achieve their respective goals was extensive. This chapter attempts to detail some of the methods that were openly employed, leaving for separate discussion some of those that were clandestine.

Accusations and counter-accusations

There is little doubt that Oetoyo and Indoff received official recognition but that was not enough. In the fierce competition for influence and accreditation among the Indonesians residing in Singapore, Oetoyo faced an uphill task. To achieve that, the obvious step to take was to respond to the needs of the Indonesians, and chief among these was the dire pecuniary deprivation faced by some. However, Indoff was itself strapped for cash, and anyway, there is no evidence that Oetoyo viewed his organization as a welfare institution. The British authorities in Singapore also sensed this reluctance or inability to help. By 1949, any matters concerning indigence among Indonesians in Singapore were referred to the Netherlands consulate[1] and not brought to the attention of Indoff.

In support of its claim to represent and advance the interests of the Republic, Indoff was of course responsible for finding ways and means to undermine the influence of the Dutch. However, because it was an official organization, there were limits to the kinds of action it could take.

Examples could be cited. Indoff faced a credibility gap. It was committed to upholding Sjahrir's diplomatic negotiations with the Dutch, including bearing the burden of explaining why the route taken was so pockmarked with potholes. In contrast, the PKBI-PI simply refused to support the negotiations that ultimately led to the Linggajati Agreement because it declared it could not trust the promises of the Dutch as colonialists (Nasution 1978a:316).

---

[1] PG 558, CGDN, No. 91-49, Singapore, Report by P.A. van der Poel, 25-5-1949.

As an official organization, Indoff also experienced difficulties dealing with individuals. Many individuals with good intentions would seek the help of Indoff with plans of their own to undermine Dutch authority, but Indoff could not accede to all such demands for assistance. Mohamad Mustaza was one such individual nationalist who approached Oetoyo sometime before March 1948 and asked for financial assistance to start an underground movement in Singapore. The purpose of his movement was to weaken the British should they support the Dutch. Oetoyo refused to have any part in it, replying that funds were not available for such an undertaking.[2]

Therefore, in his dealings with individuals, Oetoyo was left with projecting himself as one who could give political guidance but not material assistance. He eventually found himself skating on thin ice in his relations with the British, who were the ultimate arbiters of power in Singapore. When relations with the British were friendly, as they were before 1948, Oetoyo largely had a free hand. But in that year, circumstances changed. The communist threat of armed rebellion loomed in Malaya, and British authorities in Singapore began to frown on overtly political activities conducted by groups that maintained external links. The support the British gave to Oetoyo declined when the communist threat to their position in Malaya became more explicit. Increasingly, British relations with the Dutch in Singapore began to warm because the two colonial powers had come to share information about the movement of communist cadres within the archipelago.[3] The British came to fear external interference in the internal affairs of Malaya.

It was this fear that Oetoyo unwittingly aroused when, on 9 April 1948, he declared in Kuala Lumpur that there should be no objections to Indonesians in Malaya taking part in local politics, including making demands for citizenship. His opponents sensed an opportunity to discredit Oetoyo. Alarmed that the British might crackdown on their activities, they argued that such advice, if taken, would make Indonesians suspect in the eyes of the British. And if caught dabbling in Malayan politics, they would be arrested, detained, and surrendered to the Netherlands East Indies government, and not Indoff, to handle.[4] Then again, in the same month, while preparing for the opening of an Indoff branch in Penang, Oetoyo is reported to have said: 'I hope Indonesians living in Malaya will regard Malays as people of Indonesia, because this is one way to attract them to the Republic's cause. Malaya is part of the Republic' (*Indonesian intentions* 1964:6). Such advice was given in an attempt to project Indoff as the representative of the Republic, but it immediately backfired because it was ill timed and could be easily misunder-

---

[2] PG 168, CGDN, No. 185-48, Singapore, Report by R.W. van Lier, 2-11-1948.
[3] *Officiële bescheiden*, VII:415.
[4] PG 168, CGDN, No. 97-48, Report by S. van Hulst, 17-4-1948.

stood. Indoff issued a clarification, explaining that Oetoyo might have been misrepresented. His statement was not directed at those Indonesians who had been living in Malaya for generations and who regarded Malaya as their home.[5] Their credentials as genuine Malayans would not be suspect despite any pro-Republican sentiments they might harbour.

Opponents of Oetoyo exploited the bad publicity over his ill-considered statement. The issue whether Indonesians residing in Singapore and Malaya should participate in politics (in Malaya or Indonesia) had been in the minds of many. There were some Indonesians who had resided in Malaya for years and who felt they had a right to take part in Malayan politics. Others were fearful they would antagonize the British colonial authorities. Oetoyo's statement, made in 1948 when Malaya was under siege by communists and threatened with violence, caused even more confusion – a point that was exploited by his opponents (*Rahsia perdjuangan* 1948:139-43).

The British authorities in Malaya were also embarrassed. An ordinary person without Oetoyo's standing would have risked arrest under the state of emergency that was then in force. At the first opportunity, the British consul-general in Jakarta complained to the Republican foreign minister, Hadji Agoes Salim, who called for a report on the incident. The primary sources are silent on the precise response from the Republican side, but the fact that Oetoyo continued to serve could be interpreted as insufficient justification for any stiff measure against him.[6]

On the flip side of Indoff's attempts to claim official status were the attacks launched against it by its opponents, principally the PKBI-PI. However, it is necessary at the outset to stress that the PKBI-PI itself was not a monolithic or homogeneous organization in opposing Indoff, and one principal bone of contention within the PKBI-PI was how to conduct relations with that body. Its members were divided over the right of the president, Tobing, to decide on inter-organizational relations that affected them. Others felt that the bad feelings between the PKBI-PI and Indoff could be eliminated if another person replaced Tobing as president.[7] Resentment towards the aggressive confrontation strategy of Tobing had been aroused back in 1948. At a meeting on 15 August that year, a group of younger members led by Martinus Indra in fact captured the PKBI-PI leadership from Tobing.[8] This unexpected result was possible because the meeting was only moderately attended and most of the attendees were not influential in the PKBI-PI. Martinus Indra therefore

---

[5] PG 304, *Utusan Melayu*, 16-4-1948.
[6] FO 810/20, 'Report on visit to Indonesian Republic' by British Consul-General (F.M. Shepherd) in Jakarta, 13-9-1948.
[7] PG 558, CGDN, No. 24-49, Singapore, By P.A. van der Poel, 3-2-1949.
[8] PG 304, No. 276/G/III, Letter from S. van Hulst, Secretaris voor Speciale Diensten, to Procureur-Generaal, 4-11-1948.

realized that he was in a weak position and tried to secure the support of the former president, Tobing. On 19 August 1948, Indra wrote Tobing a letter in which he cast blame on the ousting of Tobing by Indoff agents and stated that he had seized the leadership of the PKBI-PI in order to prevent the organization from falling into the wrong hands. Therefore, in order to save the PKBI-PI, everybody now had to work together. Tobing ignored the olive branch altogether. The former PKBI-PI executive carried on as if business was usual. They refused to hand over the PKBI-PI premises, the archives, and the treasury. Since most of the influential members continued to support Tobing, there was little that Indra could do. In one last vain attempt, Indra and some supporters registered themselves as the Ikatan Bangsa Indonesia (IBI) on 20 January 1949, hoping to attract the attention of the PKBI-PI that had looked upon them with disdain, but this also failed and the IBI fizzled out.[9] This abortive attempt to unseat Tobing was only the first major incident. The Indoff-PKBI-PI controversy continued to take its toll on the PKBI-PI members who were forced to decide whether to follow Tobing's strategy.

To be sure, there were attempts at reconciliation between the PKBI-PI and Indoff. On 13 September 1948, for example, at a meeting at 15 Oxley Road, the mess for junior personnel of Indoff, a discussion took place between Indoff and the PKBI-PI to resolve differences. Oetoyo was not present but Zain was there. He complained that in the last few months, Indoff had been the target of a hate campaign. It was eventually agreed that the PKBI-PI would henceforth pose no obstacle to Indoff and the two organizations would even collaborate to build a clubhouse.[10] This meeting was important not because of its results, which were meagre, but for the way in which Zain defined Indoff's role. In the course of the discussions, Zain reiterated certain positions that Indoff had already taken. He reaffirmed that the organization did not want to interfere with the operations of Indonesian organizations in Malaya because it had neither the mandate nor the funds from the Republican government for such work. Indoff also had no funds to fulfil its welfare role. Indoff's task was to manage the foreign relations of the Republic and to protect its foreign trade.[11] To be sure, these views meant that Indoff's function was much less

---

[9] PG 170(I), CGDN, 571/G/III, Martinus Indra contra S.L. Tobing, Singapore, 4-12-1948, To Procureur-Generaal from S. van Hulst, Secretaris voor Speciale Diensten; the letter of 19-8-1948 from Martinus Indra to S.L. Tobing can also be found attached; see also PG 558, CGDN, No. 23-49, Singapore, By P.A. van der Poel, 2-2-1949. According to a Malaysian White Paper detailing Indonesian operations in Singapore in the immediate post-war period, the IBI was formed in 1948 to train its members in unarmed combat in support of the interests of the Indonesian Republic. An Indonesian intelligence agent even sat on its committee (*Indonesian intentions* 1964:7).

[10] PG 168, CGDN, No. 166-48, Singapore, Report by S. van Hulst, 23-9-1948.

[11] PG 166, 546/G/III, Letter from S. van Hulst addressed to Procureur-Generaal, Geheim: Poging tot verzoening van Ind. Office en Persatoean Indonesia, 2-12-1948. In this source, the date of the reconciliation meeting of 13-9-1948 was given as 12-9-1948.

general and less extensive than was deemed suitable for an organization that purported to be the Republic's representative. It confirmed the views of its opponents in Singapore that it was not good enough and hence reconciliation was a pipe dream at best.

In 1949, the divisions surfaced again. Tobing had proposed in June 1948 that Oetoyo should be de-recognized as representative of the Republic. At that time the proposal alarmed many Indonesians in Singapore who felt that the PKBI-PI was fomenting disunity and neglecting the reputation of the Republic. This matter was further discussed on 6 February 1949, when it became clear that Tobing's proposal was not received unanimously.[12] In contrast, Indoff was confident of its own position, and refused to be sidetracked by the attacks coming from the PKBI-PI.

To unseat Oetoyo, Tobing decided that any campaign against the Indoff leader could not be anchored solely in the PKBI-PI. In the search for a wider platform, he formed the Indonesian Community Committee, with himself as president, at the end of October 1948 in a bid to incorporate Indonesian leaders from all over Singapore in a joint effort.[13] A long list of grievances against Indoff was drawn up wherein Tobing's view was stated that Indoff was in fact empowered by the Republican government only to promote trade and shipping.[14] Oetoyo was accused of not enjoying the confidence of the British authorities in Singapore. When it came to trade, the Dutch and the British carried out discussions with the Chinese businessmen and Oetoyo was left out in the cold. Indoff also did not enjoy the sympathies of the international community in Singapore, as Indonesian representatives were not invited to official functions and there was no international representation at Indoff-sponsored receptions. There were also indications that Indoff was involved in opium and gold smuggling. After listing all these grievances, Tobing then called for the replacement of Oetoyo and his deputy, Zain.[15]

This list of complaints, submitted to the Minister of Foreign Affairs on behalf of the Indonesian Community Committee, was one of the more legitimate means by which Tobing hoped to draw official attention to the deficiencies of Oetoyo. He admitted to the fact that he had had another plan which he

[12]   PG 558, CGDN, No. 27-49, Singapore, By P.A. van der Poel, 8-2-1949.
[13]   PG 304, No. 276/G/III, Letter from S. van Hulst, Secretaris voor Speciale Diensten, to Procureur-Generaal, 4-11-1948.
[14]   PG 304, No. 001/PR, Letter from Sjamsoedin Loebis and S.L. Tobing, writing in their capacity as secretary and president of the Indonesian Community Committee respectively, to the Minister of Foreign Affairs, in Djokja, 3-11-1948; See also PG 304, No. 276/G/III, Letter from S. van Hulst, Secretaris voor Speciale Diensten, to Procureur-Generaal, 4-11-1948.
[15]   PG 304, No. 001/PR, Letter from Sjamsoedin Loebis and S.L. Tobing, writing in their capacity as secretary and president of the Indonesian Community Committee respectively, to the Minister of Foreign Affairs, in Djokja, 3-11-1948; See also PG 304, No. 276/G/III, Letter from S. van Hulst, Secretaris voor Speciale Diensten, to Procureur-Generaal, 4-11-1948.

had later abandoned, namely, getting a gang of labourers from the Singapore Harbour Board to get rid of Oetoyo, presumably by force. Tobing threatened that if Yogyakarta did not respond, he might have to resort to organizing a mass demonstration at Indoff premises.[16]

Other Indonesians in Singapore, acting in their own capacities, also filed complaints that sounded more like wild allegations. E. Hoetagaloeng, a member of the PKBI-PI, accused Oetoyo of being a NICA agent.[17] Some business and cultural groups also wanted Oetoyo replaced. The leaders of these groups included Bachtiar Effendi (chairman of the cultural section of the Persatoean Indonesia Merdeka), K.M. Ghazali (acting chairman of the Persatoean Pedagang Indonesia Malaya, Perpim, and chairman of a political party in Singapore called Kesatoean Kebadjikan Tasik Oetara). Then there was Zubir Said, Hadji M. Ideriess (chairman of the Himpoenan Warga Negara Indonesia or Hiwarni) and Hadji Soetan Tjahi (manager of the Persatoean Saudagar Indonesia in Singapore). Their grievances were several. They maintained that Oetoyo did not understand the Indonesians residing in Singapore, many of whom originated from Sumatra. He was accused of adopting a feudal posture ('*pendiriannja keningratan*'); he was considered inaccessible.[18] Indonesian groups already in existence in Singapore before Indoff was set up were unhappy that they had been shoved aside by the new organization. In 1947, for example, there had been in existence an Indonesian Association led by A. Wahab who looked at the activities of Oetoyo with misgivings:

> He [Oetoyo] has been in Singapore for many months now but nothing is done for anyone. He just adopts a dictatorial attitude and meanders in his work [...]. This [Indonesian] Association is well established, registered, and recognized, and I cannot understand why Dr Oetoyo is trying to establish a new Indonesian association. Something must have gone wrong somewhere – seeking to meet his own ends.[19]

Some of these complaints against Indoff, however, cannot be accepted at face value. At best, some of the individuals who opposed the new presence of Indoff or Oetoyo only represented themselves, and often their own organizations were ephemeral and tenuous in existence. The case of Wahab, for example, is indicative. By his own admission, Wahab confessed that his Indonesian

---

[16] PG 304, No. 276/G/III, Letter from S. van Hulst, Secretaris voor Speciale Diensten, to Procureur-Generaal, 4-11-1948.
[17] PG 558, CGDN, No. 6-49, Singapore, R.W. van Lier, 7-1-1949.
[18] PG 170(II), Bijlage bij geheim schrijven No. 3A dated 2-11-1947 to M. Hatta, Vice-President, and other Republican leaders in Bukit Tinggi, Sumatra.
[19] PG 170(I), Letter 715/4/xvii, dated 3-9-1947 from A. Wahab of 511-J, Kampong Batak, Jalan Eunos, Singapore, to M. Ali, Overseas Association of Indonesians and Malayans.

V Contest for influence

Association could not even afford postage for regular correspondence.[20]

Nevertheless, accusations of all kinds abounded. In general, the most common one directed at Oetoyo was that he had no time for local Indonesians in Singapore and lacked contact with them.[21] This complaint that Oetoyo did not enjoy sufficient rapport with fellow Indonesians in Singapore was corroborated by later testimony from Moekarto (see Chapter VI).[22]

But the most scandalous of the attacks launched against Indoff were the rumours that slandered the good name of its principal leaders. Stories of financial malpractice and moral turpitude among Indoff officials were rife in Singapore. Zain was reported to have demanded $1.20 more for each *picul* of rubber he sold, saving the excess for his own use. During the months of September and October 1948, it was rumoured that about two thousand tons of rubber passed through his hands. The resulting windfall, it was said, enabled him to negotiate for the purchase of a house in the eastern part of Singapore.[23]

Rumours of corruption perpetrated by Indoff were so rampant that the authorities in Jambi even sent an investigator, someone by the name of Marzoeki, to Singapore in November 1948, to check. Marzoeki noted that the senior officers in Indoff received large amounts of illicit commissions from Chinese traders, concluding that, in general, Indoff was only interested in self-enrichment.[24] Oetoyo was reported to maintain a very considerable bank account in his own name at an institution known as the National City Bank in Singapore.[25]

Allegations of corruption were often overshadowed by rumours of Indoff leaders' moral turpitude. Zain was alleged to have lived in the Majestic Hotel, next to a 'taxi girl'. Before Mrs Saroso arrived in Singapore, Dr Saroso lived in the Eastern Hotel, a place with a reputation for shady business.[26]

---

[20] PG 170(I), Letter 715/4/xvii dated 3-9-1947 from A. Wahab of 511-J, Kampong Batak, Jalan Eunos, Singapore, to M. Ali, Overseas Association of Indonesians and Malayans.
[21] PG 173, Rapport van den Inlichtingendienst der Algemene Politie Riouw (RIAPR), No. 440, Singapore, By S. van Hulst, 10-6-1947.
[22] PG 385, Statement of R. Moekorto Notowidigdo of Klaten (Soerakarta) 10, Kepatian, Java, recorded by R.S. Tufnell at 0800 hours, 1-10-1948 to 2-10-1948, the witness speaking English.
[23] PG 168, CGDN, No. 197-48, Singapore, Report by J.W.J. de Haas, 20-11-1948; for another reference to corruption within Indoff, see PG 168, CGDN, No. 75-48, Report by S. van Hulst, 28-3-1948.
[24] PG 168, CGDN, No. 189-48, Singapore, Report by R.W. van Lier, 9-11-1948.
[25] PG 556, CGDN, No. 111-49, Singapore, Report by P.A. van der Poel, 15-7-1949.
[26] PG 168, CGDN, No. 75-48, Report by S. van Hulst, 28-3-1948.

Dissemination of information

One principal strategy to maintain the interest and support of Indonesians in the Republican cause was to provide news from their ancestral lands. In this field, there was no single organization or individual that monopolized the flow of information, not even Indoff. News about Indonesia filtered into Singapore through the very porous barriers that separated it from the Indonesian islands. Travellers and visitors from all walks of life and from different parts of the archipelago each had their own stories to tell. As a result, information of all kinds raged through the streets of Singapore. A centre of news dissemination, if it can be called that, was the earlier mentioned Restaurant Kita. As far as official news items, one might expect Indoff to have published them, since it had connections with the authorities of the Republic. However, Indoff itself was often starved for news. Due to lack of funds and information, Indoff was only able to issue a weekly bulletin. Traders remained critical of Indoff's ability to disseminate information, especially about those areas where considerable commercial activities were being conducted, for example Sumatra.[27] A suggestion was even submitted to Tobing to establish a separate Indonesian information and news bureau in Singapore. Lack of funds, however, prevented the proposal from materializing.[28]

Fund-raising

For all the Indonesian organizations in Singapore, one major strategy to achieve their goals was fund-raising. Lack of funds was the principal constraint on activities. Maintaining a foreign presence for the Republic, not only in Singapore but the rest of the world, required tremendous financial resources. Propaganda and information programmes were expensive. There was also the need for arms purchases. Considerable effort was therefore expended to create wealth, and the methods used by the various organizations were innovative and original. Most attention, however, will be given to Indoff, as the documentation for that body is more extensive than for others.

Inadequate financial resources haunted Indoff like a phantom. First of all, there were infrastructure needs to be met. With about thirty persons employed at Indoff, monthly operating expenses amounted to approximately $5,000. The actual number of staff on the payroll probably fluctuated,

[27] PG 558, CGDN, No. 39-49, Singapore, By P.A. van der Poel, 24-2-1949.
[28] PG 558, CGDN, No. 10-49, Singapore, By R.W. van Lier, 12-1-1949; For details on Tobing's attempts to raise funds for this project, see PG 558, CGDN, No. 15-49, Singapore, By R.W. van Lier, 19-1-1949.

falling to a low of twelve employees in 1948.[29] Payments to Indoff staff were, on occasions, irregular. On 20 January 1948, a clerk working for Indoff was compelled to supplement his income by openly selling Republican passports in Arab Street, a precinct frequented by Indonesians.[30] By the middle of 1948, Indoff finances were so bad that the staff could only be paid half salary.[31] By December 1948, Indoff employees were reported to have received only partial payment. In January 1949, the lower ranking officers did not get their pay, while the others had to be satisfied with money for food.[32] There was talk within the Indonesian community that Indoff would close for lack of funds should the negotiations between the Netherlands and the Republic collapse.[33] For the *lebaran* (Muslim New Year) celebrations in 1949, Oetoyo and his senior colleagues decided to refuse the regular allowance given to them.[34] It was also necessary to issue a general order in Indoff to exercise strict economy.[35] By March 1949, Indoff staffers were compelled to accept a pay cut.[36] In 1949, too, Indoff was forced to sell its stationery stocks in order to raise funds.[37]

It did not help that the cost of living in Singapore was high. Post-war Singapore was not a suitable place for the indigent. As representatives of an independent Republic of Indonesia, Indoff leaders were obliged to maintain a certain standard of living. In this respect, the comments of a former prime minister of Siam – Nai Pridi Phanomyong – are relevant. In March 1948, he is quoted as having said: 'Singapore is a fantastically expensive city and one cannot live in it unless one has money or can work. If one is a politician or statesman, there is no trade to which one can turn one's hand, and [one will] find the expenses mount all the time.'[38]

Indoff received a subvention from the Republican government and this amounted to $20,000 per month sometime during the middle of 1948. The subvention was not always granted in cash. Most of the time, Indoff received

---

[29] PG 304, Letter from S. van Hulst to Procureur-Generaal, 12-7-1948.
[30] PG 168, CGDN, No. 32-48, Singapore, Report by S. van Hulst, 29-1-1948.
[31] PG 385, Letter from S. van Hulst to Procureur-Generaal, No. 808A, Singapore, 26-6-1948; for a Dutch report on the salaries paid to Indoff staff, see PG 304, letter 422/H/I, from S. van Hulst (Secretaris voor Speciale Diensten) to Procureur-Generaal, 20-11-1948. This letter is also found in Inventaris van de archieven van her Consulaat-Generaal te Singapore, 1945-54, Ministerie van Buitenlandse Zaken (MBZ) 220.
[32] PG 558, CGDN, No. 4-49, Singapore, By S. van Hulst, 6-1-1949.
[33] PG 168, CGDN, No. 20-48, Singapore, Report by S. van Hulst, 17-1-1948.
[34] PG 556, CGDN, No. 111-49, Singapore, Report by P.A. van der Poel, 15-7-1949.
[35] PG 556, CGDN, No. 111-49, Singapore, Report by P.A. van der Poel, 15-7-1949.
[36] PG 558, CGDN, No. 47-49, Singapore, By P.A. van der Poel, 7-3-1949.
[37] PG 558, CGDN, No. 37-49, Singapore, By P.A. van der Poel, 22-2-1949.
[38] 'Nai Pridi leaves St John's', *Straits Times*, 23-3-1948, p. 7. Nai Pridi was staying under quarantine at St John's island off Singapore.

only goods, which were then sold to raise cash.[39] When there was a need, it was also possible to draw on overdrafts with Chinese traders on the basis of goods landed from Sumatra.[40] The money thus obtained was partly used to finance Indoff operations in Singapore, but there were also remittances to support similar offices in Penang and Bangkok during the initial months of their founding.[41] The amount of the subvention was therefore not excessive. There were also small contributions from local Indonesians in Singapore. Diamonds are mentioned in the records (*Memoar pejuang* 1992:58).

How then did Indoff finance the shortfall and any other needs? Indoff officials put up a brave front, accepting sacrifices as necessary. Zain even maintained that Indoff representatives could be self-reliant for a long time.[42] But personal discipline aside, Indoff had arranged for a tie-up with an American businessman, Matthew Fox, in early January 1948, to export Indonesian commodities in return for Fox arranging for the import of essential goods. Singapore's role – and that of Indoff – was to facilitate transhipment. The Fox plan failed, in part because Sumatran exporters could not or would not comply with the range of conditions imposed by Indoff; and in turn, Indoff lacked the personnel to handle complicated trading arrangements.[43]

One of the conditions was the levy of a commission by Indoff on the value of goods exported from Indonesia to Singapore by private merchants. Such a measure could result in an income of about $3,000 monthly,[44] depending on the size of the levy, but clearly this was not a payment that traders accepted without complaint.

Besides bilateral agreements with Fox, it is also likely that Indoff entered into business arrangements with other individual traders, dividing the profits from sales of goods. There is one report of an arrangement between a trader, T. Hanson, together with Samin (*wedana* at Rantau Prapat) on the one hand, and Oetoyo on the other, to divide the proceeds of sales 50-50, with Hanson and Samin bearing all the risks.[45]

---

[39] PG 304, Letter from S. van Hulst to Procureur-Generaal, dated 12-7-1948.
[40] PG 304, Letter from S. van Hulst to Procureur-Generaal, dated 12-7-1948.
[41] PG 385, Interrogation of Dr Oetoyo by officers of HM Customs, Singapore, 23-10-1948. During a subsequent interrogation session, Oetoyo denied that Penang was financed from Singapore as it had independent sources in Aceh; PG 385, Further interrogation of Dr Oetoyo by officers of HM Customs, Singapore, 4-11-1948. The Penang Office of Indoff was opened on 1-6-1948 and the first item on its agenda was a discussion on the export levy of two per cent on goods from Penang to the Republic. See PG 170(II), Penang Kantoor van Mr Oetoyo, unsigned, undated.
[42] PG 556, CGDN, No. 111-49, Singapore, Report by P.A. van der Poel, 15-7-1949.
[43] Suryono Darusman, 'Singapore and the Indonesian Revolution 1945-1950', typescript. On the Fox contract, see Homan 1983:128-31.
[44] PG 385, Statement of R. Moekarto Notowidigdo of Klaten (Soerakarta) 10, Kepatian, Java, recorded by R.S. Tufnell at 0800 hours, 1-10-1948 to 2-10-1948, the witness speaking English.
[45] PG 304, De Residentie Riouw over de periode 16-10-1947 tot 31-10-1947.

In general, quite apart from the arrangements with Fox and other private traders, Indoff had in place a battery of regulations by early 1948 that would ensure a regular flow of essential goods to Indonesia and at the same time provide funds to Indoff. Upon the arrival of a *tongkang* from Sumatra[46] in Singapore, all the goods carried in that vessel was to be reported to the Trade and Finance Department of Indoff.[47] The trader concerned was required to submit all licenses issued by Republican port authorities, a declaration of the ports from which the goods were exported, and the import permits issued by the Registrar of Imports and Exports in Singapore. This provision was essential to enable Indoff authorities take follow-up action on the goods that would be transported from Singapore to the Republican territories in return. The trader was required to sell goods to Republican territories up to at least 75 per cent of the total worth of goods exported. The goods to be sent to Republican territories must in turn be approved by Indoff's Trade and Finance Department. Finally, and most important, any license of approval issued in Singapore would cost the trader one thousandth of the total worth of the goods to be exported.[48] Trade (or 'smuggling', as the Dutch called it) must have been Indoff's most important source of income (*Memoar pejuang* 1992:58).

There were also other methods without Indoff itself getting directly involved in trade administration. For example, it appointed agents in Singapore to receive from and then sell cargo to Indonesia, in return for which the agents were required to make payments to Indoff.[49]

Another strategy adopted by Indoff was to raise loans. One obvious source was Acehnese traders, but these refused to lend.[50] Acehnese traders were suspicious of Indoff, fearing that their trade would fall under its control. Attempts by Indoff to mobilize the Acehnese to support their work led to efforts to organize the Persatoean Saudagar Indonesia in Penang, where the Acehnese traders were particularly active. This came to nothing because the traders were reluctant to cooperate.[51]

---

[46] Trade regulations were mainly directed at the flow of goods between Singapore and Sumatra since it was unlikely that goods could originate from Java, given the more effective presence of the Dutch in Java and its reputation as an import-dependent area.
[47] To administer the trade that passed through Singapore, Indoff had established what was initially a Trade and Finance Department. It was at first controlled by Saroso, an appointee of the Republican Ministry of Finance, but from 1-6-1948, as a result of misunderstandings concerning who had authority over the use of funds, it passed to Oetoyo's control after Saroso left. See PG 304, Letter from S. van Hulst to Procureur-Generaal, 12-7-1948. Also, interview with Darusman in Jakarta on 20-3-1992. It is not clear whether the department was reorganized as and renamed the Trade Department of Indoff at that time.
[48] PG 170(I), Trade Regulations Announcement No. 1.
[49] PG 385, Interrogation of Dr Oetoyo by officers of HM Customs, Singapore, 23-10-1948.
[50] PG 168, CGDN, No. 134-48, Report by S. van Hulst, 25-6-1948.
[51] PG 168, CGDN, No. 130-48, Report by S. van Hulst, 8-6-1948.

Indoff was also quick to seize ad hoc opportunities to accumulate funds and at the same time serve the Republican cause. Such an instance was the agreement with Gian Singh and Company to export one thousand tons of much-needed rice to Java for humanitarian reasons, but this could not be implemented, Java being subject to more effective Dutch control. A second agreement was concluded in 1949, this time with M.S. See Hoy Yan (operating from Cecil Street in Singapore), to buy out Gian Singh and then export the rice to other territories (for example Aceh in Sumatra[52]) within two months. Profit for the sale was fixed at fifteen per cent per *picul*, with the net gains divided between the contracting parties.[53] The Chinese firm had no difficulties finding the capital to purchase the rice. The problem lay in the possibility that the Dutch would seize the rice shipment before it reached its destination in Aceh. Who then would be responsible? Zain's assurance that the Republic would be responsible cut little ice. The Chinese firm then advanced an ingenious idea. It proposed that the Netherlands consulate in Singapore be approached for a guarantee of safe passage for the rice. The consulate would be expected to give a vague answer and then refer the matter to Batavia. Indoff could then complain that the delay would lead to the deterioration of the rice quality, and to resolve that problem, propose that the rice be sold in Singapore to prevent further loss,[54] presumably with the profits divided between Indoff and the Chinese firm.

At first impression, this proposal seemed to smack of commercial gain and selfish interests, but the idea was in fact quite practical. It was unlikely that the Dutch would agree so easily to the transhipment of rice across the Straits of Malacca to Aceh or anywhere without adequate safeguards. Negotiations on these would have been time-consuming and meanwhile, the rice would rot away. There was a report in the *Straits Times* of 9 May 1949 that Zain had sought the help of British authorities to persuade the Dutch to lift the blockade of Sumatra, where the rice was also urgently needed.[55] Evidently, solutions were not readily at hand. Indoff wanted to control the

---

[52] The destination, Aceh, was chosen because it was the only major region in Indonesia that was not occupied by the Dutch during the Second Military Action. However, it was not certain that the rice could be landed in Aceh, where the rice harvest had brought the price down to $11-12 per *picul* while the rice to be shipped from Bangkok was expected to fetch a price of $25 per *picul*. This would influence the price of rice in Aceh. See PG 558, CGDN, No. 58-49, Singapore, By P.A. van der Poel, 24-3-1949.

[53] PG 556, CGDN, No. 110-49, Singapore, Report by P.A. van der Poel. 12-7-1949; Details on the terms of the contract can be found in PG 556, CGDN, No. 111-49, Singapore, Report by P.A. van der Poel, 15-7-1949.

[54] PG 558, CGDN, No. 52-49, Singapore, By P.A. van der Poel, 16-3-1949; PG 380, Letter 1301/I/I, from P. A. van der Poel, Secretaris voor Speciale Diensten, to C.W.A. Schürmann, Ambassador at Bangkok, 18-3-1949.

[55] PG 558, CGDN, No. 86-49, Singapore, Report by R.W. van Lier, 11-5-1949.

disposition of rice but had no capital. The Netherlands consulate and the British authorities were insistent that the rice should not generate profit but should be sold as cheaply as possible, while Indoff wanted to retain as much profit as possible.[56] Zain is reported to have approached the Anglo-French Bendixsens Company for help to transport the rice to Republican territories at $32 per *picul*. This was considered too high, and a 'reasonable' price was estimated at $26.[57] But even at the rate of $32 per *picul*, the risks were considerable.[58]

One aspect of the desire to raise funds was the opium controversy – whether Indoff was involved in the trafficking of opium for sale in Singapore, and attempts by other individuals to serve Republican interests by selling opium. As the documentation on this subject is fairly substantial, it will be treated in a later chapter.

The above sections all deal with people and groups who were pro-Republican. Not every Indonesian in Singapore, however, was like them. There were others who used the uncertainties of the post-war period to pursue their own private goals and on these attention must now be focused.

Riau Sultanate movement

In May 1946, the Djawatan Kuasa published a newspaper, the *Dewan Rakjat*, which outlined the objectives of the Riau Sultanate movement. It would support the legitimate demands of Indonesia. It pledged not to install a sultan till the status of Indonesia was clarified. Riau would remain a part of the future Indonesia. The sultan to be installed would not be a despot but would be subject to the will of the people. The movement also pledged not to make a distinction between ethnic groups.[59] The leader of the Djawatan Kuasa was Radja Hadji Abdoellah bin Osman. He thought that cooperation with the Netherlands Indies government was in the interest of the people of the Riau archipelago.[60]

There was more at stake than the fate of a former dynasty. The descendants of the old royal family of Riau felt that the position of the Riau Malays had been shoved aside by the arrival in Riau of more and more non-Riau

---

[56] PG 558, CGDN, No. 63-49, Singapore, Report by P.A. van der Poel, 31-3-1949.
[57] PG 558, CGDN, No. 82-49, Singapore, Report by P.A. van der Poel, 3-5-1949.
[58] PG 558, CGDN, No. 84-49, Singapore, Report by P.A. van der Poel, 6-5-1949.
[59] RI 561, Nota G. Diest Lorgion, Commissaris van Politie eerste klasse, 31-3-1947, Batavia.
[60] RI 552, Tweewekelijksche berichtgeving van de Residentie Riouw over de periode 15 t/m 30-9-1947, By J. van Waardenburg, Resident, Tandjong Pinang, 13-10-1947; For a list of objectives, see RI 551, Tweewekelijksche berichtgeving der Residentie Riouw over de periode 1 t/m 15-5-1946, By J. van Waardenburg, Resident, Singapore, 17-5-1946.

Indonesians. The position of the sultanate supporters would surely be more secure, or at least protected, if greater responsibility in the Riau civil administration was given to the Riau Malays. This was a sore point because many non-Riau Malays (Minangs, Bataks, and others from Palembang) were occupying the higher ranks of the administration. It was the Djawatan leader, Radja Abdoellah, who aroused the ethnic feelings of the Riau-Malays against these newcomers.[61]

The Djawatan Kuasa forwarded a memorial to the lieutenant governor-general on 17 June 1946 urging the restoration of the Sultanate of Riau-Lingga and the establishment of the Riau Raad, or Council of State.[62] The memorial argued that the person who should be elected sultan should be one of the lawful descendants of the last sultan of Riau-Lingga, the late Sultan Abdoelrahman Moeazam Shah, who was exiled from Riau in 1911[63] and died in Singapore in 1929. The senior surviving lawful descendant of this late sultan living in Singapore was Tengku Ibrahim bin Tengku Omar, son of the late Tengku Besar of Riau and a grandson of the late sultan. He was born in Penyengat (an island in the Riau archipelago) in 1906 and left Riau with his grandfather, the sultan, in 1911. The memorial met with no response from the lieutenant governor-general and the Djawatan Kuasa decided to send a delegation to Jakarta.[64]

With hindsight, the Sultanate movement of the Djawatan lacked popular support. The *Utusan Melayu*, a prominent mouthpiece of the Malays in Malaya, was probably right when it attacked Abdoellah, saying that he never had contact with the people [of Riau] and therefore could not claim to be acting in accordance with the will of the people. According to the *Utusan*, he only had supporters from Karimun island, who did not understand that circumstances had changed. The paper then went on to note that the Sultanate movement was not even recognized by the [Dutch] Resident of Riau, and it could be said that the Dutch even opposed it.[65] The aim of the royal descendants, it alleged, was to recover from their penurious condition, using the opportunities provided by the existing turmoil. The newspaper even compared the *modus operandi* of the Djawatan to restore the Sultanate as

---

[61] RI 561, Nota G. Diest Lorgion, Commissaris van Politie eerste klasse, 31-3-1947, Batavia.
[62] H.M. Hassan, 'The Singapore heir to the Rhio islands', *Straits Times*, 11-12-1947, p. 6.
[63] By 1911, the Sultanate was a far cry from any signs of a golden age that the Djawatan may choose to recall. The sultan was already seriously in debt to the tune of 135,000 NEI guilders. Financial matters were in a mess, although attempts had been made earlier to separate his private income from official revenues. See Memories van Overgave Riouw, AA229, Memorie van Overgave van den Resident van Riouw en Onderhoorigheden, G.F. de Bruijn Kops., 3-3-1914, Tandjong Pinang, p. 208.
[64] H.M. Hassan, 'The Singapore heir to the Rhio islands', *Straits Times*, 11-12-1947, p. 6.
[65] RI 551, Tweewekelijksche berichtgeving der Residentie Riouw over de periode 16 t/m 30-9-1946, By P.A. van der Poel, Commissaris van Politie I, 1-10-1946.

a conspiracy of thieves out to rob the Republic of its rights.[66]

Although there was little popular support, there was some financial interest shown in the movement by Chinese traders. A group of these, led by a Singkep tin-miner, Koh Peng Kuan, got together to form a committee at one of the meetings of the movement held on 10 August 1946. In return for traders' support for the movement, one of the committee's first pronouncements was the hope that trade would be unhampered.[67]

Abdoellah promised Koh that with the restoration of the Sultanate, he would be made the sole contractor for projects in Riau.[68] He was also promised a monopoly on tin exploitation at Singkep. In anticipation of these favours, Koh (either alone or in cooperation with other Chinese[69]) reportedly made a contribution of $16,000 to $20,000 by February 1946 to the Sultanate movement.[70]

Sometime during the first half of June 1946, both Abdoellah and his Chinese supporters agreed on the nomination of a claimant to the throne, the above-mentioned Tengku Ibrahim. He turned out to be a poor choice. Although his lineage gave him some kind of claim to the Sultanate succession, Tengku Ibrahim had in fact already declared that he had nothing to do with the Sultanate movement. The only tenuous link was his participation at a tea party organized by the movement and the fact that he was a lodger in Koh Peng Kuan's house.[71] According to a report in the *Straits Times*, Ibrahim was known to be 'dumb' (Dutch: *dom*). When this was pointed out to Abdoellah, he agreed but said that this made him malleable.[72] At best, Ibrahim was a shadowy figure. According to another report, he cut off links with the Djawatan Kuasa because he opposed its practice of borrowing money from the Chinese. (Up till 1947, Abdoellah's organization was indebted to the Chinese for about $70,000.)[73]

---

[66] RI 551, Tweewekelijksche berichtgeving der Residentie Riouw over de periode 1 t/m 15-10-1946, Singapore, 16-10-1946.
[67] RI 561, Nota G. Diest Lorgion, Commissaris van Politie eerste klasse, 31-3-1947, Batavia.
[68] RI 552, Tweewekelijksche berichtgeving van de Residentie Riouw over de periode 15 t/m 30-9-1947, By J. van Waardenburg, Resident, Tandjong Pinang, 13-10-1947.
[69] The primary sources reveal that there were other Chinese in Singapore who supported the Sultanate movement, but it is not clear whether they were merely following Koh or offering support on their own initiative. Three names were mentioned: Lim Tie Beng, Auh Siak Eng, and Tay Tiang Chua. See RI 552, Tweewekelijksche berichtgeving van de Residentie Riouw over de periode 1 t/m 15-8-1947 by J. van Waardenburg, Resident, Tandjong Pinang, 28-8-1947.
[70] RI 551, Tweewekelijksche berichtgeving der Residentie Riouw over de periode 16 t/m 30-9-1946, By P.A. van der Poel, Commissaris van Politie I on 1-10-1946.
[71] RI 561, Nota G. Diest Lorgion, Commissaris van Politie eerste klasse, 31-3-1947, Batavia.
[72] RI 552, Tweewekelijksche berichtgeving van de Residentie Riouw over de periode 15 t/m 30-9-1947, By J. van Waardenburg, Resident, Tandjong Pinang, 13-10-1947.
[73] RI 552, Tweewekelijksche berichtgeving van de Residentie Riouw over de periode 1 t/m 15-10-1947, By J. van Waardenburg, Resident, Tandjong Pinang, 23-10-1947.

The prospects for the Djawatan dimmed further when it became clear that as a businessman, Koh was interested in having his slice of bread buttered on both sides. His support for the Sultanate movement was not unequivocal. Koh's own interests demanded that his relations with the Republic were not sacrificed at the same time as he supported the Djawatan. After all, his trade links extended from Singapore and Riau to Republican-held territories in Sumatra. Koh also extended hospitality to visitors from Riau who were pro-Republican. Despite efforts to establish its influence in Riau by carrying out propaganda everywhere, the Sultanate movement was unsuccessful and did not have much support. It was seen as merely trying to resurrect the past. Koh performed some deft footwork by trying to mend his fences with the Republican side. During the second half of December 1946, Tengku Ibrahim broke off links with the Sultanate movement, probably at Koh's behest.[74]

As an organization, the Sultanate movement scrupulously avoided displaying pro-Republican sympathies, refusing to fly the red-and-white flag on 17 August 1946 at the movement's office on Cecil Street. In turn, the Republicans in Singapore accused the movement of being pro-Dutch. The movement, however, felt that the Dutch could not be ignored. In its view, Riau had already fallen under the control of the Dutch and only the Dutch could help. It therefore submitted a petition to the Dutch in Jakarta for the restoration of the Sultanate. But it was to be disappointed. There is no indication that Van Mook was prepared to countenance any requests to restore the political fortunes of former sultans. In fact, when he organized the Malino Conference (1946) to discuss the future of territories lying outside of Java, he decided not to invite a representative from Riau to attend but instead appointed a Sumatran, Moh Saleh, to represent the islands.[75] At the Malino Conference, Moh Saleh argued that Riau should be merged with Sumatra, and the Sultanate movement took exception to that statement.[76] In December 1946, it sent a delegation to meet the lieutenant governor-general to secure a definitive solution to the request for restoration of the Sultanate. In Jakarta, however, the delegation took the opportunity to meet with Republican leaders, Sjahrir and Hadji Agoes Salim. Discussions with the latter must have convinced the delegation that there were really only three choices – rule by the Dutch, a self-governing principality (which would exercise maximum autonomy in which links with the Dutch would be maintained), and incorporation into the Republic. Quite naturally, the choice fell on the second option. From January 1947 onwards, the code of the movement was a self-governing principality – not a Sultanate – in

---

[74] RI 561, Nota G. Diest Lorgion, Commissaris van Politie eerste klasse, 31-3-1947, Batavia.
[75] RI 561, Nota G. Diest Lorgion, Commissaris van Politie eerste klasse, 31-3-1947, Batavia.
[76] RI 551, Tweewekelijksche berichtgeving der Residentie Riouw over de periode 1 t/m 16-8-1946, By J. van Waardenburg, Resident.

An aerial picture of Clifford Pier with a view of Indonesia in the distance. Clifford Pier was one of the gateways for Indonesians arriving at Singapore (National Archives, Singapore).

Commodities to be smuggled from Singapore to Indonesia – two automobiles with engines taken apart, two motorcycles, tyres, electric motors, medicine, etc. (ARA Dirvo 74, 91014 AA4)

A Dutch naval officer inspecting a vessel for smuggled goods (KITLV 14.092)

One of John Lie's smuggling boats (ARA Dirvo 74, 91014 AA1)

Although this is a picture of Boat Quay (Singapore) during the 1930s, it is likely that the same scene was typical of the 1940s and 1950s as well (KITLV 25.596). Given the crowded mooring, it would have been difficult to distinguish between boats used for smuggling and vessels conducting legitimate trade.

Oetoyo (right) with Foreign Minister H Agus Salim (*Memoar pejuang* 1992:213)

Suryono Daroesman (top left). In front of him was Tahir Karim Loebis.
(*Memoar pejuang* 1992:77.)

Tony Wen – a photograph taken before his opium smuggling days (ARA PG 188)

Zain (left) with Dr Hatta on the right (Straits Times (Singapore) 13 November 1949)

Happy World amusement park where many an Indonesian agent went for recreation (National Archives, Singapore)

Raffles Place – where the Indonesia Office was located (National Archives, Singapore)

which the royalty would naturally still have an important role.⁷⁷ This second option was not exactly the Djawatan's most attractive course of action, but all told, given the weakness of the organization, it was an option forced on the Sultanate movement, especially when it realized that the inhabitants of Riau were not wholly supportive of the Sultanate's restoration.⁷⁸

The anti-Sultanate camp was also active. It organized itself as the Badan Kebangsaan Indonesia Riouw (Indonesian National Committee of Riau) with branches all over Riau, for example Lingga, Singkep, Karimun, and the small island of Tembalan. It sent a delegation to Singapore to counter the propaganda of Sultanate movement supporters. The delegation argued that the Riau-Lingga archipelago should be part of the Republic of Indonesia and that support for the sultanate was confined to Bintan.⁷⁹

To maintain what little momentum the movement still had, the Djawatan held a meeting on 26 October 1947 at its headquarters at Cecil Street. Present were Radja Hadji Abdoellah, Lim Tee Choy (a Chinese businessman or *towkay*), the earlier mentioned Koh, one other Chinese representative, and, interestingly enough, three *tengku* from Trengganu who were male descendants of the last Malay sultan of Riau-Lingga. The meeting decided that Abdoellah and the three *tengku* should visit Tanjung Balai (Karimun) to go on a propaganda tour through the Riau islands.⁸⁰ (The involvement of the three royal members from Trengganu was probably prompted by the need to jettison Tengku Ibrahim, whose interests did not seem to coincide with those of the Djawatan.)

The death knell for the Sultanate movement came with evidence that Republican influence was increasing, even in the Riau Council, which was set up by the Dutch to counter Republican influence in the archipelago. When it was first established, it consisted of fifteen members – nine Indonesians, four Chinese, and two Dutch. Of the nine Indonesians, one was an appointee of the Dutch Resident. The Chinese were chosen by the Chinese community. The two Dutch representatives were appointees of the Resident. Thus the Indonesian population was only empowered to elect eight representatives. As it turned out, one of the eight was pro-Dutch and so, together with the four Chinese who were also pro-Dutch, the Dutch had a narrow majority of one in the Riau Council. The Dutch had argued that the Riau Council was the competent authority to decide whether the sultanate should be restored.⁸¹

---

⁷⁷ RI 561, Nota G. Diest Lorgion, Commissaris van Politie eerste klasse, 31-3-1947, Batavia.
⁷⁸ RI 551, Tweewekelijksche berichtgeving der Residentie Riouw over de periode 1 t/m 15-11-1946, By L.B. van Straten, Assistent-Resident, Tandjong Pinang, 22-11-1946.
⁷⁹ 'Rhio nationalists oppose restoration of sultan', *Malaya Tribune*, 23-1-1947, p. 7.
⁸⁰ RI 552, Tweewekelijksche berichtgeving van de Residentie Riouw over te periode 16 t/m 31-10-1947, By J. van Waardenburg.
⁸¹ RI 552, Tweewekelijksche berichtgeving van de Residentie Riouw over de periode 16 t/m 31-10-1947, By J. van Waardenburg.

But as four of the eight elected Indonesian members of the Council belonged to a fiercely pro-Republican faction,[82] the signs were clear that the Sultanate movement would not find the future plain sailing at all. Even the *assistent-resident* of Tanjung Pinang, J.B. van Schendel, did not rate the prospects of the Sultanate movement too highly, and he thought that was why its supporters were making plans in October 1947 to go to Jakarta to make one last plea.[83] The nemesis came sometime during early November 1947, when the Djawatan broached a plan with Indoff to establish a Riau coordination bureau in which the Djawatan would cooperate with the Republic. Oetoyo agreed to supervise its formation,[84] and with that the chapter on the Sultanate's restoration came to a close, and the movement returned to the fold of the Republic.

As the saga of the Djawatan was about to end, a new organization emerged that extended the life of the Sultanate movement for a short while more. This was Persatoean Melayu Riouw Sedjati (Association of the Indigenous Riau Malays). Established on 3 March 1947 when it was clear that the Djawatan was not going to succeed,[85] it was led by one Tengku Abdoellah bin Omar, and its claimant to the Riau throne was none other than Tengku Ibrahim,[86] the same person who had been chosen by the Djawatan. In October 1947, Tengku Abdoellah paid a visit to Tanjung Batu in the Riau islands to try and get the *penghulu* to support the return of Ibrahim as sultan. He pointed out that the Trengganu royal claimants that had visited the Riau islands earlier under the auspices of the Djawatan had no grounds for claiming the throne.[87] It was doubtful if the Persatoean Melayu Riouw Sedjati had any better chances of success than the Djawatan. The latter had already tested the waters in Riau and the people had been found to be lukewarm at best to the restoration of the Sultanate. Further visits to champion the cause of the royal descendants would only be impositions on the hospitality of the Riau islanders.

The foregoing and the material presented in the next two chapters represent the strategies adopted by the Indonesian organizations in Singapore to advance the aims of the Indonesian revolution in ways most appropriate,

[82] RI 561, Nota G. Diest Lorgion, Commissaris van Politie eerste klasse, 31-3-1947, Batavia.
[83] RI 552, Tweewekelijksche berichtgeving van de Residentie Riouw over de periode 1-11-1947 to 15-11-1947, By J.B. van Schendel, Assistent-Resident, Tandjong Pinang.
[84] RI 552, Tweewekelijksche berichtgeving van de Residentie Riouw over de periode 1-11-1947 to 15-11-1947, By J.B. van Schendel, Assistent-Resident, Tandjong Pinang.
[85] RI 552, Tweewekelijksche berichtgeving van de Residentie Riouw over de periode 15 t/m 30-9-1947, By J. van Waardenburg, Resident, Tandjong Pinang, 13-10-1947.
[86] RI 552, Tweewekelijksche berichtgeving van de Residentie Riouw over de periode 1 t/m 15-10-1947, By J. van Waardenburg, Resident, Tandjong Pinang, 23-10-1947.
[87] RI 552, Tweewekelijksche berichtgeving van de Residentie Riouw over de periode 16 t/m 31-10-1947, By J. van Waardenburg; for details about the Persatoean Melayu Riouw Sedjati, see letter to the *Straits Times*, 4-1-1948, copy enclosed in Directie Verre Oosten, 198.

given their resources. These strategies could only be implemented in the context of tacit support from Chinese traders and British colonial officials. Many threads were thus interwoven in the fabric of the Singapore connection.

CHAPTER VI

Clandestine activities

Operation Mariam Bee was a gun-smuggling scheme to equip the IV Indonesian Naval Command at Tegal in Java. The manoeuvres began shortly before Christmas 1945, when a Singapore-registered *tongkang* called the *San Giang* sailed out of Tegal harbour. On board were an Indonesian official called Suryono Darusman and a colleague. Their orders were simple. On the outward journey, they would carry a cargo of one hundred tons of sugar for sale in Singapore. Then, using the proceeds of the sale, they were tasked with the assignment to purchase weapons for the return journey. Such seemingly straightforward instructions seem clear enough, but the execution of the task was fraught with problems. The disposal of the sugar was easy and once that was done, the search for weapons to purchase began. Since the latter part of the task could not be completed immediately, there was temptation to use the waiting period to invest the cash available from the sale of sugar for some private business venture. Such diversions, however, would only delay the completion of the task further. Meanwhile, Darusman made exploratory trips to various parts of the Malay Peninsula to look for arms caches that could be purchased in fairly large quantities. The key was to find the right contact. Success was eventually achieved. Through Abdul Samad, Darusman managed to make a deal with a Chinese in Singapore known as Captain Joseph Loh, who had previously been active in the anti-Japanese underground movement called Force 136. Loh arranged for an arms shipment from the British naval dump in Changi to be stored on a ship, the *Mariam Bee*. In early September 1946, the *Mariam Bee* began its voyage to Indonesia with its precious cargo of contraband. The route that it took was circuitous. The ship sailed along the north shores of the Karimun islands, Bangka, and Billiton, and then eastward to South Borneo before changing direction southwards for Tegal. The entire operation was a success and the Indonesian Republic was strengthened by the acquisition of 1,400 rifles with ammunition, six anti-aircraft guns, one field hospital, and other equipment for an entire field regiment.[1] The *Mariam*

---

1 Suryono Darusman, 'Operation Mariam Bee', *Indonesian Observer*, 17-10-1988; for a Dutch account which more or less fits in with the one above given by Darusman, see PG 378, Letter

Bee was involved in smuggling, pure and simple.

Smuggling was an ambiguous term packed with emotions during those days of the Indonesian revolution. Much of its meaning depended on the perspective taken to describe the movement of goods. To the traders in Singapore, free market forces determined the direction of flow of goods. To the Dutch, smuggling was an act of evasion. Trade was regarded as smuggling when the activity lay outside of Dutch control. It was also unfair exchange, because the smuggled goods usually fetched a price in Singapore that was allegedly only about twenty per cent of their real value.[2] The Indonesians viewed it differently. The Dutch had imposed controls on exports, but Indonesians felt it was legitimate (and patriotic) to evade the controls.

It was during the Japanese occupation that the infrastructure for smuggling was put in place. Economic dislocations during those trying years gave rise to a group of traders who worked on a small scale as individuals ferrying goods in boats from one place to another. The kind of goods depended on demand. The destinations too were demand driven. Capital was small, trading journeys were irregular, and a lot depended on traders' personal contacts. The traders were mainly Chinese and the trade was called *danbang* (Twang 1998:97). Only a thin line separated this means of livelihood from its later metamorphosis, smuggling.

In this study, the term 'smuggling' is used to denote those trading activities in which goods were secretly transported from one place to another with the intention of dodging the controls exercised by various authorities. Smuggling flourished in proportion to the severity of controls on imports and exports. When trade was free, there was no incentive to smuggle.[3] The irony is that as more rules were applied to control trade, more smuggling took place.

The goods that were smuggled belonged to two broad categories: conventional commodities and contraband, discussed below in that order. But whatever the meanings and attributes, smuggling played a crucial role in advancing the Republican cause. It was a role that particularly suited Singapore, entrenched as it was in the trade with Indonesia, and equipped with a storehouse of expertise represented in the myriad Chinese firms found on the island. In Singapore, the 'smugglers' cove' was the Boat Quay and Beach Road areas. In these two places, a great number of boats moored there sailed to and from West Borneo, Riau, Bangka and Billiton, and other parts of Sumatra.[4]

Given the secretive nature of smuggling, there are no statistics to indicate

---

from P.A. van der Poel (Secretary for Special Duties, Netherlands Consulate-General Singapore) addressed to Mr E.A.G. Blades, Special Branch, Singapore, dated 11-5-1949.
2   Directie Verre Oosten, 89, Untitled document.
3   'Smuggling', *Straits Times*, 24-4-1946, p. 2.
4   PG 380, Letter 1702-K-VII, from P.A. van der Poel, Secretaris voor Speciale Diensten, to Procureur-Generaal, 4-5-1949.

its extent although there are many estimates. One source claims that the Java-Singapore smuggling trade was worth $10 million.[5] The amount of goods smuggled also varied from month to month, depending on the opportunities. Figures for the 1945-1946 period are difficult to obtain or unreliable. Later, calculations made by the Netherlands consulate in Singapore became more sophisticated as better statistics were made available. It was worked out that from September to December 1948, the value of goods smuggled from Sumatra to Singapore was Straits $10,142,266. The value of goods smuggled from Singapore to Sumatra was Straits $13,258,315.[6]

Several factors combined to promote the smuggling of conventional trading commodities like estate products and consumer goods. The uncertain political situation in Indonesia was important because government attention was diverted to the struggle for political control, leaving traders unsupervised. To the delight of Indonesia's smugglers, it was not only this political situation that was in the dark. Indonesia's coastline was also left unlit. According to estimates provided by Dutch authorities, over half of Indonesia's pre-war total of 246 lighthouses had been rendered non-functioning during the last six months of hectic political and military turmoil. As for harbour lights, seventy per cent of the pre-war fittings were not working. Only sixty lights were operating.[7]

British measures to promote trade

The British themselves unwittingly promoted smuggling when their military administration tried to restore trade connections between Singapore and the neighbouring islands soon after the Japanese surrendered. The authorities realized that trade was essential in order to inject economic viability into Singapore. Towards this end, it released a number of army landing craft at very reasonable prices to the public for use as trading vessels. These boats could land anywhere, and were thus useful in providing access to many parts of Southeast Asia. Rubber importers immediately purchased them, as they were very versatile for collecting cargoes from remote locations.[8] By the end of 1946, such craft could be seen sailing near Palembang, loaded down

---

5   '$10 million Java-Singapore smuggling trade', *Malaya Tribune*, 25-6-1946, p. 2.
6   Directie Verre Oosten 85, 'Economisch Overzicht Malaya January 1948-April 1949', Compiled by CGDN Singapore, 15-5-1949. Other accounts estimate the extent of smuggling by weight. See, for example, Twang 1998:200.
7   'Darkness aids smugglers', *Malaya Tribune*, 5-4-1948, p. 4.
8   Archief Consulaat-Generaal Singapore 1946-51, Map 5, Singapore Overseas Chinese Importers and Exporters Association, Singapore Cons. Gen. 1946-54 (Singapore).

so heavily with rubber that Plimsoll would have turned in his grave.[9] The voyage between Singapore and Palembang usually took two days in good weather. Capable of eight knots per hour, the landing craft enjoyed a tremendous advantage over the slow-sailing junks. Some of these craft made two trips per month from Singapore to Sumatra, returning with rubber on each journey.[10]

The naval base in Singapore also sold speedboats. These were snapped up by Chinese businessmen and then resold to Indonesian contacts. Like the landing craft, these speedboats were ideal for the waters connecting Singapore with the Indonesian islands.[11] Such sales worried the Dutch because they believed the speedboats aided Chinese traders in their smuggling activities. In an attempt to deny British responsibility, the Secretary for Economic Affairs (A. Gilmour) stressed that complete speedboats were never sold, except for vessels that were small and slow. Sometimes the Chinese were only able to buy hulls of speedboats. After the necessary repairs, and the installation of an old motor cannibalized from elsewhere, the entire collection was resold to Indonesians or others for much profit. Gilmour assured the Dutch that for every sale, the buyers were screened. If there were complete speedboats available for sale, the offer would first be made to the Singapore harbour service or police, where there was a shortage of such equipment.[12]

From the surplus military stores, there was a range of goods that would come in handy for trade or smuggling. These included cooking utensils, furniture, harbour craft, bulldozers, vehicles, and radio sets. Bicycles also had to be smuggled (Coast 1952:165).

Even British army uniforms were suitable for smuggling; they were in demand because the Indonesian army was short of uniforms for its soldiers. Six Indonesians were arrested and charged for exporting textiles without a permit. Suspicion was raised when their motorboat raced at full speed for the open seas shortly after sundown from their anchorage off Beach Road. The destination: Tembilahan (on the coast of Sumatra). An alert Singapore police patrol gave chase. The sea was rough and it was not until the fugitive boat was about to clear the harbour breakwater that it was caught by the police launch. Searching the vessel, the police found a large quantity of cloth and military uniforms concealed in the engine room. According to the manifest, the vessel

---

[9] 'Impressions of Indonesian rule; Malaya's western neighbour; From a special correspondent', *Straits Times*, 4-11-1946, pp. 4 and 6.
[10] 'LCTs used for trade with Sumatra', *Straits Times*, 13-7-1946, p. 3.
[11] PG 173, Rapport van den Inlichtingendienst der Algemeene Politie (Singapore), No. 525GE, Singapore, By S. van Hulst, 27-8-1947.
[12] PG 185, Letter No. VIII-A-7323/163 from A.M.L. Winkelman to Minister of Foreign Affairs, 23-3-1948.

was only authorized to carry 7,000 jute sacks and cooking utensils. The crew was fined sums from $100 to $750 or rigorous imprisonment in lieu of.[13]

Shipping regulations not enforced

The vessels used for smuggling often melted into the colony of boats moored at Boat Quay and Beach Road, where as many as half the boats tied up were unmarked or inadequately marked. This made identification almost impossible, and helped smugglers to evade the authorities. If there were registration numbers, at least some effort could be made to identify ships that were used for smuggling. The master attendant (harbourmaster) in Singapore was confronted with many ships whose registration numbers were unknown or incomplete, and therefore little could be done to separate the smugglers from the non-smugglers. While many had no numbers, others had names but no registration numbers. Those with numbers displayed them in places that could be easily removed; indeed the numbers were so small in size that they could not be read from a distance. Some numbers were hastily scribbled while others were written over old numbers. There seemed to be no authority in Singapore that checked on shipping documentation. Certainly, the authorities themselves were not altogether certain of the regulations regarding the proper display of registration numbers. Officials remembered that the numbers must be sealed in, but when asked by Dutch authorities to confirm, no one could provide the complete set of conditions.[14]

This concern for proper identification numbers was not given the same emphasis by British authorities in Singapore. To them, the registration number was not important; what mattered was whether the ships had declared their cargo properly.[15] As far as ensuring every vessel was properly tagged with a registration number, enforcement was lax.[16]

Shipping papers were no different. They were either false or falsified. However, the prevailing laws made prosecution difficult because any detained vessel had to be released within 24 hours unless there was a *prima facie* case, and it was difficult to establish one within such a short time. It was also necessary to prove that the holder of false papers knew that they were false, and apparently many were not aware that their papers were not in

---

[13] 'Army uniforms being smuggled to Indonesians', *Straits Times*, 18-7-1946, p. 1.
[14] PG 380, Letter 1702-K-VII, from P.A. van der Poel, Secretaris voor Speciale Diensten, to Procureur-Generaal, 4-5-1949.
[15] PG 380, Letter 1978-K-VII, from P.A. van der Poel, Secretaris voor Speciale Diensten, to Procureur-Generaal, 7-6-1949.
[16] PG 380, Letter 3049-K-VII, from P.A. van der Poel, Secretaris voor Speciale Diensten, to Procureur-Generaal, 19-10-1949.

order or were not convinced that proper documentation was important.[17]

Customs officials in Singapore were also too lowly paid compared to the value of the goods they were supposed to inspect. Corruption and bribery of those in authority was easy enough.[18] The police could also be bribed so that smugglers could learn which places in Singapore goods could be unloaded without fear of detection.[19] Smuggling ships were known to have entered Boat Quay between two and four in the morning, and pay between $100 and $200 to the local marine police to evade arrest and avoid registration in the arrivals book.[20]

On the Dutch side, enforcement action was also severely hampered by lack of ships to conduct checks. Knowing this, several prauws (usually weighing not more than twenty tons each) would sail in large convoys to Singapore. If these prauws encountered ships of the Netherlands navy, only a few of them could be detained. Seizure was a time-consuming exercise. The seized prauws had to be escorted to the nearest Dutch-controlled harbour. There, the cargo would be seized. Since the navy did not have enough ships, the remaining prauws would proceed unhindered to Singapore at the sacrifice of a few.[21] Searching the cargo holds of seized ships for smuggled contraband was almost impossible. Cargo was piled high and there was no warehousing space to conduct a proper search. Weapons and ammunition were stuffed in all kinds of places. Ships often took in smuggled goods after the legal declarations were filed.[22]

However, a favourable environment played only a limited role. The crown jewel of the smuggling activity was the opportunity to acquire Straits dollars, a very desirable currency compared to the NEI guilder. Dollars were in demand because they paved the way for the smuggler to purchase the kind of goods he wanted on the Singapore market. In contrast, legal trade using guilders was risky, considering that the value of the guilder was subject to fluctuation.[23]

---

[17] PG 380, Letter 2512-K-VII, from P.A. van der Poel, Secretaris voor Speciale Diensten, to Procureur-Generaal, 11-8-1949.
[18] PG 380, Letter 1702-K-VII, from P.A. van der Poel, Secretaris voor Speciale Diensten, to Procureur-Generaal, 4-5-1949.
[19] PG 380, Letter 2168-K-VI, from P.A. van der Poel, Secretaris voor Speciale Diensten, to Procureur-Generaal, 28-6-1949.
[20] PG 417, Letter 1867-K-V, from P.A. van der Poel, Secretaris voor Speciale Diensten, to Procureur-Generaal, 21-5-1949.
[21] PG 285, Report by W.R. Kerkhoff to Hoofdcommissaris van Politie te Batavia, No. 2306/VID/R, dated 27-12-1947. Onderwerp: Exporthandel der Republiek.
[22] Directie Verre Oosten 336, Report No. S227/G/7/16 by Rear-Admiral G.B. Salm to First Government Secretary, 13-9-1947.
[23] Directie Verre Oosten 85, 'Economisch Overzicht Malaya Jan 1948-April 1949', Compiled by CGDN Singapore, 15-5-1949. An account of early currency fluctuations in Indonesia can be found in Cribb 1981:113-36.

The smugglers

Smugglers from Indonesia consisted of many types. Some were experienced, and pulled off many successful deals. Others were just a little wet behind the ears. They came to sell small quantities of rubber, obtained principally from Sumatra. Never having lived in a big city before, they were easy prey for confidence tricksters in Singapore, who made all kinds of offers to them to cheat them of the proceeds of their sales, including even the offer of dancing lessons at $120 per week.[24] Smugglers took advantage of the many opportunities to enrich themselves. This misuse of funds was so widespread that an army major from the Republican army unit in West Sumatra was sent to Singapore to investigate why there were so many cases of cheating by persons who were sent to Singapore with goods for sale.[25] Clearly there were some who claimed to represent the Republic but managed to invest their wealth in luxuries while in Singapore (Nasution 1978a:321).

The inexperience of these new arrivals must be contrasted with the phalanx of Chinese firms who were suspected of dabbling in smuggling behind the façade of legal business. These smugglers, all of them Chinese, had a relatively extensive network that included representatives stationed in Sumatra and elsewhere. Their business volume can be calculated in terms of the number of smuggling boats per firm arriving in Singapore daily. Some specialized in certain commodities. The names of some of these firms are listed below.[26]

Wan Tong Trading Company, 62 Cecil Street, with a branch of the same name in Tanjung Pandan (situated in Belitung island off the southeast coast of Sumatra).

Gian Lee and Company, 44 North Boat Quay, believed to be the biggest smuggler in tin ore and pepper. It had a representative in Pangkal Pinang (situated in Bangka island off the southeast coast of Sumatra).

Mui Heng, 40 Boat Quay, dealt in pepper smuggling. It also had a representative in Pangkal Pinang.

Leong Huat and Company, 62 Boat Quay. The proprietor was Gui Oh Nua, who was also involved in opium smuggling, as mentioned earlier.

Sen Long and Company, 43 Boat Quay. It was also represented in Pangkal Pinang.

Foong Huang, 80 Boat Quay. It had a representative at Sungai Liat.

[24] PG 168, CGDN, No. 75-48, Report by S. van Hulst, 28-3-1948.
[25] *Officiële bescheiden*, VI:455
[26] PG 841, Letter 3424-K-VII, from P.A. van der Poel, Secretaris voor Speciale Diensten, to Procureur-Generaal, 7-12-1949. Additional names can be found in PG 417, Letter 1524/L/II dated 11-4-1949 to Procureur-Generaal from P.A. van der Poel, Secretaris voor Speciale Diensten, where there is a list of Chinese firms in Singapore receiving smuggled copra and rubber from West Borneo.

Hiap Hoe Guan, 50 Church Street. It operated a shop at Pakan Baru under the name of Hiap Teck and did good business using a single vessel weighing three tons.

Heng Ham and Company, 50A Chulia Street, which had links with Singkawang in West Borneo.

Modus operandi

Discussion on the routes used by smugglers and the methods employed runs the risk of applying structural constructs to what must have been a disorganized web of contacts between individuals and companies. Nevertheless, in order to facilitate digestion of historical details, the risk of distorting reality will be necessary. In the discussion that follows, smuggling activities are described in terms of geographical segments. This seems to be the most convenient approach available. However, it should be remembered that the smuggling environment changed continuously. Favoured ports and stretches of coast replaced one another in rapid succession, depending on the intensity of checks exercised by the Dutch.[27]

The Sumatra sector

Palembang

Very soon after the end of the war, Singapore's trade with Sumatra revived, and one of the first places to benefit was the Palembang region in the south. The Japanese occupation had deprived the area of many goods, and in order to attract traders to send goods there, it was the policy of the Republican governor of South Sumatra, A.K. Gani, not to levy import duties. As a result, many ships stopped at Palembang before sailing up the Musi River from Singapore. By March 1946, supplies to the region became so plentiful that when the Indonesian general Oerip Soemohardjo arrived at Palembang from Java, he and his entourage were immediately given new uniforms and their bags were filled with gifts when they left. Palembang continued to be an important destination for ships from Singapore until the subsequent anti-Chinese riots frightened away the Chinese traders, who then preferred to stop at Jambi (see below).

Ships on the Singapore-Palembang route were supposed to dock at Tanjung Pinang in the Riau islands[28] for clearance. Some did not comply, and

---

[27] For the 'rise and fall' of ports (in Java and Sumatra) in response to changes in strategic situations, see Twang 1998:209.

[28] Smuggling from Singapore to the Riau islands was a night operation; during the day, the

instead sailed from somewhere within the myriad of islands near Tanjung Pinang during the night to another destination, Jambi.[29]

Jambi

Jambi was a nodal point for smuggling. In the early years of the revolution, oil, rubber, and copra were exported to Singapore from Jambi in exchange for textiles, canned food, and cigarettes (Sutter 1959, II:439, note 62). Trade was actively promoted to compensate for the years of deprivation during the war, drawing on the estate products found inland. The Dutch suspected that these export commodities were stolen from the Dutch-owned estates in the vicinity, but this was difficult to verify. Only a small detachment of four hundred Allied soldiers arrived in Jambi after the war to maintain security, and the good relations between the battalion and the local population meant that there was no outbreak of incidents (Nasution 1977:238). This kind of accommodation enabled Jambi's role as a trade centre with Singapore to increase further, especially after anti-Chinese feelings surfaced in nearby Palembang,[30] causing Chinese traders from Singapore to look for a more 'friendly' port.

In the vicinity of Jambi, cargo was discharged at Kampung Laut or Muara Sabak before continuing on to Palembang. These smuggling ships relied on coolies working on the *kelong* (fishing stakes) along the Sumatra coast to alert them to danger. During the day, flags would be used to serve warning of approaching Dutch patrol ships, and during the night, lamps were used.[31] These *kelong*, usually the ones located at strategic points between Labuan Bilik and Jambi, would light two red lamps at night or fly two flags during the day if a Dutch navy ship was in the neighbourhood. The all-clear signal was one red lamp at night or one flag during the day.[32] Documents were falsified to show that the ships arriving at Palembang from Jambi did not start their journeys there. *Chinchew* were often in possession of counterfeit stamps and declaration forms. The procedure of requiring ships to call at Tanjung Pinang for clearance was not foolproof either. Smuggling ships from Sumatra

---

ships would hide in one of the many islands. See PG 169(I), Halfmaandelijksche berichtgeving van den Secretaris belast met Bijzondere Diensten verbonden aan het Consulaat-Generaal, over de periode 1 t/m 14-9-1947, No. 544A, Singapore, By S. van Hulst, Secretaris voor Speciale Diensten, 15-9-1947.
[29] RI 552, Tweewekelijksche berichtgeving der Residentie Riouw over de periode 15 tot 31-12-1947, By J. van Waardenburg, Resident, Tandjong Pinang, 12-1-1948.
[30] *Officiële bescheiden*, VII:610.
[31] RI 552, Tweewekelijksche berichtgeving der Residentie Riouw over de periode 15 tot 31-12-1947, By J. van Waardenburg, Resident, Tandjong Pinang, 12-1-1948.
[32] RI 552, Tweewekelijksche berichtgeving van de Residentie Riouw over de periode 1 tot 15-11-1947, By J.B. van Schendel, Assistent-Resident, Tandjong Pinang.

would make their approach in the dark, unloading contraband before proceeding for checking. After inspection, the contraband was reloaded for the onward journey to Singapore. This evasion was possible because of the myriad mooring places around Tanjung Pinang.[33]

Pakan Baru

For the Sumatra sector, the smuggling trade between Pakan Baru and Singapore drew much attention because the same routes were used by gun smugglers to meet Republican needs for weapons. From the Sumatra side, motorboats were used to transport estate products like coffee, tea, and quinine to Sungai Apit, a village lying at the mouth of the Siak River. Then, during the night, the products were shipped by prauw to Selat Panjang, and from there motorboats from Singapore completed the journey. The crossing from Selat Panjang to Singapore was the most dangerous. There was even an Indonesian navy guard post at an island called Pulau Rangsang, where a lamp was placed to indicate that the passage was unsafe. This lamp could be seen from Selat Panjang. For the Singapore-Sumatra route, small boats carried goods from Pasir Panjang in western Singapore to Pulau Pisang, where the cargoes were loaded onto bigger boats originating from Selat Panjang. The goods eventually ended up as far away as the town of Pakan Baru.[34]

Another smuggling route from Singapore to Sumatra ran within British territorial waters along the western coast of Malaya till around Port Swettenham. Then, at night, the ships attempted a crossing to Labuan Bilik.[35]

For the smuggling operations between Singapore and Bagansiapiapi, firms in Singapore, upon learning that goods from Java had reached Bagansiapiapi, would send one or two motorboats there. Goods like tea, coffee, batik, rubber, sugar, peanuts, and peanut oil were available. These goods were brought over to the Singapore boats by small prauws and then hidden among the cargo that was legally permitted. Bribery was needed to induce guards to look away while the loading took place. By morning, the Singapore boats were well on their way home.[36]

The captains of the smuggling vessels used on the Singapore-Sumatra route were usually Malays or Chinese with passports certifying they were British subjects. In that way, the vessels would not be seized should the

[33] RI 552, Tweewekelijksche berichtgeving der Residentie Riouw over de periode 15 tot 31-12-1947, By J. van Waardenburg, Resident, Tandjong Pinang, 12-1-1948.
[34] PG 168, CGDN, No. 199-48, Singapore, Report by J.W.J de Haas, 30-11-1948.
[35] PG 169(I), Halfmaandelijksche berichtgeving van den Secretaris belast met Bijzondere Diensten verbonden aan het Consulaat-Generaal, over de periode 1 t/m 14-9-1947, No. 544A, Singapore, By S. van Hulst, Secretaris voor Speciale Diensten, 15-9-1947.
[36] PG 558, CGDN, No. 70-49, Singapore, Report by P.A. van der Poel, 9-4-1949.

Dutch navy detain them for carrying contraband. Only the *chinchew* would be responsible for the cargo.³⁷

Riau archipelago

One important feature of the smuggling trade in the Sumatra sector was the use of the Riau islands as a point of departure. This was a natural thing to do. Despite the separation of the Riau islands from the territorial jurisdiction of the British in Singapore and Malaya, the Chinese traders and the Malay inhabitants probably ignored this legal distinction and treated the Riau islands as part of Singapore for purposes of trade. One important instrument in trade was of course the use of currency, and in this regard, the Riau islands were to all intents and purposes part of the trade network of Singapore. Thousands of Straits dollars were circulating in the Riau islands as long ago as 1914. The currency enjoyed the trust of Chinese traders and the indigenous population. It prompted the Dutch Resident of Riau at that time, G.F. de Bruijn Kops, to make the very valid remark that:

> As far as concerns trade and shipping, the Riau islands are, at the least, a part of, if not exclusively dependent on Singapore. Everything was linked to Singapore. Everything, except a portion of gambier, was exported to Singapore. Indeed, there were direct connections from and to Singapore with each of the various islands. As a result, it was not possible to make mention of [the existence of] an important trade centre [in Riau]. The administration or owners of the majority of the investments in trade and shipping were established in Singapore. Communication with the famous emporium is heavy. Apart from the extensive prauw traffic, there were many daily or less frequent steamship connections with Singapore. Given this heavy influence of Singapore, it is difficult to avoid using Singapore standards in measuring the value of goods, although these values might have been expressed in [Dutch] guilders.³⁸

The border-free relationship between Singapore and Riau must therefore be factored into any discussion of the phenomena of 'smuggling'. If in 1914, when Dutch control over the Indonesian archipelago was in a much stronger position and Riau was already economically part of Singapore, how much more so in the period after 1945 when that same authority was severely challenged.

In fact, during the Japanese occupation, the Riau islands were 'Little Syonan', comparing them to Syonan, the Japanese name for Singapore. Karimun, one of the Riau islands, served as an entrepot and a collection point for

---

³⁷ RI 552, Tweewekelijksche berichtgeving van de Residentie Riouw over de periode 1 t/m 15-10-1947, By J. van Waardenburg, Resident, Tandjong Pinang, 23-10-1947.
³⁸ Memories van Overgave Riouw AA229, Memorie van overgave van den Resident van Riouw en Onderhoorigheden, G.F. de Bruijn Kops, Tandjong Pinang, 3-3-1914, pp. 187-8.

smugglers, black market operatives, and firms and agents of dubious reputation. Rice was then such an important trading commodity that the Japanese authorities were forced to tolerate the smuggling of rice between Karimun and Singapore (Twang 1998:94-6).

The Borneo sector

With respect to Borneo, the Singapore connection was also important. And again, as in the case of Riau, it would be useful to preface any discussion with an examination of pre-war patterns of trade.

Pre-war connections

The part of Borneo that enjoyed most trade contacts with Singapore was the western coastal areas. There, rubber was the principal export commodity. The slabs were sent in great quantities to Singapore, where they were remilled into sheets and then exported, mainly to America and partly to Europe. To encourage local rubber remilling, a special export tax was levied on 1 June 1934. As a result, the export of raw rubber to Singapore declined but purchasers of sheet rubber began to show up in Borneo. On the whole, good quality sheets were directly exported from Borneo to user countries but poorer quality sheets were sent to Singapore to be resorted and sold. Singapore was still an attractive market because a rubber exchange market had been established there and it was possible to find a buyer for each type of rubber. As for other types of goods, Borneo depended heavily on Singapore for its imports. This was especially true of the period before 1929. The Chinese traders in both territories had family relations with each other. Proximity was another factor. However, in the 1930s, licensing and other regulations were enforced, which strengthened the European import houses established in Java. The result was a shift of trade from Singapore to Java.[39] The war disrupted this pattern and during the post-1945 period, when the European import houses had not yet resumed their previous trading positions, the natural inclination was to look to Singapore for the goods that were in demand. By early 1946, this trade had clearly brought tremendous benefits to the region of West Borneo where, as noted by the Dutch authorities, the economy was clearly stronger than many other parts of the Indonesian archipelago.[40]

---

[39] Memories van Overgave Westerafdeling van Borneo, AA203, Algemeene Memorie Westerafdeling van Borneo van Resident J. Oberman, Pontianak, 30-8-1938, pp. 44-7.
[40] *Officiële bescheiden*, III:457.

Camouflage and corruption

A considerable proportion of this trade must have consisted of smuggling, in view of the elaborate efforts made to camouflage the activities. Vessels would ply from Singapore and upon reaching the small islands lying between Mempawah and Singkawang, would lie in wait while a scout was sent ahead to Singkawang or Pemangkat. When the coast was clear, a flashlight was used to send a signal. A white light meant safe passage. A red light indicated danger.[41] The vessels that came from Singapore were small motorboats not heavier than sixty tons each. These were mainly fishing vessels. The boats were registered in Singapore or Malaya. This facilitated movement because such boats could sail freely from Singapore to British-controlled Sarawak or in the general direction of Borneo with scarcely more than a permit, or even no papers at all. On the other hand, an Indonesian-registered boat would need guarantees of various kinds.[42]

From the Borneo side, small *sampan* would assemble at Pemangkat. Laden with rubber, the vessels would moor in little creeks waiting for smuggling boats from Singapore. When these were sighted, the *sampan* would move towards them for unloading once the all-clear signal was given.[43] Such operations had to be swiftly executed and were therefore labour-intensive. As many as forty coolies, working between 20.00 hours and midnight, were required.[44]

A common feature of the Singapore-Borneo run was bribery. Although the Dutch were relatively strong in Borneo compared to Sumatra and enforcement was in force, as for example in Pemangkat, boats could still leave if bribes had been paid to the customs officers, police, harbourmaster, and patrol officers.[45] Police patrols were bribed at the rate of one thousand guilders per smuggling boat. Police officers who performed night duty were paid one thousand guilders each, while gangland members were employed to keep a watch on the coasts.[46] Dutch reports insisted that a Chinese smuggler, Sin Thong Hin, stationed at Pemangkat, had an agreement with patrol vessel no. 47 to allow smuggling boats to pass unhindered.[47] Another patrol vessel,

---

[41] PG 556, CGDN, No. 112-49, Singapore, Report by P.A. van der Poel, 19-7-1949.
[42] PG 417, Letter 1867-K-V, from P.A. van der Poel, Secretaris voor Speciale Diensten, to Procureur-Generaal, 21-5-1949.
[43] PG 417, Letter 1524/L/II, from P.A. van der Poel, Secretaris voor Speciale Diensten, to Procureur-Generaal, 11-4-1949.
[44] PG 417, Letter 1867-K-V, from P.A. van der Poel, Secretaris voor Speciale Diensten, to Procureur-Generaal, 21-5-1949.
[45] PG 558, CGDN, No. 71-49, Singapore, Report by P.A. van der Poel, 11-4-1949.
[46] PG 417, Letter 1867-K-V, from P.A. van der Poel, Secretaris voor Speciale Diensten, to Procureur-Generaal, 21-5-1949.
[47] PG 417, Letter 1524/L/II, from P.A. van der Poel, Secretaris voor Speciale Diensten, to Procureur-Generaal, 11-4-1949.

no. 38, was even known to have given direct assistance to a smuggling boat. On the night of 7-8 May 1949, at 01.00 hours, a small sailing vessel weighing seven or eight tons and laden with goods was ready to sail to Singapore from Pemangkat. Because of the lack of wind, the vessel could not move and the smuggling firm in charge, Sin Thong Hin and Company, asked patrol vessel no. 38 for help to tow the boat to sea. The fee paid was 1,200 guilders.[48]

However, not all the patrol vessels were venal. The most feared patrols were the *Slamet* and the *Columbia*. The captain of the latter was a Dutchman. When it was his turn to patrol the seas at Singkawang or Pemangkat, the smugglers would move to Sukadana near Pontianak to ship their rubber.[49]

If arrests were made, the smugglers are also known to have made provisions for such eventualities. The smuggling vessels sometimes had on board a straw man or *chinchew palsu*, who acted as the person responsible for the cargo in the event of any trouble with the authorities. He was paid $100 or five hundred guilders per trip. In addition, he was paid $10 per day during his stay in a foreign port. The real *chinchew* stayed behind the scenes. The *chinchew palsu* had to take the rap for any legal charges. He also had to be prepared for imprisonment. If that happened, money was provided to maintain his family.[50]

Further east

The web of smuggling activities centred on Singapore did not stop at Borneo. In December 1948, the Minister of Justice of the Dutch-backed state of East Indonesia headquartered at Makassar, Soumokil, reported to its parliament that for the past two years, as much as eighty million guilders worth of goods had been smuggled out of East Indonesia, mostly to Singapore. One firm in Makassar reportedly made a net profit of a million guilders in less than a year. The products that were smuggled made their way from inland areas to the sea by truck or buffalo cart, and then by prauw to larger ships at sea, which then sailed to Singapore. There were even prauws that made the long voyage direct. For bigger shipments, smugglers used an uninhabited island off the coast of Celebes to assemble coffee, copra, and similar products.[51]

---

[48] PG 417, Letter 1867-K-V, from P.A. van der Poel, Secretaris voor Speciale Diensten, to Procureur-Generaal, 21-5-1949.
[49] PG 417, Letter 1867-K-V, from P.A. van der Poel, Secretaris voor Speciale Diensten, to Procureur-Generaal, 21-5-1949.
[50] PG 417, Letter 1867-K-V, from P.A. van der Poel, Secretaris voor Speciale Diensten, to Procureur-Generaal, 21-5-1949.
[51] 'Smugglers sail to Singapore', *Straits Times*, 10-12-1948, p. 1.

Smuggling by air

Smuggling contraband was not limited to sea-lanes. In June 1947, an attempt was made to export quinine by air from Yogyakarta to Manila. In October 1947, the same plane was used to drop Republican parachutists into those parts of Borneo occupied by the Dutch. The Dutch were helpless. The skies were even more difficult to patrol than the seas. However, an opportunity came in December 1947 when bad weather forced the same plane to divert to Singapore while flying between Yogyakarta and Sumatra. This time the plane carried a foul-smelling coffin containing the decomposing body of a junior Republican soldier whose rich Sumatran family had arranged for the air passage after his death in Yogyakarta. Acting on information received from the Dutch consul, the Singapore police searched the coffin for contraband. The body was transferred to the local morgue where air-conditioning was available, while technicians worked on the plane's engine. To avoid publicity, the plane was allowed to leave at five the next morning.[52] The incident reveals Dutch suspicions of every form of transport between Indonesia and Singapore.

The efforts of the Dutch to control smuggling became more effective in the second half of 1948. By that time, out of ten prauws, or small boats at sea, at least six or seven were detained by patrols for investigations. As a result, smugglers were compelled to be more cautious. Goods like copra began to pile up in godowns, to be released only in small amounts when circumstances were favourable. When the Second Military Action ended in January 1949, the number of smuggling craft arriving in Singapore showed a marked decline.[53] This is a reflection of the fact that surveillance by Dutch patrols had been strengthened. Previously 'safe' routes between Singapore on the one hand and places like Borneo and Indragiri (Sumatra) on the other were no longer usable.[54]

In general, the rate of smuggling always increased when vigilance fell, or when it was expected that vigilance would increase in the near future. If an agreement between the Dutch and Indonesians seemed imminent, and more peaceful conditions were expected to lead to increased vigilance, Chinese traders would try harder to smuggle as much as possible before the agreement was signed.[55]

The above smuggling activities focused largely on smuggling of conventional commodities. Attention should now be turned to the smuggling of weapons and other unconventional commodities like opium.

[52] 'Secret take-off as police guard Indonesian plane', *Straits Times*, 16-1-1948, p. 1. An account that differs in details about the coffin can be found in *Memoar pejuang* (1992, Chapter VII).
[53] PG 558, CGDN, No. 29-49, Singapore, By P.A. van der Poel, 10-2-1949.
[54] PG 558, CGDN, No. 43-49, Singapore, By P.A. van der Poel, 1-3-1949.
[55] PG 556, CGDN, No. 123-49, Singapore, Report by P.A. van der Poel, 27-8-1949.

Weapons

To defend the Republic's sovereignty, the acquisition of weapons was of paramount importance. After the Japanese surrendered, a lot of weapons were stashed away in remote parts of Southeast Asia. The Philippines was a major source. For a time, there was a steady flow of weapons from the 'Lost 93rd', a Chinese nationalist division stranded in Burma's Shan states after the war (Rowan 1949:49-52). From Bangkok, military attachés reported that they did not think large amounts of automatic weapons were obtained in Siam. Some could have ended up in the market but most were sold to the Shan State of Kengtung in the north, where many inhabitants were threatened by the communists and had to resort to arms. In southern Siam, Chinese businessmen could get access to a number of fire weapons, but it was not believed that these constituted a large source.[56] Near Singapore, a favourite hideout for weapons was the state of Johore, where the largest arms dump was located and its discovery was only reported as late as February 1949. Found southwest of the abandoned Senai Kulai airfield, the arms consisted of aircraft machine guns, Japanese light anti-aircraft guns, a Lewis gun, Thomson submachine guns, shotguns, hand grenades, and other assorted arms.[57]

Many of these weapons were destined for the scrap heap or were to be thrown into the sea.[58] However, there were many middlemen who aspired to lay their hands on the weapons before they reached that inglorious end, for purposes of resale to those who needed them, like the pro-Republican units fighting the Dutch. At a trial of an alleged gun smuggler (Carlton Hire) in Tanjung Pinang in 1948, it was claimed that weapons were openly offered for sale by newspaper advertisers in Singapore, but a police permit was needed to import arms.[59] If the claim could be substantiated, this was true only of the situation before 1948. By June of that year, very stringent controls were enforced in the wake of an armed revolt launched by the communists in Malaya.

The arms smugglers

Who were these traders in weapons? Because operations were conducted in a cloak-and-dagger fashion, hard evidence is not easily available. The journalist with *Utusan Melayu*, A. Samad Ismail, was one who smuggled arms to Indonesia, although his operations were so secretive that even his wife did

---

[56] Directie Verre Oosten 74, Ambassador in Bangkok (C.W.A Schürmann) to Consul-General (Singapore), No. 2872, 2-8-1949.
[57] 'Largest arms dump found', *Malaya Tribune*, 21-2-1949, p. 3.
[58] PG 378, Letter from P.A. van der Poel (Secretary for Special Duties, Netherlands Consulate General Singapore) addressed to Mr E.A.G. Blades, Special Branch, Singapore, dated 11-5-1949.
[59] 'Hire tells of his arrest', *Malaya Tribune*, 21-1-1948, p. 1.

not know at the time that he was involved (A. Samad Ismail 1987:1). Another arms smuggler was Rais Abin, who later rose to the rank of general in the Indonesian army and became ambassador to Kuala Lumpur. Rais Abin and A. Samad Ismail worked together in arms smuggling deals.[60]

Sources from the PKBI-PI suggest that those who came to Singapore to purchase arms were of different types. Most were unfamiliar with the intricacies of wheeling and dealing in Singapore. Some came with goods to trade for weapons. Others brought cheques that could be cashed in Chinese shops in Singapore. Many worked alone. Often, they disappeared among the inhabitants once they landed in Singapore and became 'mystery men', not revealing their whereabouts. Some feigned innocence but were surreptitiously at work trying to identify weapons sources. In contrast, there were others who assumed an image of wealth, openly flouting their money. Still others forgot their mission and got sidelined by the world of prostitutes (*Rahsia perdjuangan* 1948:33-5). Lack of experience was a serious limitation. An emissary with the rank of colonel and empowered by the president of the Republic himself would arrive in Singapore to purchase speedboats and torpedoes to attack Dutch ships. Such a mission sounded so important, but was unsophisticatedly simple. Others tried to establish a branch of Bank Indonesia, but such an objective would have been difficult to achieve (Nasution 1977:314). A.H. Nasution, then a Republican military officer, summed it all up when he complained: 'While the TRI [Republican] soldiers suffered on the battlefield, the weapons-hunters enjoyed themselves in Singapore'.[61] (A common meeting place of weapons smugglers was Restaurant Kita,[62] where notes were exchanged and experiences recounted.)

The vigilance of the Singapore police in weapons also made transactions in arms difficult. When caught, arms dealers faced imprisonment. T. Hoetoegaloeng was sentenced to five years' jail upon conviction of illegal possession of small arms, kept in Paya Lebar district in an innocent-looking wicker basket.[63]

Lest the impression be given that most of the weapons smugglers were failures, it should be noted that there were exceptions like Abdoel Latif from Kuala Tungkal, who operated three motorboats, the *Melati*, *Rose*, and *Bunga*. These boats sailed between Singapore and Jambi, carrying weapons hidden in steerage compartments in the *tongkang* that were towed by these boats. For

---

[60] *Samad Ismail* 1987:1. See also *Memoar pejuang* 1992:40.
[61] Nasution 1977:314. An engaging account of deceit, deception, and corruption can be found in Tantri (1960, Chapter XXXV).
[62] PG 168, CGDN, No. 172-48, Singapore, Report by J.W.J de Haas, 7-10-1948.
[63] 'Discovery of arms cache; Indonesian sent to jail', *Malaya Tribune*, 15-1-1947, p. 5.

these purposes, the compartments were fitted with false board covers.[64]

The Chinese were also participants in arms smuggling. One example is Tan Chi Ku, a Chinese trader from Selat Panjang in Riau. Along with others, he survived the Japanese occupation by smuggling rice from Singkep to Selat Panjang. During the early days of the Republican administration, he started a business in Selat Panjang, but in 1946 this was terminated and he became leader of a Chinese dockworkers' organization. Because of poor remuneration, he resigned after only four months and returned to smuggling. By 1948, he had become well known to the Republican authorities in Pakan Baru, Bukit Tinggi, and Jambi as a weapons smuggler. In all, he was responsible for smuggling to Pakan Baru two Bren-guns, one Vickers machine gun, twenty carbines, and twenty thousand cartridges. The weapons found their way to a Mobile Police Brigade stationed at Bukit Tinggi. Republican army officers who came to Singapore to purchase weapons were known to be always in touch with Tan Chi Ku.[65]

The Republican army in Pakan Baru was well supplied with military material from Singapore. At a parade in 1946, some one thousand Republican army personnel were able to don British uniforms, all sequestered from Singapore. There was a report that men dressed in British military garb attacked a Dutch post, and this was extremely confusing to the defenders, who were not sure about the identity of their opponents. The uniforms were delivered courtesy of a Chinese businessman from Singapore. He operated a huge landing craft that carried not only new British uniforms but also Japanese military helmets, gas masks, and tyres.[66]

Often it was difficult to distinguish between weapons smuggling and trade in approved commodities. Seemingly innocuous ventures by innocent traders were invariably involved in some degree of weapons smuggling. There is the case of a motorboat that left Tanjong Katong in the eastern part of Singapore ostensibly bound for Pemangkat in Borneo to trade. At least that was the impression of one crew.[67] But when the first steersman came on board, he carried a container. Once at sea, the container was opened, revealing six revolvers, three hand grenades, and one hundred cartridges. On the way, the motorboat stalled near the island of Sumaja, and the first steersman

---

[64] RI 551, Tweewekelijksche berichtgeving der Residentie Riouw over de periode 16 t/m 30-6-1946 by J. van Waardenburg, Resident, Tandjong Pinang, 6-7-1946.
[65] PG 168, CGDN, No. 199-48, Singapore, Report by J.W.J. de Haas, 30-11-1948.
[66] RI 551, Tweewekelijksche berichtgeving der Residentie Riouw over de periode 1 t/m 16-8-1946 by J. van Waardenburg, Resident.
[67] PG 166, Proces-verbaal, Interrogation of Tan Tjein Loh, 35 years, b. Canton, van beroep barbier, 243 Middle Road, by J.W.J. de Haas, Inspecteur van Politie der eerste klasse, CGDN, in presence of CID detective Tan Tong.

went on shore with the container. When he returned, the container was no longer with him.[68]

Prices for weapons varied. In 1948, Singapore-based smugglers could barter two carbines and a thousand cartridges for a ton of tea; one machine gun and a thousand cartridges were worth 2.5 tons of tea; six anti-aircraft guns and a thousand cartridges could be bartered for six tons of tea.[69] However, the market for weapons was not usually a barter system; vendors preferred cash or gold. American automatic rifles in Singapore fetched $400 each, light and heavy machine guns cost $1,000 each, the price of light field-pieces varied, with light anti-aircraft guns costing $1,500 apiece and four-inch guns $1,200 each. Ammunition for all types of weapons were transacted, including those for heavy machine guns at 0.70 cents each, and those for four-inch guns at nine Straits dollars each. The prices were negotiable but the total value involved must have run into fairly sizeable amounts.[70]

Once purchased, the weapons were loaded onto speedboats with a capacity of forty tons and a speed of fourteen to fifteen knots. The actual transhipment route for most of the caches ran through the islands surrounding Singapore, usually keeping clear of British-controlled waters so as not to alert the police, leaving only the Dutch blockade to be negotiated.[71] Smugglers also used speedboats to make the eight-hour journey from Singapore to Indragiri.[72] Other landing points for weapons brought in from Singapore during the early days of independence, before the Dutch got wise to the weapons smuggling, included Tanjung Balai (Asahan), Pakan Baru, and Bengkalis (*Rahsia perdjuangan* 1948:36).

Indoff's complicity

Did Indoff incorporate weapons acquisition as part of its strategy in Singapore? This was an extremely controversial matter. The clandestine nature of weapons purchase made it difficult to ascertain with accuracy the extent of Indoff involvement. However, it was known that military representatives from Sumatra made regular forays into Singapore to seek assistance for arms purchase, sometimes descending on Indoff for assistance. An example

---

[68] PG 166, Proces-verbaal, Interrogation of Tan Tjein Loh, 35 years, b. Canton, van beroep barbier, 243 Middle Road, by J.W.J. de Haas, Inspecteur van Politie der eerste klasse, CGDN, in presence of CID detective Tan Tong.
[69] *Officiële bescheiden*, XIII: 574.
[70] PG 771, 'International firearms dealers in Singapore negotiating transactions, large quantities transacted, but shipments by-pass Singapore', *Sin Chew Jit Poh*, 6-4-1948.
[71] PG 771, 'International firearms dealers in Singapore negotiating transactions, large quantities transacted, but shipments by-pass Singapore', *Sin Chew Jit Poh*, 6-4-1948.
[72] *Officiële bescheiden*, XIII:574.

was Major Ali Rashid, who was referred by friends to Oetoyo. Rashid was a senior officer (second-in-command) with the Indonesian intelligence service stationed at Bukit Tinggi. He had come in September 1947 to purchase weapons, for which he was prepared to pay with a shipment of rubber already available at Pakan Baru.[73] According to a Dutch report, the major was also the commandant of the 5th battalion of the 3rd division of the Republican army at Pakan Baru. He was empowered to take charge of all Republican (or perhaps Sumatran?) interests in Singapore and Malaya.[74] Oetoyo advised against his using Singapore as a base to buy weapons because the risk of discovery was very high.[75] This reluctance to comply with the request to help, however, tarnished Oetoyo's reputation. Rashid was a Sumatran and the rumour circulated that Oetoyo would only help the Javanese.[76]

Publicly, Oetoyo denied that Indoff was involved in the illegal purchase of weapons. He claimed that Sjahrir had issued specific instructions not to get involved. However, given Singapore's close proximity to arms supplies, it was unavoidable that Oetoyo should receive requests to purchase arms. In another instance, the police in Sumatra sought his assistance to acquire weapons for their task of maintaining law and order. He asked for a letter of authority to deal directly with the British government on the matter and Oetoyo was in fact given such a mandate in early 1948. This mandate did not result in any material achievements, allegedly because he did not have the funds.[77]

However, the Dutch supplied incriminating evidence to the Malayan Special Branch (police in charge of security) in order to taint Oetoyo's testimony. In one document that was sent to the British, Oetoyo was alleged to have written:

> We must be v. careful in letting Pemudas organize arms supplies for they are not cunning enough. I, myself, with the aid of British officers, have sent arms to Sumatra already several times. I would like to cooperate with Pemudas if only they knew how to hold their tongues.[78]

The weapons trade was an explosive issue in Singapore and the Federation of Malaya. In June 1948, a state of emergency had been declared by the

---

[73] PG 173, Rapport van den Inlichtingendienst der Algemeene Politie (Singapore), No. 507GE, Singapore, By S. van Hulst, 9-8-1947; PG 304, 'Indonesian agencies in Malaya', Secret (109) in M.S. 815, Written by H.Q. Malayan Security Service, 23-6-1948.
[74] *Officiële bescheiden*, IV:215.
[75] PG 173, Rapport van den Inlichtingendienst der Algemeene Politie (Singapore), No. 510GE, By S. van Hulst, 12-8-1947.
[76] PG 173, Rapport van den Inlichtingendienst der Algemeene Politie (Singapore), No. 517GE, Singapore, By S. van Hulst, 16-8-1947.
[77] PG 304, Letter from S. van Hulst to Procureur-Generaal, dated 12-7-1948.
[78] PG 304, 'Indonesian agencies in Malaya', Secret (109) in M.S. 815, Written by H.Q. Malayan Security Service, 23-6-1948.

British to control communist activities. Since the communists had embarked on an armed struggle against British colonial rule, the supply of weapons to them was a matter of critical importance. The Netherlands government tried to prove that there were close links between communists operating in Indonesia, Burma, China, and Malaya. The evidence was flimsy. At the United Nations, the Netherlands representative submitted two documents that demonstrated a link between the communists in Indonesia and Malaya. The first document was issued by the Commander of the Banteng Division of the Republican army and addressed to the Republican Indonesian representative in Kuala Lumpur in May 1948. In it, he wrote,

> On the strength of the agreement between the high command of the Army and the Indonesian communist leaders, I give my assent to your cooperation with Malayan communist leaders throughout Malaya because they have considerable influence in Malaya and Singapore.

The second document originated from the Indonesian communist party in Sumatra. This time, the link with the communists in Malaya was even more tenuous. It contained a statement that 'All the KMT rascals will soon be put in a concentration camp [...] we are going to take revenge on them like the Communists in Malaya'.[79] From the records, the evidence on communist links between Malaya or Singapore and Indonesia was sparse.

It was likely that Oetoyo had no hand in the smuggling of firearms from Singapore to Indonesia, for the reason that he was the political representative and could not be expected to get involved in such activities.[80] But even if Oetoyo was not involved, he could have been unwittingly drawn into providing indirect help to weapons smugglers in his official capacity as the person in charge of Indoff. On 29 December 1947, a Dakota aircraft made a forced landing at Changi airstrip in Singapore. The plane carried 29 Indonesians, none of them with travel documents. Oetoyo undertook to provide surety for them in Singapore until such time as they were able to depart. On 1 January 1948, 27 of these left Singapore by train on their way to Port Swettenham from where, according to Oetoyo, they would return to Indonesia. As far as is known, the 27 dispersed at the first opportunity and their whereabouts were unknown.[81] They were suspected by the British authorities to be people interested in purchasing weapons.

---

[79] 'Malayan Reds in Java link: Dutch', *Straits Times*, 21-1-1949, p. 3.
[80] PG 385, Statement of Moekarto (alias Sowigno) son of Motowidigdo, Javanese, aged 37, living at 17 Pakoelaman, Djokjakarta, Java. Recorded by Inspector Yusoff at Special Branch on 2-10-1948 and 3-10-1948. For John Coast's press interview denying Indoff's complicity, see Coast 1952:184.
[81] PG 304, 'Indonesian agencies in Malaya', Secret (109) in M.S. 815, Written by H.Q. Malayan Security Service, 23-6-1948.

Successful attempts at arms smuggling

If the evidence against Oetoyo was not conclusive, there was at least one Indoff official who confessed to being personally involved in the weapons smuggling activities. This was Darusman, whose exploits in Operation Mariam Bee were mentioned above.[82] In 1946, the Ministry of Defence in Yogyakarta also established its own agency in Singapore to source for weapons. Major Ali Daeng Prawiro was put in charge and he was able to maintain a logistics facility of seven seaworthy vessels that plied between Singapore and Sumatra. Details of the goods carried by the ships are not available, but the reticence of Major Ali to mix with Indonesian expatriates in Singapore suggests that something clandestine was going on. His activities ended in September 1948, when his agency was placed under Indoff's jurisdiction, and it was decided then to discontinue Major Ali's undercover work so as not to compromise Indoff's official role (Darusman 1992:28).

John Lie (Jahya Daniel Dharma) was another important arms smuggler (Darusman 1992:29). Senior Republican officials entrusted him to contact Oetoyo regarding the purchase of ammunition especially in mid-1949, when guerrilla war against the Dutch had to be intensified and weapons were most in need. However, there was little or no money for payment.[83]

As a smuggler, John Lie's exploits were legendary. His network of operations spread to Manila, Penang, Bangkok, Rangoon, New Delhi, and of course Singapore. Singapore was only one sector; many of John Lie's operations were connected to the Penang, Aceh, and Bangkok sectors.[84] According to one account (Rowan 1949:49-52), Lie's career as a smuggler was like a religious conversion. He had been praying that his country would be transformed from a wild jungle into a Garden of Eden. However, he declared vehemently there would be no Dutchmen there. Lie said,

> When I was a boy, I did wrong. The Lord told me to move on, and I went to sea. I spent fifteen years on Dutch ships sailing between Durban and Shanghai. But I saw the Dutch did wrong, so once again I moved on. I went to the Holy Land. There, God told me to go home and help make Indonesia a Garden of Eden.

---

[82] Suryono Darusman, 'Singapore and the Indonesian Revolution 1945-1950', typescript.
[83] PG 380, Letter 2262-G-I, from P.A. van der Poel, Secretaris voor Speciale Diensten, to Procureur-Generaal, 7-7-1949.
[84] Five interesting photographs of John Lie are available in Directie Verre Oosten 74, 21-10-1949, Br./N 6963 Smokkelaffairs John Lie. The photographs show pictures of John Lie's boat and smuggled goods (automobiles, motorcycles, tyres, electric motors, medical goods), and the bridge of the ship for his smuggling missions in which John Lie hung the plate 'Have faith in God'. The same folder contains an article, 'Marine vangt John Lie's smokkelschip van Siam naar Atjeh met de bijbel op de brug', *Nieuwsblad van Sumatra*, 4-10-1949, as well as a report on the chase to capture one of John Lie's boats near Aceh.

VI Clandestine activities

In 1949, Lie was 39 years old. He bought five ships from the British but all were shelled, strafed, and bombed, leaving only one that was never caught.[85]

The Mariam Bee operation, Major Ali's contributions, and John Lie's activities are probably the most outstandingly successful, but this was not the case with other operations. However, I do not wish to give the impression that weapons smuggling was a major achievement of the revolution in Singapore. There were more failed or aborted missions than successes. Often, greed triumphed over nationalist passion; this was a major stumbling block to the successful completion of any weapons smuggling mission. Supplies of arms could be negotiated in Singapore, and officials in charge of dumping them in the seas were prepared to hand them over to Republican agents instead. However, those in charge of the disposal insisted on cash payments. Republicans could not comply with such conditions. Also, the Republican policy was to pay only after the goods had landed,[86] and this did not contribute towards ensuring cooperation.

Aborted operations

There were a few aborted operations that failed for the reasons mentioned above and possibly others. Project Siam was one of these. Siam was one of those places in Southeast Asia where large caches of arms could be found. As an ally of the Japanese during the Pacific War, Siam was required to destroy a quantity of weapons that included light firearms as well as field guns. But through a Siamese vice-admiral, a plot was hatched to store the arms in rice ships and transfer them in mid-voyage to ships of the Soon Hong *kongsi* (firm) waiting off Singapore. For this purpose, Darusman was supposed to proceed to Bangkok for the arrangements, but for unclear reasons the project was cancelled.[87]

Another location where weapons were available was Johore. The weapons there had been left behind or hidden by the resistance movement known as Force 136 during the Japanese occupation. The problem was how to get these weapons shipped to Indonesia. Various attempts to smuggle them into Singapore for transhipment were aborted.[88]

---

[85] Directie Verre Oosten 74, 21-10-1949, Br./N 6963 Smokkelaffaires John Lie. John Lie gave an account of the adventures he encountered running the blockade, how he survived attacks by Dutch patrols, and other exploits. See *Memoar pejuang* 1992, Chapter X.
[86] PG 378, Letter from P.A. van der Poel, (Secretary for Special Duties, Netherlands Consulate-General Singapore) to E.A.G. Blades, Special Branch, Singapore, 11-5-1949.
[87] PG 378, Letter from P.A. van der Poel (Secretary for Special Duties, Netherlands Consulate-General Singapore) addressed to Mr E.A.G. Blades, Special Branch, Singapore, 11-5-1949.
[88] PG 378, Letter from P.A. van der Poel (Secretary for Special Duties, Netherlands Consulate-General Singapore) addressed to Mr E.A.G. Blades, Special Branch, Singapore, 11-5-1949.

The case that received most publicity was the Airabu weapons smuggling ring. In a most colourful drama that had the makings of a Hollywood movie, Singapore detectives disguised as Indonesian soldiers boarded a ship in the Riau archipelago in September 1948 and seized forty cases of arms and ammunition. The arrest was made outside Singapore, the weapons originated from the Philippines, and the weapons were not intended for shipment to Indonesia but to plantation owners in Malaya who wanted to defend themselves from bandits in the jungles. Moreover, Indonesians were not involved. However, the case received much news coverage in Singapore and there were almost daily reports in Singapore of the trial in Tanjung Pinang.[89] There was such wide publicity because the Airabu trial posed issues that were far wider than the innocence or guilt of each individual accused of complicity in gun smuggling. Regardless of the verdict, the trial showed that arms smuggling existed in Southeast Asia on a vast scale.

But why did it exist? The trial, of course, did not consider that question. It existed because of the political conditions that were allowed to develop. The police could snare individual gun smugglers, but there would always be others to take their place as long as there was a market. There was an unstated assumption behind the wide public interest in the trial. If it was permissible for Britain and the United States to supply arms and training to the Netherlands, then the Republic was morally justified to buy arms from anybody who would sell them. The Dutch military actions were carried out using British and United States equipment. This created a situation in which the Republic had to resort to gun smugglers to fight for survival.[90] There were therefore ideological and moral reasons for the wide publicity given to the Airabu trial, but there was also a practical perspective. Evidence during the trial implicated an American businessman in Manila by the name of George C. Murray. When Murray was murdered in the Philippines, documents were found in his house describing a million-dollar smuggling ring selling guns to the Indonesians (Rowan 1949).

Another source of weapons was China, then in the throes of a civil war. Indonesian agents used Singapore as the launching pad for operations involving China. One of these agents was Colonel Oemar Slamet. By his own account, he entered Singapore at dawn in early December 1946, by motor sampan from Karimun. In Singapore, he established contact with the Malayan Communist Party (MCP), and through that organization, he

---

[89] Details on the Airabu smuggling case are found in the following reports: 'Airabu island seizure; Police dressed as Indonesian soldiers', *Straits Times*, 25-9-1948, p. 1; 'Handed over to Dutch, charge; Remarkable case, says Counsel', *Straits Times*, 3-11-1948, p. 7; 'Airabu guns trial starts today', *Straits Times*, 16-12-1948, p. 1; 'Dutch seized Malaya arms says pilot', *Straits Times*, 18-12-1948, pp. 1 and 3; 'Americans gaoled for gunrunning', *Straits Times*, 5-1-1949, p. 1.
[90] 'Carlton hire', *Malaya Tribune*, 29-1-1949, p. 4.

was able to ascertain the supplier of weapons from China. Oemar Slamet subsequently moved to Hong Kong, and Singapore was never a base of operations, strictly speaking. He did not have kind words for the activities of the Indonesians in Singapore. He thought Singapore needed to be cleared of traitors who passed themselves off as supporters of the Indonesian independence movement but were really enriching themselves. However, the colonel admitted that the cost of residing in Singapore was high. Since he had to establish contact with international representatives in Singapore, he was forced to maintain a decent standard of living.[91]

Oemar Slamet's account, however, was contradicted by Dutch investigations. Only two facts were corroborated – that he slipped into Singapore and that he tried to smuggle weapons. According to Dutch documents, he was a fraud. Oemar Slamet was not an active colonel. He had deserted from the Republican army, and arrived in Singapore claiming falsely that he was empowered by President Soekarno to purchase weapons. Only Tobing believed him sufficiently to write a letter of recommendation (in September 1947) for Oemar Slamet. In this letter, it was explained that he had no credentials to show, as they had been destroyed when he slipped through the Dutch blockade. In Singapore, he was suspected of counterfeiting Siamese currency notes to buy weapons in Bangkok, apart from his attempts to establish contacts in China through the MCP. Dutch authorities described him as 'a great swindler'.[92] If he succeeded in smuggling any materials of value to Indonesia, these were confined to trucks that were off-loaded in international waters outside Singapore to avoid alerting the Dutch.[93] Reports on Oemar Slamet's subsequent activities border on fantasy. In August 1947, he called a meeting at a hotel in Singapore to convince various Indonesians to fund his weapons purchases. The audience sought an endorsement from Oetoyo, but Oetoyo refused and the plans fell through. Subsequently, the mystery deepened. Oemar Slamet wanted to travel to Bangkok where a communist coup was expected. Once the Soviet Union had established an embassy there, he would make Bangkok the big anti-colonial base of Southeast Asia.[94]

Many other operations probably failed because they involved a cash deposit, and the Republican authorities were only prepared to pay up after

---

[91] PG 190, CMI document No. 5467, 13-4-1947.
[92] PG 181, Letter No. 1017/X/GB16, from H.W. Felderhof (Procureur-Generaal) to Colonel K. Drost (Base Commander, Batavia), 25-2-1948. The letter of recommendation issued by S.L. Tobing is also enclosed in the same file.
[93] PG 181, Report by Director, Malayan Security Service, 11-4-1947.
[94] PG 181, Letter, No. PS/10117 from Elink Schuurman to Tijdelijk Zaakgelastigde Bangkok, 14-11-1947; PG 181, Letter from S. van Hulst (Commissaris van Politie II) to Onderhoofd van den Dienst der Algemeene Recherche, Batavia.

the goods were delivered.[95] Only if there was the kind of goodwill involved in operations like the Mariam Bee would there be some chance of success.

As for the PKBI-PI, its involvement in weapons smuggling was only very minimal. However, one of its executive members, Herman Simandjoentak, was arrested for having links with a weapons smuggler who was caught red-handed at Karimun (*Rahsia perdjuangan* 1948:44). Dutch reports give a slightly different version of the arrest. According to them, Simandjoentak was arrested as a result of close cooperation with the British police. He was detained after returning from Palembang, where he delivered two tommy guns, 26 revolvers, and five thousand cartridges.[96] Apart from that isolated case, there do not seem to be any other instances.

The records show that there were individual cases of successful weapons smuggling in the early months after the end of the war, but there were no extensive schemes in operation. With hindsight, the Netherlands consul-general in Singapore thought the concern over weapons smuggling was excessive. The officer in charge of patrolling the seas between Singapore and Indonesia, Vice-Admiral A.S. Pinke, said major weapons smuggling attempts were never confirmed. The Netherlands navy never caught a ship carrying a large amount of weapons. Dutch sources also quote an admission by A.A. Maramis, Republican Minister of Finance in 1948, to Netherlands authorities in Bangkok that there was much discussion on weapons smuggling but the outcome had not been significant.[97]

Opium smuggling

Diplomacy, welfare, and weapons did not come cheap. After attempts to raise money through trade failed, the Republican government (of Amir Sjarifoeddin) made the decision in July 1947 to sell its stock of opium.[98] The Dutch blockade of Republican ports made it very difficult for the Republicans to export produce like rubber, sugar, and tobacco. The Republican government had not yet signed any convention or international agreement governing the sale of opium.[99]

---

[95] PG 378, Letter from P.A. van der Poel (Secretary for Special Duties, Netherlands Consulate-General Singapore) addressed to Mr E.A.G. Blades, Special Branch, Singapore, dated 11-5-1949.
[96] RI 551, Tweewekelijksche berichtgeving der Residentie Riouw over de periode 16 t/m 31-7-1946; By J. van Waardenburg, Resident, Tandjong Pinang, 6-8-1946.
[97] Directie Verre Oosten 74, A.M.L Winkelman (Consul-General Singapore) to Minister of Foreign Affairs, VIII-m-1/27753/621, 22-11-1949.
[98] PG 385, Statement of R. Moekarto Notowidigdo of Klaten (Soerakarta) 10, Kepatian, Java recorded by R.S. Tufnell at 0800 hours, 1-10-1948 to 2-10-1948, the witness speaking English. Soekarno himself confirmed that opium was smuggled out of Indonesia. See Adams 1965:235-6.
[99] PG 166, Statement of Moekarto recorded on 2-10-1948 and 3-10-1948.

At the time of the Japanese surrender, there was about 22 tons of raw opium stored in Batavia for medicinal purposes. Arrangements were quickly made to transport the opium by train to Republican territory to prevent its seizure should the Dutch return.[100] The opium was then placed under the charge of the Republican Opium and Salt Board, with Raden Moekarto Notowidigdo as head. (During the colonial and Japanese period, he used to work for the Salt and Opium Monopoly from 1937 till 1945.) Opium was a small, easily transportable commodity that could fetch high prices. It therefore served the needs of a government that was strapped for cash with no prospect of developing alternative sources of funding.

Opium smuggling exposed

Details about opium smuggling between Singapore and the Republic surfaced after the arrest of Moekarto on 10 August 1948 in connection with opium deals he was trying to close. Aged 37, he had been appointed on 26 July 1948 as the financial coordinator of the Republic of Indonesia for Southeast Asia and Australia. His duties included the supervision of trade in Southeast Asia (Singapore, Bangkok, Delhi) and Australia (Sydney); and financing Republican offices in London, New York, Egypt, Pakistan, and elsewhere. He arrived in Singapore to make arrangements for his work, during which time he met with Indoff officials.[101]

He revealed that in May 1948, Maramis, at that time Minister of Finance, had made an agreement with one Tjioe Men Leong to let him sell 2,017 kilograms of raw opium in Singapore. The net proceeds were expected to be $900,000, but this sum was never paid to any Indonesian official. Moekarto also confessed that around 10 July 1948, he delivered about 1,500 kilograms of raw opium to one Lee Kwet Jin.[102] It was agreed that the sale amount,

---

[100] PG 377, Report by the government of the Netherlands on seizure of the illicit traffic in opium in Indonesia in accordance with Article 23 of the Geneva Convention (1931) for limiting the manufacture and regulating the distribution of narcotic drugs. According to another source, there was about 80 tons of raw opium available in Batavia at the time of the Japanese surrender. PG 385, Statement of R. Moekarto Notowidigdo of Klaten (Soerakarta) 10, Kepatian, Java recorded by R.S. Tufnell at 0800 hours, 1-10-1948 to 2-10-1948, the witness speaking English.

[101] PG 166, Statement of Moekarto recorded on 2-10-1948 and 3-10-1948. A description of Moekarto's duties in Singapore can be found in 'Instruksi Sementara untuk Koordinator Keuangan Pemerintah RI di Singapore', PG 337, by A.A. Maramis, Ministry of Finance, Republic Indonesia, 26-7-1948. The background on how the Dutch uncovered Republican opium smuggling is found in Directie Verre Oosten 75, Government Information Service, AE 936 Batavia, 16-8-1948.

[102] PG 385, Verslag betreffende Lee Kwet Tjin by H.J. Hana, Commissaris van Politie I, 2651-0948-2823. Lee Kwet Jin was doing business in sugar during the Japanese occupation. Sometime in March 1948, he arrived at Singapore; PG 385, Statement by Mrs Bong Soei Kim – spouse of Lee Kwet Jin – made before C.O. Williams, 2005 hours, 13-8-1948. There is a photo of Lee Kwet Tjin in PG 385.

estimated at $675,000, would be paid to Moekarto. Moekarto also revealed that another person by the name of Tony Wen was given five hundred kilograms of raw opium to sell.[103] Altogether, the Republican government appointed five agents including the three named above for the sale of opium in Singapore. By arrangement with Maramis, payment for the opium was to be made in Straits currency either to Maramis or Moekarto or, in their absence, to Oetoyo. The Singapore price was fixed at $450 per kilogram.[104] The Republican government was not concerned with the ways and means of selling the opium or the expenses incurred by the agents. All in all, Tony Wen reimbursed a total of $225,000 for his sales, but the other four agents are not known to have made any payments. If this figure is correct, the sales proceeds were only a fraction of the total profits reaped, because the value of the amount of opium consigned to the five agents was estimated at $308 million.[105]

Smuggling opium to Singapore

Altogether, 8.5 tons of opium was smuggled out of Yogyakarta, but not all landed in Singapore.[106] By the middle of 1948, an estimated amount of two tons of opium had been smuggled to Singapore for sale. The *modus operandi* usually involved the use of aircraft since opium was relatively compact. It was wrapped in crepe rubber and flown by a Catalina aircraft[107] from Java to a rendezvous at sea (usually the Karimun islands), where the goods were unloaded onto a *tongkang* or speedboat for the final journey to Singapore itself.[108]

---

[103] PG 385, Verslag betreffende Lee Kwet Tjin by H.J. Hana, Commissaris van Politie I, 2651-0948-2823. On Tony Wen, see also Cribb 1988:714-5.

[104] Reports on prices varied. By 1948, each kilogram could fetch a price of about $1,600. See PG 385, Letter from S. van Hulst to Procureur-Generaal No. 808A, Singapore, 26-6-1948. Customs officials in Singapore gave the estimate that 7 tons of opium could fetch $3.75 million on the market. See PG 385, Interrogation of Oetoyo by officers of HM Customs, Singapore, 23-10-1948. In Singapore, the Indonesian opium was made available to traffickers with brand names such as 'Red and White Paper' and their prices were reported at $430 per pound. See PG 166, a Report to R.S. Tufnell (Singapore Customs), 24-11-1948. According to Moekarto, the consignments that reached Singapore were sold for $900 per kilogram. PG 385, Statement of R. Moekarto Notowidigdo of Klaten (Soerakarta) 10, Kepatian, Java recorded by R.S. Tufnell at 0800 hours, 1-10-1948 to 2-10-1948, the witness speaking English.

[105] PG 166, Statement of Moekarto recorded on 2-10-1948 and 3-10-1948.

[106] PG 385, Statement of R Moekarto Notowidigdo of Klaten (Soerakarta) 10, Kepatian, Java, recorded by R.S. Tufnell at 0800 hours, 1-10-1948 to 2-10-1948, the witness speaking English.

[107] British personnel (including ex-RAF pilots) piloted the planes. The pilots were prepared to take the risks for a fee. PG 385, Statement of Raymond Herbert Godwin Coombs, a British subject, age 27 years, of Mitre Hotel, No. 145 Killiney Rd, Singapore. Recorded by C.O. Williams at 15.20 hours, 25-9-1948 to 28-9-1948, the witness speaking English, Singapore Police Force-Statement.

[108] PG 385, Letter from S. van Hulst to Procureur-Generaal, No. 808A, Singapore, 26-6-1948. See also PG 385, Verslag betreffende Lee Kwet Tjin by H.J. Hana, Commissaris van Politie I,

In Karimun, the principal agent was Gui Oh Nua, an influential businessman stationed at Tanjung Balai who enjoyed good relations with all the Dutch government officials.[109] On the Indonesian side, Gui Oh Nua also had good friends. He was well known in Tanjung Balai as the philanthropist who had equipped the town with electricity.[110] In 1947, he was even decorated by the Republican Resident of Riau.[111] Police personnel were also familiar with Gui, who had been operating in Karimun for a long time, perhaps too long for them to conduct any objective investigations as far as Gui was concerned.[112] Thus Gui exercised considerable influence in Karimun. He also operated a branch office at Boat Quay along the Singapore River. From Karimun, the opium was shipped in small trading vessels. Often the contraband was camouflaged as ordinary cargo or passed off as bales of rubber.[113] An ex-RAF pilot, who was later questioned in Singapore, described one consignment of the cargo as '20-25 packages, some small some large, all wrapped in sheets of smoked rubber. The largest of these packages was about 200 pounds as it took 3 persons to lift. The smallest was about 85 lbs.'[114]

Opium smugglers operating in Singapore

Over in Singapore, the principal receiving agent was the proprietor of a business in Telok Ayer district.[115] This was an establishment called Chop Kim Yeng Kee located at 73 Telok Ayer Street. The proprietor was one Mr Cheong, who had worked as a detective before the Pacific War. Cheong was probably only a facilitator. The principal agents operated in their individual capacities and not in the form of business establishments. The chief of these agents was Tony Wen,[116] and he was probably linked to Gui Oh Nua in Karimun through his brother Boen Kin Kioen, who himself was the son-in-law of Gui.[117]

2651-0948-2823; PG 377, Report by the government of the Netherlands on seizure of the illicit traffic in opium in Indonesia in accordance with Article 23 of the Geneva Convention (1931) for limiting the manufacture and regulating the distribution of narcotic drugs.
109 PG 385, Information regarding Indonesian opium made to R.S. Tufnell on 11-11-1948.
110 PG 166, A Report to R.S. Tufnell (Singapore Customs), 24-11-1948.
111 PG 166, Letter 400/K/IV/X, from S. van Hulst to Procureur-Generaal, 17-11-1948.
112 PG 166, Letter from S. van Hulst to Procureur-Generaal, No. 400/K/IV/X, 17-11-1948.
113 PG 385, Information regarding Indonesian opium made to R.S. Tufnell on 11-11-1948.
114 PG 385, Statement of R.H.G. Coombs (continued); Recorded by R.S. Tufnell commenced 1200 hours on 27-9-1948 to 29-9-1948.
115 PG 385, Information regarding Indonesian opium made to R.S. Tufnell on 11-11-1948.
116 Other agents were Lee Kwet Tjin, Tjoe Meng Liong, Sie Tek Soen, and one agent identified only as Tjan. See PG 385, Statement of Moekarto (alias Sowigno) son of Motowidigdo, Javanese, aged 37, living at 17 Pakoelaman, Djokjakarta, Java. Recorded by Inspector Yusoff at Special Branch on 2-10-1948 and 3-10-1948.
117 PG 166, Letter from S. van Hulst to Procureur-Generaal, No. 400/K/IV/X, dated 17-11-1948.

Tony Wen was important. He received recognition many years later. Adam Malik, then a leading *pemuda* leader and many years later a Foreign Minister, identified him as one who had performed yeoman service for the Republic. Perhaps Wen's role received special recognition because, of all the agents in Singapore, he was the only one who was known to have forwarded some of the proceeds of his sales to the Republican authorities.[118] But Wen also possessed some pro-Republican credentials. He was born in Bangka[119] and educated in Shanghai before the war. During the Japanese occupation, he worked for the Perserikatan Rakjat dan Boeroeh Tionghoa (Association of Chinese People and Labour) in Surakarta as manager of the sports department. By the time of the Japanese surrender, he had become vice-president. He had made clear his pro-Republican inclinations as early as April 1946, when he led his organization to announce its loyalty to the Republican government (Sutter 1959, II:417). On the basis of these nationalist credentials, the Republican Ministry of Internal Affairs recognized him as the Chinese liaison officer in March 1947. He was well qualified for the job because it required him to use his contacts to maintain harmony between the Chinese and Indonesians as well as to defend Chinese interests within the Republican government structure. He virtually became a spokesman for the Chinese in Surakarta, making broadcasts weekly from Radio Jogya. He spoke English, Chinese, Indonesian, and a little Dutch.[120] The work was exacting but the pay low. To survive, he was forced to participate in some private trading through a firm called Tio Siong Lim in Tuban (Java). Using his official position, he was able to obtain licences for the firm to deal in sugar and tobacco export to Surabaya and other Dutch-held territories.[121] He also entered into a partnership with another Chinese from Surakarta, called See Teck Soon. A firm, the Victory Trading Company, was set up with agencies throughout Southeast Asia under different names. It was Wen's job to obtain from the

---

[118] PG 385, Statement of Moekarto (alias Sowigno) son of Motowidigdo, Javanese, aged 37, living at 17 Pakoelaman, Djokjakarta, Java, Recorded by Inspector Yusoff at Special Branch on 2-10-1948 and 3-10-1948.

[119] PG 385, Statement of R. Moekarto Notowidigdo of Klaten (Soerakarta) 10, Kepatian, Java recorded by R.S. Tufnell at 0800 hours, 1-10-1948 to 2-10-1948, the witness speaking English. A photo of Tony Wen making a speech is found in the letter from P.A. van der Poel (Secretaris voor Speciale Diensten) to Procureur-Generaal, 1761-K-II, 9-5-1949, PG 385. A photo of Tony Wen is also enclosed in Directie Verre Oosten 75. For brief notes on Tony Wen, see also Suryadinata 1995:221.

[120] PG 385, Statement of R. Moekarto Notowidigdo of Klaten (Soerakarta) 10, Kepatian, Java recorded by R.S. Tufnell at 0800 hours, 1-10-1948 to 2-10-1948, the witness speaking English. For details on Wen's political views, see PG 385, Enige gegevens omtrent de persoon van Tony Wen. For a physical description, see PG 385, letter 909A dated 7-8-1948 from S. van Hulst, Secretaris voor Speciale Diensten, to Procureur-Generaal. There is a photograph of Tony Wen making a speech in PG 166, Letter 1761-K-II, dated 9-5-1949, from P.A. van der Poel, Secretaris voor Speciale Diensten, to Procureur-Generaal.

[121] PG 385, Statement by Tony Wen made to R.S. Tufnell, completed 17-9-1948.

Republican government export licences for the disposal of sugar, tobacco, and vanilla to Singapore and China. His influence was therefore twofold: on behalf of the Republicans with the Chinese and on behalf of the Chinese with the Republicans.[122] His work enabled him to become acquainted with many Indonesian officials, 'from the President down'.[123] By 1948, he was feeling the strain of his job. It was becoming increasingly difficult especially after the Republican troops began to withdraw to Central Java. At the same time, the influx of undisciplined troops into the Solo area must have made the maintenance of harmony between the Chinese and the Indonesians difficult at best.

He decided to move to Singapore and stay with his brother (Boen Kin Kioen). Sensing the possibility of profit, he purchased 650 bags of sugar and four thousand pounds of vanilla beans at a good price from dealers who were selling out in view of the deteriorating political situation. His brother had advised him to resell these goods for a profit. When it was learned that he was going to Singapore, a former colleague then employed in the Ministry of Finance asked him to help an official (Soebino) who was being sent to Singapore to collect funds on behalf of the Indonesian government, amounting to $288,000, owed by Chinese firms. Wen's job, essentially, was to keep a check on Soebino so that the funds would not be siphoned off. The journey to Singapore was made by boat via Karimun. At the Singapore Immigration Office, he was given a one-month visa. The sale of his goods resulted in a net profit of $42,000, a princely sum that even enabled him to keep a cabaret hostess as mistress. (Wen was married and there was much domestic turmoil when his wife arrived unannounced in Singapore from Batavia to find him cavorting with another woman.) In the course of his business dealings, he maintained contact with Indonesian officials in the Republic (for example Maramis and Moekarto), Indoff officials, and a host of business contacts including those accused of gun running. His association with opium smuggling surfaced when Moekarto was arrested in Batavia for trafficking in opium and implicated him under interrogation.[124]

Wen's arrest took place in September 1948 at the urging of the Dutch authorities in Singapore. However, on the eighteenth of that month, a magistrate released him for lack of evidence on which to base a charge, whereupon the Singapore authorities decided to detain Wen under the state of emergency regulations that were then in force. However, the detention was brief – lasting only a few days – before Wen was again released. The Colonial

---

[122] PG 385, Statement of R. Moekarto Notowidigdo of Klaten (Soerakarta) 10, Kepatian, Java recorded by R.S. Tufnell at 0800 hours, 1-10-1948 to 2-10-1948, the witness speaking English.
[123] PG 385, Statement by Tony Wen made to R.S. Tufnell, completed 17-9-1948.
[124] PG 385, Statement by Tony Wen made to R.S. Tufnell, completed 17-9-1948.

Secretary explained that the goal of the emergency regulations was the crippling of subversive activities perpetuated by extremists, communists, bandits, and those engaged in violence. Wen could not be classified as such. The Dutch consul-general protested but the Colonial Secretary explained that the continued detention of Wen would raise questions in the Legislative Council. It would not do to give the impression that the British were cooperating with the authorities in Batavia. Also, Wen's lawyer was a member of the Council and he would know how to make public this detention. The British government was not prepared to give the impression that the emergency regulations had been abused or arbitrarily applied. Already, in July and August 1948, that is prior to the detention of Wen, there had been various cases of people detained under the emergency regulations who had to be released. What was unclear was whether Wen was released because he had agreed to turn 'crown witness' by providing relevant information regarding Indoff's role in opium smuggling.[125]

Upon release, Wen immediately fled to China on 9 November 1948.[126] The Dutch consul-general maintained that Wen was an arch-smuggler who was also a communist and former commandant of the International Brigade, a communist front organization. If he had to be released, so the argument went, he should have been deported to the Netherlands East Indies and not simply set free without prior consultation with the Dutch. Indeed, neither the police, nor immigration nor customs were informed. The Dutch consul-general noted that other individuals with lighter 'crimes' had been surrendered to the Dutch authorities in the past. He continued that since Wen was a Netherlands East Indies subject – a piece of information that the Colonial Secretary denied knowing – there would have been no difficulty or political complications if he had been deported and placed in Dutch hands.[127] Wen was released on a technicality. The extradition formalities were not in order. There was a delay of 3.5 months before the proper document was submitted, and then, the supporting evidence was not attached.[128]

What then were Wen's connections with Indoff? Under interrogation by British customs officers about opium smuggling, Oetoyo confessed that he met Tony Wen in Singapore sometime in April 1948. At that time, Oetoyo showed Wen a letter authorizing him (Oetoyo) to collect $42,000 from Wen

---

[125] PG 385, Letter from A.M.L. Winkelman (Consul-General) to T. Elink Schuurman, No. VIII-P-2 26091/356, 12-11-1948.
[126] PG 385, Letter from S. van Hulst, Secretaris voor Speciale Diensten, to Procureur Generaal, No. 323/K/II, 10-10-1948, Singapore.
[127] PG 385, Letter from A.M.L. Winkelman (Consul-General) to Chef Directie Verre Oosten te Batavia, No. 27453/365, 17-11-1948, Singapore.
[128] Directie Verre Oosten 75, Brutton and Company (legal firm in Hongkong) to Netherlands Consul-General (Hongkong), 7-4-1949.

to purchase a boat. Oetoyo said they never liked one another because Oetoyo knew he was an agent for the Japanese and Oetoyo never thought highly of Japanese agents.[129] He described Wen as very secretive and not at all communicative.[130]

Oetoyo's complicity in opium smuggling

Oetoyo denied he himself was ever involved in opium smuggling. Oetoyo's alleged involvement first became public in June 1948. Two newspapers in Java published accounts that Dutch officials had accused him of receiving five hundred kilograms of opium in Singapore, and then remitting $72,000 as part of the proceeds of sales to the Indonesian ambassador in London. Oetoyo denied he had any knowledge about opium smuggling until he learnt it from press reports.[131] He also denied Moekarto's statement implicating him in opium transactions[132] and all the while, during his contacts with Republican officials from the Republic, Oetoyo was under the impression that they were dealing in sugar or sisal or vanilla.[133] Moekarto's statement to his interrogators incriminated Oetoyo: 'Dr Oetoyo thought it [opium sales] a fine idea as a means of building up foreign credit abroad'.[134] That was May 1948 but, according to Moekarto, Oetoyo knew about the opium sales probably in March or April 1948, when he met Tony Wen. In the course of time, Wen paid $112,000 to Oetoyo as revenue[135] and Indoff channels were used to maintain telegraphic and written communication between the Republican authorities in Java and the opium agents in Singapore.[136]

Oetoyo continued to insist that Indoff funds were obtained from trade turnover with Sumatra and Java, not opium smuggling. He revealed that imports from Sumatra totalled $6 million a month and exports to Sumatra were worth $4 million monthly. One-fifth of all goods from Sumatra was

---

[129] PG 385, Interrogation of Dr Oetoyo by officers of HM Customs, Singapore, 23-10-1948. The report is also found in Directie Verre Oosten 75.
[130] PG 385, Interrogation of Dr Oetoyo by officers of HM Customs, Singapore, 23-10-1948.
[131] 'Slander, says Dr Oetoyo', *Straits Times*, 31-8-1948, p. 1.
[132] PG 385, Interrogation of Dr Oetoyo by officers of HM Customs, Singapore, 23-10-1948.
[133] PG 385, Interrogation of Dr Oetoyo by officers of HM Customs, Singapore, 23-10-1948.
[134] PG 304, Letter GD 4/14156, VIII-C-3, 23700/327, from J.B. Haverkorn, de Consul belast met de waarneming van het Consulaat-Generaal, to T. Elink Schuurman, Chef Directie Verre Oosten van het Ministerie van Buitenlandse Zaken, Batavia, dated 14-10-1948.
[135] PG 304, Letter GD 4/14156, VIII-C-3, 23700/327, from J.B. Haverkorn, de Consul belast met de waarneming van het Consulaat-Generaal, to T. Elink Schuurman, Chef Directie Verre Oosten van het Ministerie van Buitenlandse Zaken, Batavia, dated 14-10-1948; PG 385, Statement of R. Moekarto Notowidigdo of Klaten (Soerakarta) 10, Kepatian, Java recorded by R.S. Tufnell at 0800 hours, 1-10-1948 to 2-10-1948, the witness speaking English.
[136] PG 377, Report by D. van den Dool, Commissaris van Politie tweede klasse bij de Dienst der Algemene Recherche, Batavia, 22-2-1949.

assigned to Indoff for sales to raise its funds. The proceeds were even sufficient to support the Bangkok representatives.[137]

To the charge that Indoff was involved in the clandestine smuggling of opium, it delivered the following official response:

> Dr Oetoyo, Indonesian Republican Representative in Singapore, has issued the following statement: – 'The Indonesia [Office] in Singapore knew only from news publications round about the Third Anniversary of the Republic (Aug 17 1948) of the sale of opium alleged by the Netherlands East Indies Government, of being conducted by Indonesian officials in Java. In anticipation of an official comment from Republican government, the Indonesia Office wishes to make it clear that it is not intimate with facts surrounding these charges nor is it in any way linked-up with the alleged affair. The Indonesia Office stresses that its funds are acquired through legal channels and sources.[138]

This denial by Indoff was not quite corroborated by the version given by Darusman. Thanks to the disclosures in the recollections of Darusman, it could be confirmed that Indoff personnel working individually, if not together as an organization, were engaged in smuggling of weapons and opium. Darusman said with a chuckle years after that Oetoyo could not but know what was going on, although he could not confess to it.[139] According to Darusman, there were also a number of what he called 'field officers' who were brave men willing to risk their necks to smuggle goods across the seas from Singapore.[140] Of these 'field officers', the most prominent was John Lie. A devout Indonesian nationalist and a committed Christian missionary, he was a key figure in a vast weapons-smuggling network that stretched from the Philippines to India, with operations in Manila, Bangkok, Penang, Singapore, Rangoon, and Delhi.

Darusman also recalled that even innocent travellers to Singapore had opium squeezed into their luggage. Upon arrival, the opium would be handed over to a fieldworker, Bagdja of Indoff's trade and finance department. He was then instructed to pass the opium to a designated person. Darusman described Bagdja as one 'who usually was put in charge of similar shady operations'.[141]

According to Darusman, these unsuspecting 'traffickers' were blithely

---

[137] 'NEI trade not opium for funds', *Straits Times*, 8-9-1948, p. 5.
[138] PG 304, 3998/APO3, Letter from J. B. Haverkorn van Rijsewijk, Consul belast met de waarneming van het Consulaat-Generaal, to Minister van Buitenlandse Zaken, 2-9-1948. See also PG 304, 'Persconferentie Mr Oetoyo, Aneta,' No. 1059, 31-8-1948.
[139] Interview with Darusman in Jakarta on 20-3-1992.
[140] Interview with Darusman in Jakarta on 20-3-1992.
[141] Suryono Darusman, 'Opium and RI's fight for Independence', *Indonesian Observer*, 14-5-1989.

unaware of the dangerous commodity they were carrying. In December, a group of ladies belonging to the Indonesian Women's Organization was travelling to Delhi to attend the Inter-Asian Women's Congress. Since they were travelling by way of Singapore, a quantity of opium was hidden among their luggage. Apparently, no one who could be used as a 'trafficker' was spared. Darusman even alleged that opium was smuggled in the hand luggage of a group of high-level Indonesian officials – including at one time Soetan Sjahrir and Oetoyo – who were all travelling to Singapore, and on a United Nations aircraft at that.[142]

In connection with the allegations about Indoff's involvement in opium smuggling, it is interesting to note that at the end of June 1948, Indoff was so low in funds that its staff could only be paid half their salaries. Oetoyo, however, told them not to worry at all about the payment of the rest, because 'in a very short time he would have sufficient funds at his disposal'.[143] At a time when normal trade and smuggling were being throttled by the Dutch blockade, this assurance allegedly given by Oetoyo could only point an incriminating finger at Indoff's complicity.

Indoff's complicity became more entangled when Yogyakarta fell into Dutch hands in December 1948 and the Dutch captured documents allegedly implicating Indoff in smuggling eight tons of opium into Singapore. The state attorney's office in Batavia accused Indoff of cooperating with Tony Wen to receive and distribute the eight tons sometime during May to July 1948. That office also charged Indoff with chartering an Australian flying boat to smuggle five tons of opium into Sumatra.[144]

Opium smuggling was an illegal activity in Singapore. The bad publicity generated against the Republicans led to increased police vigilance. Several key agents in the opium trade were deported from Singapore and the operations centre was forced to move to Bangkok.[145]

Intelligence gathering

'Intelligence' was a fashionable word to use in those heady days of the Indonesian revolution in Singapore. Many Indonesians came to Singapore under the guise of 'intelligence' and surrounded their movements in a veil

---

[142] Suryono Darusman, 'Opium and RI's fight for Independence'', *Indonesian Observer*, 14-5-1989. It should be mentioned that Sjahrir took the precaution of bringing along a medical practitioner who could vouch that the opium was used for medicinal purposes. See Cribb 1988:713.
[143] Directie Verre Oosten 75, No. 898H, S. van Hulst, Director of Special Services, to Director, Malayan Security Service, explaining Singapore's role in opium smuggling, 3-8-1948.
[144] '"Jogja men in Singapore opium racket" say Dutch', *Malaya Tribune*, 24-3-1949, p. 8.
[145] 'Indonesian opium agents flee from police to Bangkok', *Straits Times*, 4-9-1948, p. 5.

of secrecy. Many of them, however, were mere adventurers who took advantage of this emotive word in order to impress the Indonesians in Singapore to extend hospitality to them.[146]

Tahir Karim Loebis

At the very least, collecting intelligence must have been a difficult task. Nevertheless, many individual Indonesians claimed to be involved in it. Tahir Karim Loebis, the former manager of the trading firm Noesantara Agency, was one. He was allegedly planning to steal papers belonging to Lord Killearn, but was caught in July 1947[147] and sentenced to eighteen months' imprisonment. Loebis was originally sent by Governor Hassan of Sumatra to Singapore to serve as liaison for the development of trade relations, among other duties. He was involved in a business deal with an American of Swiss descent who offered to ship rubber and palm oil from the Republican territories in Sumatra to America in return for a supply of ships and jeeps.[148] The British suspected that Loebis's trading firm was only a front for intelligence activities.[149]

Loebis was able to gain access to Lord Killearn's papers with the help of Rachmat bin Ahmat, who was in charge of duplicating materials in Killearn's office. The trial of the Indonesians involved in the case was conducted *in camera*.[150] Apart from those individuals, no other Indonesian organizations like Indoff or the PKBI-PI were incriminated. All the accused denied any links with the Republican authorities and maintained that the Republican government did not sanction their actions. Loebis was deported from Singapore and Malaya after serving his term in prison, and it is interesting that he tried to obtain a meeting with Oetoyo before he left Singapore but the latter steadfastly refused to meet him (*Rahsia perdjuangan* 1948:92-3).

Information about other intelligence-gathering activities is necessarily scarce, especially when they escaped detection or merely fizzled out. There was an agent by the name of Lamara who arrived in Singapore on 17 April 1947 from Pakan Baru, sent by a TNI (Indonesian army) division. His task was to expose the Netherlands intelligence network as well as bring together

---

[146] PG 861, Tweewekelijksche berichtgeving der Algemeene Politie Riouw, Nederlandsch Consulaat-Generaal, Singapore, over de periode 13 t/m 26-5-1947, Rapport No 422A, p. 1, Singapore, By S. van Hulst, Commissaris van Politie II, 26-5-1947.
[147] Indonesians in the pay of the Dutch betrayed Loebis. See Nasution 1978a:47. See also *Memoar pejuang* 1992:55.
[148] *Officiële bescheiden*, VII:186.
[149] PG 304, Letter from S. van Hulst to Procureur-Generaal, 12-7-1948.
[150] 'Official secrets convictions in Singapore; Indonesians go to prison', *Straits Times*, 8-7-1947, p. 1.

all the intelligence organizations of the Republic in Singapore. Intelligence, however, was only one activity. He had also been given $500 to defray costs and he used this as capital to set up a roadside business at Change Alley, smack in the centre of the Singapore business district.[151] It is difficult to determine which activity received priority.

The PKBI-PI claimed that it had been sending out agents since early 1946 to sow the spirit of struggle among the population in Indonesia itself; the organization even reported that it had infiltrated the Dutch army and police till the NICA was confused (*Rahsia perdjuangan* 1948:47). Details are, however, lacking except for the attempt by Kilian Simandjoentak to infiltrate Lingga via Sumatra from Singapore in mid-1946. But it is not clear whether the entire operation (presumably to start an uprising against the Dutch) was managed by the PKBI-PI. In any case, it came to grief when Simandjoentak was himself arrested by military police in Tembilahan (*Rahsia perdjuangan* 1948:48-51).

The clandestine activities to advance Republican interests described above were linked to Indonesian organizations or individuals residing in Singapore. However, in themselves, they are not complete and in some respects, they constitute only the top layers of an Indonesian *kueh lapis* (multi-layered cake) or the outer layers of an onion. At the base or core, other important activities were going on, with participants who were non-Indonesians. These were the traders of Singapore, especially Chinese traders, whose goals were not specifically directed at advancing the interests of the Republic but were closely related to their own economic well-being. Such different aims did not necessarily conflict. Many Republican officials in fact found that the activities of Chinese traders dovetailed with their own objectives. For that reason, it is also necessary to consider the role of the traders in Singapore in the Indonesian revolution, especially in respect of officially sanctioned trade.

---

[151] PG 168, CGDN, No. 111-48, Report by S. van Hulst, 12-5-1948.

CHAPTER VII

Commercial relations, or the 'Singapore squeeze'

Trade between Indonesia and Singapore had existed since Singapore's founding in 1819. The kind of trade practised in Singapore was the type described in the literature as 'entrepot trade'. Entrepot trade had served Singapore well. It attracted traders from the west and Asia to flock to Singapore. It was responsible for the wealth that accrued to traders in Singapore. To many traders active in pre-war Singapore, this was the kind of trade that had to be restored in 1945. The entrepot trade of Singapore involved two categories of activities, one simple and the other complex. At the simple level, goods were merely handled in transit and were not processed. The bulk goods were also not broken. The merchant's gain was limited to charges for storage, handling, and transhipment. At the complex level, machinery was used for sorting, grading, treatment, and processing according to the requirements of the market. Bulk imports from the west were also broken down to meet Asian demands. For both kinds of activities, certain conditions were essential for the viability of the entrepot trade. There should be no restriction for entry of goods to Singapore from any source. There should be no restriction on the distribution of goods from Singapore to any destination. Finally, a financial mechanism must be available whereby settlements could be made.[1] As far as trade between Singapore and Indonesia was concerned, the conditions listed above did not exist once the Dutch were able to re-establish their presence more effectively after 1946.

Trade conditions before 1947

By the mid- and late 1940s, trade between Singapore and the Indonesian islands had resumed its small-scale, disorganized operations that characterized the earlier periods of the maritime history of the archipelago. The best

---

[1] 'The entrepot trade', *Straits Times*, 20-2-1946, p. 2. The ideas on the restoration of entrepot trade were developed in a paper drafted by the British military administration that ruled Singapore after the Japanese surrendered (see *Entrepot trade*, 1945).

survey of the trade links existing up to about 1947 is the one written by R.M. Margono Djojohadikoesoemo, president-director of Bank Negara Indonesia, BNI (the *de facto* central bank of the Republic of Indonesia). In a wide-ranging report submitted after a fact-finding visit to Singapore in March-April 1947,[2] he expressed concern that the activities that were described as trade between Singapore and Indonesia were mere manifestations of dilettantism. Margono began the report by stating that given the state of war, there was no such thing as regular trade between the two territories. Commercial relations up till the time of the visit did not exist in the true sense of the word; all activities took place in the form of barter conducted in secrecy by people and organizations free from control by the Republican government.[3] In fact, for the period before August 1946, all commercial dealings between Indonesia and Singapore were controlled by agencies of the Indonesian navy and army.[4] The institution represented by Margono did not seem to have any part in the activities going on. No records were kept and any profits registered would most likely have been siphoned off somewhere or the other. Given the confused conditions, many dishonest practices prevailed. Traders from Singapore, some even with letters of authority issued by Oetoyo, would visit various parts of Sumatra offering to transport much-needed consumer goods in return for the right to export valuable commodities. The Sumatran officials who approved such deals were not always paid in full or at all. Their complaints to Oetoyo also led them nowhere. Oetoyo denied knowing anything about the transactions.[5] Oetoyo confirmed that before August 1948, there were no records of goods that came to Singapore from Sumatra and their values.[6] According to him, Indoff was not then in charge. The income before August 1948 was very irregular and when control thereafter was transferred

[2] Margono was ordered by the prime minister of the Republic of Indonesia to settle financial matters in connection with commercial dealings between Indonesia and Singapore. For this purpose, he was instructed to liaise with Oetoyo. This visit gave an official imprimatur to Oetoyo and Indoff, but quite apart from that, the report submitted after the visit also provides a first-hand account of the prevailing commercial links between Singapore and Indonesia. For the report, see AS 2/1072, Report of the 'Bank Negara Indonesia' on the Singapore journey from 31-3-1947 up to 10-4-1947, By President Director Bank Negara Indonesia, R.M. Margono Djojohadikoesoemo, Batavia, 15-4-1947.
[3] AS 2/1072, Report of the 'Bank Negara Indonesia' on the Singapore journey from 31-3-1947 up to 10-4-1947, By President Director Bank Negara Indonesia, R.M. Margono Djojohadikoesoemo, Batavia, 15-4-1947.
[4] AS 2/1072, Report of the 'Bank Negara Indonesia' on the Singapore journey from 31-3-1947 up to 10-4-1947, By President Director Bank Negara Indonesia, R.M. Margono Djojohadikoesoemo, Batavia, 15-4-1947.
[5] For some examples of such complaints involving Oetoyo, see PG 170(I), Rapport over de kaboepaten L. Batoe en Zuid-Asahan, from S. van Hulst, Secretaris voor Speciale Diensten, Consulaat-Generaal der Nederlanden aan de Procureur-Generaal, No. 393f-VI, 16-11-1948.
[6] PG 385, Interrogation of Dr Oetoyo by officers of HM Customs, Singapore, 23-10-1948.

to Indoff, the books were in deficit.⁷

Although Oetoyo's comments relate to the 1948 period, they are also valid for the earlier years. Such untidy trade relations prompted Margono to propose a review. He thought: 'In our relations with Singapore we have to turn a new page, drawing up a thoroughly considered plan.'⁸ He recommended that, pending the establishment of an Indonesian-owned bank in Singapore to control remittances, to channel profits, and provide credit, the first step was to enter into an agreement with a local Singapore bank. He recommended that the Overseas Chinese Banking Corporation (OCBC) – a major Chinese institution in Singapore – be authorized to act as the agent of the BNI in Indonesia. (Towards this end, the OCBC opened an account in the name of the BNI on 7 April 1947.) Next, it was necessary to establish an office called the 'Research Branch' of the BNI to conclude a monetary agreement between Indonesia and Singapore.⁹ In turn, the Indonesians would be required to abolish all the various trade bodies operational in Singapore and recognize one organization that would be controlled by the Republican government's Welfare Department. (These trade bodies would include the various trading firms already established in Singapore, for example, Namsoco.) But, recognizing the difficulty of implementing this step and also not wanting to diminish the role the various trade bodies had played, Margono delicately noted that the latter had 'suffered a lot and took many risks and we must not forget what they have done. But exploration and experimentation changed into drainage-politics, carried on by traders at Singapore with the help of our people.'¹⁰

Extent of trade

What was the extent of the trade between the Indonesian islands and Singapore? Statistics are notoriously unreliable but ballpark figures could be gleaned from broad estimates made available from various sources. Reports for the January-July 1947 period suggest that the value of exports from Indonesia to Singapore exceeded $67 million, or more than one-third

---

7   PG 385, Interrogation of Dr Oetoyo by officers of HM Customs, Singapore, 23-10-1948.
8   AS 2/1072, Report of the 'Bank Negara Indonesia' on the Singapore journey from 31-3-1947 up to 10-4-1947, By President Director Bank Negara Indonesia, R.M. Margono Djojohadikoesoemo, Batavia, 15-4-1947.
9   AS 2/1072, Report of the 'Bank Negara Indonesia' on the Singapore journey from 31-3-1947 up to 10-4-1947, By President Director Bank Negara Indonesia, R.M. Margono Djojohadikoesoemo, Batavia, 15-4-1947.
10 AS 2/1072, Report of the 'Bank Negara Indonesia' on the Singapore journey from 31-3-1947 up to 10-4-1947, By President Director Bank Negara Indonesia, R.M. Margono Djojohadikoesoemo, Batavia, 15-4-1947.

of Indonesia's total exports for that period. The exports from Singapore to Indonesia during the same period were only one-seventh of Singapore's total exports, which amounted to $93 million (Nasution 1978a:60).

Official figures for December 1947 show that the value of goods exported from Jambi via Tanjung Pinang (Riau islands) to Singapore was three times the amount flowing the other way. If the value of goods that evaded detection, namely contraband, were available and included, the magnitude of the trade would be even more astounding.[11] Figures for that are not available but most of Riau's business was done with Singapore because the enforcement of strict regulations by the Netherlands authorities made trade between Riau and Java-Sumatra almost impossible. Principal obstacles were problems of communication and the difficulties of gaining access to foreign exchange. As a result, that trade was almost nonexistent and large quantities of rubber, copra, fish, sago flour, firewood and charcoal, tin, and so on were shipped from Riau to Singapore while the return traffic brought manufactured goods and textiles.[12]

Oetoyo estimated the trade realized from the sale of goods originating from Sumatra from August till October 1948 at $100,000.[13]

Dutch control measures

If the Chinese traders in Singapore thought it was possible to achieve a restoration of entrepot trade like that before the war, they were sorely mistaken. Many reports filtered into Singapore about the dangers to be encountered on the high seas. Although some may have been exaggerated or embellished, the main features were repeated from one report to another. Below is one such account:[14]

> A thin veil of mist hung like a cold curtain over the waters of the Banka Straits off Sumatra. It was just before dawn on 2 August 1946. A Singapore landing craft, PC 2300, was pushing its squat nose past Pulau Nanka when the silence was shattered by the crackle of machine-gun fire that lasted for five long minutes. A stream of bullets hit the iron and woodwork of the ship before ripping into the sea. The Malay cook (Abdullah bin Mohamd Zain) was sleeping near the stern air pump when he felt and heard bullets screaming past him.
> The crew consisted of 35 Malays and Chinese. For a while, confusion reigned.

---

[11] RI 552, Tweewekelijksche berichtgeving der Residentie Riouw over de periode 15 tot 31-12-1947, By J. van Waardenburg, Resident Tandjong Pinang, 12-1-1948.
[12] PG 170(II).
[13] PG 385, Interrogation of Dr Oetoyo by officers of HM Customs, Singapore, 23-10-1948.
[14] 'Singapore crew tells story of Dutch piracy; By Tribune staff reporter', *Malaya Tribune*, 10-9-1946, p. 3.

Then a Dutch patrol boat, the *Krokodil*, emerged from the mist and five Dutch officers accompanied by Ambonese ratings boarded the PC 2300. An Ambonese rating slapped the cook and appropriated his supply of cigarettes. When the cook asked a Dutch officer the meaning of this outrage, he was told that anybody killed by the machine-gun fire would be thrown overboard. The Dutch and Ambonese then proceeded to take away the personal possessions of the crew, including cigarettes, medicines, and writing pens.

PC 2300 was on the way to Lampung, but instead, it was towed to Muntok on Banka island. At Muntok, the Dutch dismantled the oil pumps to prevent the ship from sailing away. The PC 2300 was carrying 510 bags of salt. The cargo was not confiscated when the ship was released on 4 September 1946.

The Dutch were the first to take steps to control the trade. As long as the turmoil and confusion of war prevailed and the colonial authorities had little chance to exercise their writ, the Dutch could do little but tolerate the trade connections. However, once the Dutch (in particular, their navy) were able to establish their presence, restrictions of all kinds came into existence. The Dutch had all along suspected that much of this trade was illicit. They wanted to check whether the goods exported, especially the estate commodities, originated from Dutch and foreign-owned enterprises whose stocks had been confiscated by the Japanese during the occupation. Estate produce – as opposed to indigenous produce – should be returned to the rightful owners before being exported. In the absence of accurate information, confiscation of cargo was the option the Dutch seized upon in the early months after the Japanese surrendered. In January 1947, the Dutch court in Karimun allowed the cargo of a seized vessel to be stamped as the property of HVA and Goodyear (Western enterprises operating in Indonesia) since the ownership was not disputed.[15]

Control over the movement of such goods was therefore important. Regulations were needed but enforcement measures were difficult. Moreover, Dutch shipping companies were quickly resuming their services in the Pacific and Malayan waters. The KPM was working towards control of the inter-island shipping routes between Singapore, Java, Sumatra, Borneo, and Celebes. By the end of 1947, the company had ninety vessels engaged in the carrying trade. In the next two years, it expected to launch two hundred ships, including small craft.[16] There was thus added commercial pressure to control the inter-island trade.

Problems first arose during the July-August 1946 period. During those months, the Dutch seized no less than eighteen Singapore-registered ships (motor launches, *tongkang*, and lighters), together with their cargo estimated

[15] 'Dutch on seized cargoes', *Straits Times*, 18-1-1947, p. 5.
[16] 'Increase in Dutch shipping', *Straits Times*, 15-1-1948, p. 4.

at $16 million. As reported by Kwek Soan Loh, chairman of the Singapore Overseas Chinese Importers and Exporters Association, the Dutch navy gave no warning. Operating from Muntok, Tanjung Pinang, Belawan, and Tanjung Balai, ships with cargoes of sugar, rubber, and tin ingots were seized even if they held proper import and export permits. Kwek assured the Dutch that Chinese traders would observe any legitimate conditions that had to be obeyed but feared that such seizures would compel fifty per cent of his members to close business. This would impact tremendously on the trade between Singapore and the Indonesian islands as his association represented sixty per cent of the importers and exporters in Singapore.[17]

The 19 August 1946 control measures

It was not long before the Dutch authorities in Batavia produced a set of regulations that constituted the template on which modifications were made later but from which the Dutch never really departed in spirit or principle. On Monday, 19 August 1946, an advertisement appeared in the *Straits Times* (a leading local newspaper) giving some details of a new Dutch export scheme. Essentially, the Dutch decreed that with the exception of indigenous produce originating from the Riau archipelago, the export of goods from Indonesia could only be carried out if a permit was granted. Since not all areas of Indonesia were under Dutch jurisdiction, ships proceeding from areas under Republican control were required to call at certain specified Dutch ports to apply for export permits. Patrol vessels would check to ensure that this policy was followed. At the time of the announcement, the ports included Belawan (Deli), Tanjung Balai (Karimun island), Gunung Kijang or Tanjung Pinang (Bintan), and Muntok (Bangka). Export goods sent to Indonesia required approval at the above-named ports after checks for prohibited articles were conducted.[18] The list of these ports was augmented in the succeeding months as the Dutch were able to restore better control over the sea-lanes.

Among the first Chinese traders to fall foul of the new regulations were the owners of the 250-ton Singapore-registered motor vessel, the *Beng Huat*. On the outward journey from Singapore, the vessel was detained at Semarang for eight days and searched. Nothing irregular was detected. However, on the return journey, it was detained again and this time, the Dutch seized one hundred and ten tons of rubber and tea.[19]

The application of these control measures was not designed to discrimi-

---

[17] 'Temporary cessation of island trade; Chinese say cargoes have been seized', *Straits Times*, 16-8-1946, p. 5.
[18] 'Indonesian trade with Singapore; Dutch export scheme announced', *Straits Times*, 19-8-1946, pp. 1 and 6.
[19] 'Singapore cargo seized by Dutch', *Straits Times*, 30-1-1947, p. 7.

nate against Chinese traders. An American ship, the *Martin Behrman*, was caught loading off Ceribon. Meanwhile, the Dutch destroyer, *Kortenaar*, was blocking access to the open seas to prevent the *Martin Behrman* from leaving.[20] Detaining the *Martin Behrman* was politically explosive. The Dutch might well have wished that the case would blow away. The ship was forced to proceed to Batavia, where the master made a formal protest and invoked the assistance of the American consul-general. In Batavia, the Dutch declared the cargo (rubber) to be looted property and seized it. In response, the master (perhaps schooled in the tradition of Yankee clipper skippers in the nineteenth century) walked off the ship and dumped the whole affair squarely onto the lap of the Dutch.[21] There is more documentation about the *Martin Behrman* case because of the international publicity that was generated. In substance, this case was no different from the seizures of the Chinese vessels registered in Singapore and their cargoes, followed by howls of protest. If there was any difference, it can be found in the approaches employed by the United States and Singapore governments together with the Chinese traders. The United States State Department protested to The Hague against the regulations, claiming that they restricted trade, but did not challenge the legality of the regulations. In contrast, the kind of arguments raised by the Singapore authorities protested the legality issue. However, this fine distinction was unimportant in the face of serious financial losses facing the Chinese.[22]

Within a month of promulgating the regulations of 19 August 1946, 22 Chinese vessels were detained. All except seven were later released.[23]

Not all Dutch authorities were agreed on how best to establish control over the thriving trade between Singapore and Indonesia. Admiral A.S. Pinke of the Netherlands navy was convinced that seizure of ships was the most efficient method. Within a few months when the Pinke strategy was applied, the Chinese in Singapore suffered a loss of $4.5 million (Nasution 1978a:60). To him, the seizures were an essential aspect of the mission of the navy, and he defined this mission as follows: to maintain law and order on the seas, to prevent infiltration by enemies of the Netherlands East Indies state, and to support landing of the Dutch army in Indonesia. He denied that the navy interfered with legitimate trade between Republican ports.[24] Pinke also tended to adopt a rather wide definition of contraband. He even regarded green textiles as contraband, as these could be turned into military

[20] 'U.S. ship to defy Dutch', *Straits Times*, 18-2-1947, p. 1.
[21] 'The N.E.I. trade issue', *Malaya Tribune*, 12-3-1947, p. 4. On the *Martin Behrman* case, see also Homan 1983:126-7.
[22] 'The N.E.I. trade issue', *Malaya Tribune*, 12-3-1947, p. 4.
[23] 'Dutch have released 14 out of 22 ships', *Straits Times*, 17-9-1946, p. 5; 'Dutch release all detained vessels', *Straits Times*, 23-9-1946, p. 5.
[24] 'Dutch not interfering with inter-isle traffic', *Straits Times*, 13-7-1946, p. 1.

uniforms.²⁵ When the Republican minister (A.K. Gani) met him to complain about the seizures off Palembang, Pinke shouted that he held power at sea in Indonesia. For good measure, he added that *bona fide* ships were only delayed by an hour as a result of checks, but vessels that were suspected of smuggling were investigated for longer periods.²⁶ Pinke's sense of duty was robust. He was described by a contemporary, the British consul-general (G. Mackereth) at Batavia, as one 'who believes every Java-bound vessel to be brimful with war material, and appears to be used by him as a justification for boarding ships on the high seas'.²⁷

The lieutenant governor-general, Van Mook, seems to have placed a slightly different gloss on the matter when he commented on the control of trade in discussions in Singapore in September 1946. He said the best system was to require all ships to call at certain ports to pay customs duties. To this, a staff member of Lord Killearn's office, the special commissioner for Southeast Asia, thought that the Chinese would not have objections provided the rules were spelt out clearly and ships were not delayed for too long. In Van Mook's view, the Dutch authorities could do little more than levy customs duties, since it was difficult to prove ownership even of the estate products, as some of these originated from Chinese-owned and not Dutch-owned estates. He also thought a list of import and export goods that would be considered contraband should be drawn up. These would include machinery and weapons.²⁸ This was an enlightened view. It would have taken the sting out of the criticisms that the Dutch were commandeering goods on the high seas. Van Mook was not known to be an ardent supporter of the foreign investors in Indonesia who held imperious aims on the basis of their investments.

The 28 January 1947 control measures

The 19 August 1946 regulations were followed by other trade control measures on 28 January 1947. These were not substantially different. They merely legalized a trade blockade on the Republic, requiring all ships carrying imports bound for the Republic to call at specific ports for inspection. All exports from Dutch-controlled areas had to be approved by the NEI Director of Economic Affairs, thus in effect restricting all commercial activities to

---

[25] FO 810/4, 'Discussions of 13-12-1946 in Jacatra between Gani and Pinke, Idenburg, Koets, Lieut. Dobbinga and Mr Heinse'.

[26] FO 810/4, 'Discussions of 13-12-1946 in Jacatra between Gani and Pinke, Idenburg, Koets, Lieut. Dobbinga and Mr Heinse'.

[27] FO 810/10, Telegram from G. Mackereth (British Consul-General at Batavia) to Foreign Office, No. 131, 14-2-1947. Another British source described Pinke as 'choleric'. See Coast 1952: 37.

[28] *Officiële bescheiden*, V:388.

VII Commercial relations, or the 'Singapore squeeze'

inter-insular trade (Sutter 1959, II:597). The control measures were further elaborated in April 1947 when Singapore vessels were given clear instructions where they would be inspected, depending on their destination in Indonesia.[29]

The SOCIEA petitioned for the early lifting of the control measures, calling them a 'blockade'. It argued that lifting the blockade would eliminate the smuggling that had caused considerable misunderstanding.[30] The Dutch authorities were almost united in denying that they had imposed a blockade. Their aim was simply to prevent the import of war materials and the export of looted factory stocks and equipment. Their system of controls did not prevent vessels from calling at Republican ports. Also, as they were quick to stress, no *bona fide* trader was denied the right to trade.[31] As a matter of fact, the Dutch studiously avoided the word 'blockade' in their internal documents. When the Director for Special Services (S. van Hulst) accredited to the consulate-general in Singapore, accidentally used it in a report, he was reprimanded and made to promise not to repeat it.[32]

The proclamation of control measures did not mean the seizures were discontinued. Apparently, either the new regulations had not been digested or Singapore traders chose to ignore them. By September 1946, a total of 22 ships and four hundred sailors had been detained. This was about ten per cent of the two hundred junks, motor *tongkang*, and landing craft tanks (LCTs) that had left Singapore for Indonesian ports. Kwek Soan Loh estimated that if these detentions continued unabated, Singapore's post-war rehabilitation problems would be aggravated by an addition of ten thousand more unemployed. Further, two hundred large Chinese firms with a fleet of six hundred vessels engaged in the inter-island trade with Indonesia would be forced to liquidate. Kwek claimed that the traders were merely performing a public duty by bringing in foodstuffs to relieve the acute food shortage in Singapore and Malaya. More seizures meant less food. Moreover, the goods were all properly approved. The vessels were registered in Singapore and flew the British flag. It was an affront to seize the ships on the high seas since the British and the Dutch were not at war.[33] Kwek did not mention this but it could also be noted that the regulations issued in August 1946 assumed a condition of affairs that did not exist – namely, that effective Dutch authority was exercised.[34]

---

29 'New shipping rules for N.E.I. trade', *Straits Times*, 10-4-1947, p. 3.
30 'Lifting of NEI blockade urged', *Straits Times*, 28-1-1948, p. 5.
31 'New NEI talks likely soon', *Straits Times*, 13-8-1948, p. 3.
32 Directie Verre Oosten 336, Letters 24540/189 (4-11-1947 and 5-11-1947) from A.M.L. Winkelman to Chief of Directie Verre Oosten. The same file contains other documents on the use of the term 'blockade'.
33 'Singapore boycott of Dutch threat; By Tribune staff reporter', *Malaya Tribune*, 31-8-1946, p. 3.
34 'Control, or piracy', *Malaya Tribune*, 31-8-1946, p. 4.

The situation at Muntok, where the boats were detained, deteriorated when it was learnt that the four hundred seamen were not allowed to buy food. They were also confined to their ships. This lasted fourteen days. When several men fell ill, all four hundred crew went ashore in one body and demanded permission from the harbour master to stay ashore for food, medicine, water, and haircuts. Faced with such pressure, the seamen were granted shore leave for two hours. The people of Muntok appeared unwilling to help. The crew had to sell their clothing to get by. Petty traders raised prices. *Chinchew* assured Muntok traders with connections in Singapore that the ship owners would reimburse them if they would extend loans to the crew, but still the Muntok traders refused to help.[35] To make matters worse, the Dutch consulate-general refused to allow a relief ship to sail to Muntok unless it was granted a permit.[36] When the relief ship finally arrived, it was a godsend because the crew were able to get a full meal and cigarettes for the first time in a week.[37]

The Chinese Chamber of Commerce in Singapore threatened a boycott of the Dutch if detained ships were not released.[38] At the same time, the Chamber's president, Lien Ying Chow, petitioned the colonial government in Singapore and pressure was brought to bear on the Dutch, who agreed to release fourteen out of the 22 ships.[39] The remaining ships were also subsequently released from detention after the *chinchew* (supercargo) swore that the cargo was not looted property. By then, the detained cargo (mainly sugar) had been looted while under inspection.[40] It is interesting to note that even the Dutch explained the release by saying that there was not always adequate evidence to prove Singapore-registered ships were involved in illicit trade. At the time of the release, the Dutch explained that 'there is sufficient doubt regarding the origin of the cargoes in question not to warrant confiscation on the strength of the prevailing law of the Netherlands Indies regarding looted property'.[41]

The threat of a total boycott was not a remote possibility. The Chinese traders argued that the British government could not ignore the Dutch seizures since it was the British government that requested Chinese merchants to pro-

---

[35] 'Chinese mercy ships sails for Muntok; Departure delayed by Dutch objection; By Tribune staff reporter', *Malaya Tribune*, 4-9-1946, p. 1; 'Detained crews victimized in Muntok; By Tribune staff reporter', *Malaya Tribune*, 24-9-1946, p. 2.
[36] 'Dutch statement on seized ships', *Malaya Tribune*, 17-9-1946, p. 1.
[37] 'Detained crews victimised in Muntok; By Tribune staff reporter', *Malaya Tribune*, 24-9-1946, p. 2.
[38] 'Chinese may boycott Dutch – if detained ships are not released', *Straits Times*, 3-9-1946, p. 1.
[39] 'Dutch have released 14 out of 22 ships', *Straits Times*, 17-9-1946, p. 5.
[40] 'Detained crews victimized in Muntok; By Tribune staff reporter', *Malaya Tribune*, 24-9-1946, p. 2.
[41] 'Dutch release all detained vessels', *Straits Times*, 23-9-1946, p. 5.

VII Commercial relations, or the 'Singapore squeeze'

cure foodstuffs for the rehabilitation of Malaya. The seizures also dealt a major blow to the prestige of the Chinese traders and their business interests.

However, punitive actions continued. Dutch naval vessels seized Chinese ships from Palembang and Cirebon accused of carrying cargo that was the property of non-Republican-owned estates to Singapore.[42] According to Dr M. Gaus, the Dutch had confiscated suspected estate produce on the high seas but the estate produce was in fact indigenous produce. Quoting a source in Sumatra, Gaus accused the Dutch of changing the markings after the confiscation. He said it was a common practice in Palembang, Karimun, and Singapore. In any case, Gaus thought the distinction between estate and indigenous produce was a dubious one. When the Dutch capitulated to the Japanese, the Japanese had carted away all the stocks. If there was any balance of estate produce left, the Republic had been responsible for taking care of it and its return could be discussed after a political agreement had been reached. Dutch regulations defined Sumatran gambier and pepper as estate produce, but Gaus explained that in Central Sumatra, Indonesian-owned estates also grew these products. Other Indonesian enterprises also produced rubber, quinine bark, palm oil, coffee, tobacco, gold, and silver. It was therefore not easy to distinguish between indigenous and estate produce.[43]

The Dutch must have realized how difficult it was to apply the distinction. So, for practical purposes, they resorted to drawing a line across Sumatra, from Bengkalis to Sibolga, and then issuing instructions that any rubber, tobacco, fibres, and gambier in blocks produced north of that line would not be recognized as indigenous produce. Similarly, it was difficult to apply the distinction between indigenous and estate produce in Java. The Dutch overcame this problem by simply declaring that quinine, coffee, rubber, tobacco, and fibres were not indigenous produce.[44]

Problems of implementing the Dutch regulations were not confined to definitions. Seizure of ships with their cargo was also political dynamite. When news broke in 1946 that Singapore ships had been detained, the colonial secretary in Singapore was interested to know whether these were ships flying the British flag that were seized outside Indonesian territorial waters. The Dutch Resident of Bangka and Billiton, J.J. Mendelaar, said it was entirely possible that some of the ships had been detained outside the three-mile territorial waters limit and then ordered to sail into a Dutch-controlled port like Muntok. However, Mendelaar added that the Dutch were employing the same powers that gave any flag nation the right to seize pirates on the high

---

[42] Sutter 1959, II:491. For a report on another seizure, this time near the Karimuns during December 1946, see RI 551, Tweewekelijksche berichtgeving van de Residentie Riouw over de periode 15 tot 31-12-1946, by J.B. van Schendel, Assistent-Resident, Tandjong Pinang, 15-1-1947.
[43] 'Sumatrans accuse Dutch of injustice', *Straits Times*, 11-2-1947, p. 3.
[44] 'Blockade by the Dutch', *Straits Times*, 8-3-1947, p. 4.

seas.⁴⁵ The failure to resolve the issue over seizures led the first governor in post-war Singapore in 1947, Sir Franklin Gimson, to request the British government to protest to the Netherlands government (Nasution 1978a:302).

This arbitrariness was a sticking point between the Chinese traders of Singapore and the Dutch. The actions of the Netherlands navy were particularly resented. A typical example of the inconveniences and delays experienced by Chinese vessels was the voyage of the *Hung Hai*. Even with all the necessary papers, the *Hung Hai* did not sail undisturbed. It left Singapore on 30 December 1946 for Tegal in Java. On 3 January 1947, it was approaching twenty miles off the Java coast when it encountered a Dutch warship. The warship signalled and was given the ship's name. The warship then cruised around the *Hung Hai*. The latter waited for twenty minutes and then proceeded on its way. On reaching the three-mile limit, the vessel was detained for two hours and searched. The cargo was opened and inspected. After that, the vessel was allowed to anchor at Tegal. The next morning, it was boarded and searched again. Then a guard was posted on the ship and it was ordered to sail to Semarang. Meanwhile, the *Hung Hai*'s master was not permitted to use the radio to contact any British authorities. At Semarang, the cargo was inspected again. After that, the vessel was allowed to return to Tegal, where it was permitted to discharge its cargo without further interference. During its return journey, the vessel was again detained several times upon leaving the three-mile limit. The master complained that at all times, the attitude of the Dutch officials was churlish, bullying, and intimidating. No reasons or explanation of their actions were given. Every move made by the Dutch was backed up by force.⁴⁶

These inconveniences continued unabated. Each time the Dutch blockaded a port to retaliate against the Republic, it was Chinese traders in Singapore who led the protests. On the occasion of the Dutch attack on Palembang, the Chinese spokesman in Singapore, Ng Aik Huan, pointed out that the Chinese were neutral in the conflict. They dealt only in goods that originated from Indonesian-controlled territories and were purchased from Indonesians. If the Dutch were powerless in such regions, they could not accuse the Chinese of thievery. He reassured the Dutch that the Chinese were honest traders

---

⁴⁵ 'Seized ships: Govt. asks for details; Colonial Secretary's letter to importers', *Straits Times*, 24-9-1946, p. 5.

⁴⁶ Archief Consulaat-Generaal Singapore 1946-51, CSO 10218/47, Map 9, Singapore Cons. Gen. 1946-54 (Singapore), Letter from T. van der Gaast to CGDN on 25-6-1947. For another example of a Singapore vessel that was detained, see Archief Consulaat-Generaal Singapore 1946-51, Map 5, Singapore Cons. Gen. 1946-54 (Singapore), letter from the Director of the Lee Rubber Company Limited, to the Master Attendant, Fullerton Building, Singapore, on 31-8-1946. Also, see Archief Consulaat-Generaal Singapore 1946-51, Map 5, Singapore Cons. Gen. 1946-54 (Singapore), Letter from W.W. Jenkins, Director, Ho Hong Steamship Company (1932), Limited, to G.J.A. Veling, Representative of the Resident of Riouw (in Singapore), dated 30-8-1946.

who suffered because they were unprotected.[47]

Threats of a boycott led the Dutch to send a mission to Singapore to interview local Chinese leaders. This time, the Dutch delegation included Teoh Thiam Chong, a political adviser to Van Mook. The delegation did not achieve a breakthrough. The Singapore Chinese side, led by Tan Kah Kee, reiterated the same demands – withdraw the restrictions on Chinese trade, release ships, cargo and crew from detention, and pay compensation.[48] The Dutch delegation offered little beyond assurances, but the threatened boycott did not materialize if only because the Chinese traders themselves would have been the worst sufferers.[49]

Again in 1947, the Singapore Motor Vessel Traders Association had complained that the Netherlands navy had recently blockaded Bengkalis, Pakan Baru, Selat Panjang, and other Sumatra ports. Vessels calling at those places were either detained or barred from entry. As a result, traders suffered great losses and inconvenience. In those areas were also many Chinese-owned sago factories, timber yards, firewood stores, and charcoal kilns, where a large number of labourers and employees were dependent on external sources of food supplies that had been prevented from landing on account of the blockade.[50]

The Dutch regulations as well as the seizures all contributed to a downturn in trade. Fear that their cargo would be seized led many Chinese traders to discontinue smuggling. As many as fifty *tongkang* were lying idle in the Singapore River for lack of work. Indeed, in February 1947, the quantity of smuggled rubber brought into Singapore showed a big drop of eight or nine thousand tons compared with the two previous months.[51] Dutch controls were achieving their effect but the situation fuelled indignation among the Chinese in Singapore. News about the experience of their compatriots in Indonesia (Java and Sumatra) also did not endear them to the Dutch. They were angered by the perceived failure of the Dutch to protect their Chinese friends and relatives in Indonesia against the violence inflicted on them by pro-Republican nationalists.[52]

---

[48] 'Dutch mission in Singapore seeks to avert boycott; Interviews with local Chinese leaders', *Malaya Tribune*, 19-2-1947, p. 5.
[49] 'Netherlands Consul "shocked" at Chinese boycott threat', *Malaya Tribune*, 6-2-1947, p. 5.
[50] Archief Consulaat-Generaal Singapore 1946-1951, Singapore Cons. Gen. 1946-1954 (Singapore), Letter from Lee Kong Chian, President, Singapore Chinese Chamber of Commerce, to Secretary for Economic Affairs, Singapore, 19-8-1947.
[51] 'Less rubber smuggled into Singapore; By Tribune staff reporter', *Malaya Tribune*, 9-4-1947, p. 1.
[52] 'Singapore protest to The Hague', *Straits Times*, 1-2-1947, p. 5.

British mediation

The British protested against the control regulations imposed by the Dutch. Lord Killearn was taken by surprise. The measures involved complicated questions of national flags, international law, and territorial limits. He thought it would have been more appropriate for the Dutch to consult with the British first, especially when he was under the impression that Van Mook had agreed to letting the Dutch consul-general in Singapore discuss with Lord Killearn how to work out a practical arrangement.[53]

Therefore, right from the start, the British did not show enthusiasm for the Dutch measures. This gave the impression to the Netherlands authorities that the British were not sincere in wanting to cooperate. They were convinced that this reluctance reflected the conviction that Singapore's growth was in large part dependent on 'robbery', that is, conniving at the trade then going on between Singapore and Indonesia.[54] The Dutch felt that there were also British officials who believed the economic growth of Singapore after the war was to a large extent artificial and dependent on Indonesia.[55] It was estimated that any attempt to enforce a trade agreement would have meant a reduction of income by as much as US$48 million in the British treasury.[56] A peaceful Indonesia was viewed as a threat. Better to leave things unorganized or messy, a situation that would surely benefit the Chinese traders and their profit motive.

British courts also considered the 'Netherlands East Indies' to be an entity without any standing in law. This was the conclusion that could be drawn from an appeal case heard in the Singapore High Court 30-31 July 1947. The counsel for the Netherlands Indies government was appealing against a decision by a lower court judge, in favour of Allied Company, on 28 November 1946.[57] While the counsel was halfway through his submissions, the presiding appeal judge interrupted and told him there was little evidence that the Netherlands

---

[53] *Officiële bescheiden*, VII: 393, note 2.
[54] Archief Consulaat-Generaal Singapore 1946-51, Map 24, Singapore Cons. Gen. 1946-54 (Singapore), Letter from P. Mijnarends (Consul der Nederlanden, Handelscommissaris voor NI) to J. Hardeman, Raad Adviseur, Hoofd 2e Afdeling, Ministerie van Overzeese Gebiedsdelen, X-B-3a, 13560, 8-6-1948.
[55] Archief Consulaat-Generaal Singapore 1946-51, Map 24, Singapore Cons. Gen. 1946-54 (Singapore), Letter from P. Mijnarends (Consul) to the Secretary of State for Economic Affairs (Batavia), X-B-3a, 13385, 5-6-1948.
[56] Archief Consulaat-Generaal Singapore 1946-51, Map 24, Singapore Cons. Gen. 1946-54 (Singapore), Letter P. Mijnarends (Consul der Nederlanden, Handelscommissaris voor NI) to J. Hardeman, Raad Adviseur, Hoofd 2e Afdeling, Ministerie van Overzeese Gebiedsdelen, X-B-3a, 13560, 8-6-1948.
[57] For Brown's judgement, see *The Malayan Law Journal* 13-2/3, Singapore, February/March 1947, pp. 20-4.

Indies government was a legal entity and therefore capable of being considered as a party to proceedings in Singapore. The High Court stuck to this position even though it conceded that there appeared to be evidence of the existence of the Netherlands Indies government. This view made it difficult to bring other lawsuits before the Singapore judiciary in the future.[58]

The 23 March 1948 agreement

This, of course, did not mean that there was no cooperation between the Netherlands and the British governments.[59] Negotiations to resolve problems had already begun in 1947.[60] But many a British diplomat was convinced that the Netherlands was too unyielding when it came to trade negotiations. One diplomat in The Hague even composed a ditty to describe what he considered the parsimony of the Dutch during what must have been an interminably difficult moment of negotiations:

> In matters of commerce
> The fault of the Dutch
> Is giving too little
> And asking too much.[61]

A trade agreement was finally concluded on 23 March 1948 in London between the Netherlands and British governments to bring some semblance of order to the murky trading arrangements then in existence between the Netherlands Indies and Singapore. The British had to overcome their initial distaste for regulations when it became clear that Dutch control over the seas was getting stronger and stronger each day, often with the effect of strangling the movement of goods. And it was a matter of prime importance for the British in Singapore to retain its transit trade of produce originating from the Indonesian archipelago as in the pre-war days. For the Netherlands, it was equally important to obtain hard currency from this transit trade. There had been some such agreement before the Pacific War. Under an earlier 1940 agreement, arrangements were enforced regarding the repatriation of

---

[58] Archief Consulaat-Generaal Singapore 1946-51, Ref. GMC/N, Singapore Cons. Gen. 1946-54 (Singapore), Letter from Rodyk and Davidson, Advocates and Solicitors, to CGDN, 5-8-1947.
[59] Archief Consulaat-Generaal Singapore 1946-51, Map 24, Singapore Cons. Gen. 1946-54 (Singapore), Letter P. Mijnarends (Consul der Nederlanden, Handelscommissaris voor NI) to J. Hardeman, Raad Adviseur, Hoofd 2e Afdeling, Ministerie van Overzeese Gebiedsdelen, X-B-3a, 13560, 8-6-1948.
[60] PG 307, 'Handelsovereenkomst met Maleise Federatie – smokkelhandel zal op krachtige wijze worden tegengegaan,' *Het Dagblad*, 3-4-1948.
[61] 'Dollar crisis', *Straits Times*, 24-6-1947, p. 6.

foreign exchange earned by imports into Malaya and Singapore from the then Netherlands Indies; but exports from Malaya and Singapore to the Netherlands Indies were not catered for in the agreement because they were considered insignificant in comparison. One aspect of the control measures of the Dutch from 1946 onwards was to ensure a fair return from the huge quantities of US dollar earnings that had left the country.[62] Significantly, neither colonial authorities in Singapore nor the Chinese traders were party to the agreement, although they were most directly involved (Gilmour 1973:22).

The trade agreement of 1948 provided that in those places where recognized banking facilities existed, in other words areas under effective Dutch control, all shipments between ports would be financed through recognized banks. In such transactions, the terms of sale were left to the merchants but subject to the approval of the government authorizing the export.[63]

However, in those places without officially recognized banking facilities, that is, those areas under Republican authority, Singapore was required to exercise control by means of a barter book system. This barter book system dated back to the pre-war period. Under this system, the Chinese Chamber of Commerce in Singapore issued licensed dealers with books. This allowed them to export (take out) currency (NEI guilders or Straits dollars) with which they could conduct their trade. The amount of currency to be taken out of Singapore was specified and accounted for in goods when the traders returned, and in Indonesia, the currency coming in was accounted for by the goods leaving the country.[64] This system worked in part because the exchange rate between currencies remained stable and was not subject to fluctuations.

The barter book would thus show the value of exports and imports of the firm engaged in the barter trade. In essence, the firm was required to balance the exports to Indonesia with the value of imports from Indonesia. The Dutch authorities would estimate the value of return goods based on the recognized exchange rate of $80 to one hundred guilders. The Dutch also reserved the right to accept or reject the values declared by the barter trading firm.[65] The difference between the value of such goods exported from Singapore and the goods returned to Singapore from Indonesia would be calculated from the records in the barter book and any difference would then be settled in

---

[62] Archief Consulaat-Generaal Singapore 1946-51, Singapore Cons. Gen. 1946-54 (Singapore), Minutes of meeting 17-7-1948 at the Nederlands-Indisch Deviezen Instituut, Batavia, on the occasion of the visit of Mr R.W.R. Oliver, representative of the Secretary for Economic Affairs in Singapore, dated 19-7-1948.
[63] 'Trade Pact with NEI; Colony and Malaya in Agreement', Straits Times, 31-3-1948, p. 6.
[64] Inventaris van de archieven van het Consulaat-Generaal te Singapore, 1945-54, Ministerie van Buitenlandse Zaken 212, Memorandum by Mr G.J. Mulder of the Netherlands Indies Foreign Exchange Control, Batavia, on exchange control in respect of trade between Malaya and the Netherlands Indies, 26-3-1946.
[65] 'Chinese decision on barter trade', Straits Times, 6-4-1948, p. 7.

favour of Indonesia.⁶⁶ This would ensure that Indonesia was given the foreign exchange it deserved.

Broadly, the post-war barter book system was different from the pre-war system in one major way. Merchants in the pre-war period were allowed to take to the Netherlands East Indies such amounts of Straits dollars as might be required for trading purposes. For the post-war period, no dollars or guilders could be carried for transactions.

Another difference was that the 1948 system of barter book arrangements would do away with the practice of using Straits dollars or guilders for transactions. Using US dollars instead, it was believed that this would overcome the problem of having to contend with the fluctuating disparity between the Straits dollar and the NEI guilder that circulated after 1945. Fluctuations in currency values would only serve to encourage smuggling.⁶⁷

The 1948 agreement also required Singapore to ensure that the goods shipped to areas without officially recognized banking facilities were actually needed by the inhabitants of those areas.⁶⁸ This ensured that unnecessary luxury items would not end up in Indonesian markets. There were reports of cheap American articles ranging from lipsticks to cigarette lighters, to sunglasses and hairpins selling at high prices in Batavia shopping districts.⁶⁹

Implementation of the 23 March 1948 agreement

The implementation of this agreement was, of course, fraught with difficulties.⁷⁰ The most obvious difficulty was the fact that the Republic of Indonesia was not a signatory. Its absence was recognized in the appendix to the agreement. Thus the following clause was inserted: 'Both Governments realise that this Agreed Minute cannot be put into full effect in respect of trade between Singapore and the Federation of Malaya and those parts of the Netherlands Indies which are not under the actual control of the Netherlands Indies

---

66   'Trade Pact with NEI; Colony and Malaya in Agreement', *Straits Times*, 31-3-1948, p. 6.
67   Archief Consulaat-Generaal Singapore 1946-51, Singapore Cons. Gen. 1946-54 (Singapore), Letter of P. Mijnarends (Consul) to the Secretary for Economic Affairs, Fullerton Building in Singapore, X-B-3, 3897, 14-2-1948. See also Archief Consulaat-Generaal Singapore 1946-51, Map 24, Singapore Cons. Gen. 1946-1954 (Singapore), Letter from A. Luytjes, Director of Economic Affairs, No. 8 to Lieutenant Governor-General, 15-1-1948. In this letter, Luytjes also stated the problem which the agreement sought to resolve as one defined by the character and volume of the imports and exports; 'Chinese decisions on barter trade', *Straits Times*, 6-4-1948, p. 7.
68   Archief Consulaat-Generaal Singapore 1946-51, Singapore Cons. Gen. 1946-54 (Singapore), Map 24, Letter from P. Mijnarends (Consul) to the Secretary of State for Economic Affairs (Batavia), X-B-3a, 13385, 5-6-1948.
69   'Dutch tighten imports control; "Rubbish dumped on market"', *Straits Times*, 20-1-1948, p. 3.
70   A summary of the main obstacles faced by traders after the 1948 agreement was implemented can be found in Directie Verre Oosten 450, *Nan Chiau Jit Pao*, 21-6-1948.

Government. Such trade will be on a barter basis and will be subject to Netherlands Import and Export Regulations. The Governments of Singapore and the Federation of Malaya will cooperate to the best of their ability to promote compliance by traders with these regulations.'[71] Under the circumstances, a declaration of intentions was the maximum that could be achieved.

Almost immediately, Dutch authorities proclaimed those waters in the Indonesian archipelago that were not under their control as still closed to trade. The ports under Dutch control were instructed to check incoming and outgoing cargoes in order to balance the barter trade. No outgoing cargo should have a higher value than the incoming cargo.[72] Chinese ships (including fishing vessels) continued to be seized, fired upon, or fined.[73] When Dutch patrol boats were fired upon at Jambi, stricter forms of retaliation were implemented. The Dutch banned all shipping from entering Jambi harbour for two weeks in June 1948. This immediately forced five Singapore motor *tongkang* (carrying $200,000 worth of textiles, foodstuffs, and sundries) to cancel their trip.[74] The Dutch also insisted that all ships out-bound from Jambi would be quarantined for one week at Tanjung Pinang when they called there for cargo inspection as required. As a result, the Singapore ship *Hong Tat* returned from Jambi only 21 days later. The normal time taken for the Singapore-Jambi-Singapore trip was one week, after allowing for loading and unloading of cargo at the Jambi River mouth. Trade pact or not, delays still ruled the day.[75]

On the occasion of the Jambi blockade, Zain from Indoff seized the opportunity to denounce the barter book system, claiming that it placed Singapore traders at the mercy of the Dutch. In contrast, there was no similar difficulty with barter trade in Republican territories.[76]

Among the Chinese traders, there was little enthusiasm for the barter book arrangement and the trade agreement in general. The chairman of the SOCIEA commented: 'Most of the merchants are disappointed and dissatisfied. They think the British had been fooled by the Dutch. The Pact will not help trade.' The vice-chairman of the Chinese Chamber of Commerce, Tan Chin Tuan, said: 'In principle, the Pact aims at encouraging trade between

---

[71] Archief Consulaat-Generaal Singapore 1946-51, Map 24, Singapore Cons. Gen. 1946-54 (Singapore), Letter from P. Mijnarends (Consul) to the Secretary of State for Economic Affairs (Batavia), X-B-3a, 13385, 5-6-1948.
[72] Archief Consulaat-Generaal Singapore 1946-51, Singapore Cons. Gen. 1946-1954 (Singapore), Map 24, Unsigned note dated 14-6-1948.
[73] 'Twenty colony ships detained', *Straits Times*, 10-4-1948, p. 7.
[74] 'Threat to colony trade; Indonesian on port closure', *Straits Times*, 17-6-1948, p. 7; Directie Verre Oosten 450, 'Merchants' view re Djambi', *Nan Chiau Jit Pao*, 14-6-1948.
[75] 'Traders' protest at shipping delay', *Straits Times*, 20-6-1948, p. 8.
[76] 'Threat to colony trade; Indonesian on port closure', *Straits Times*, 17-6-1948, p. 7; Directie Verre Oosten 450, 'Indonesian spokesman exposes Dutch intention', *Sin Chew Jit Poh*, 17-6-1948.

VII Commercial relations, or the 'Singapore squeeze'   157

the Netherlands East Indies and Malaya, but much will depend on the execution of the provisions of the Pact. In this connection, diplomacy plays an important role.' Merchants in Republican-controlled areas like Sibolga in Sumatra thought the agreement served no purpose, maintaining that goods leaving Indonesian-held territories continued to be seized and confiscated.[77] The unhappiness of the Chinese was due to the perception that the barter book system placed Singapore traders at the mercy of Dutch officials who were given the discretion to declare the value of the import and export cargo.[78] Goods arriving from Singapore at Belawan (near Medan) were not discharged because the value of the goods was too low or the trademarks of the goods failed to agree with those indicated on the papers. Where the goods were perishable, the losses were substantial.[79] This was particularly unsatisfactory when compared to the traders' relationship with Republican-held territories, where trade was conducted on a pure barter basis with no book records (and no valuation).[80] In view of the unhappiness, the Chinese representatives agreed to recommend that final adoption of the barter book system should await clarification by the Dutch authorities as to what they were prepared to concede in implementing the trade agreement.[81]

Although the Chinese Chamber of Commerce issued the barter books, it was the British authorities that were ultimately responsible for the accuracy of the barter book records. Naturally, they were not keen to be burdened with the duty of maintaining records. They wanted to transfer the administration of the barter books to a private accounting firm, Evatt and Company, so as to pass off the responsibility. But this would inevitably raise costs because of the commission that must be paid to the firm. The British also wanted to exempt the Riau archipelago from the trade agreement. This would mean, in effect, the wrecking of the agreement, because the traffic between the Riau archipelago and Singapore was estimated at about one hundred ships per day compared to a total of about one hundred and forty ships that crossed daily between Singapore and Indonesia as a whole.[82] Naturally, the Dutch were against this proposal.

The Chinese traders were not convinced that the March 1948 trade regula-

[77] Archief Consulaat-Generaal Singapore 1946-51, Singapore Cons. Gen. 1946-54 (Singapore), Attachment of letter X-B-3/7976 from P. Mijnarends (Consul) to the Secretary of State for Economic Affairs, Batavia, Map 24, Ad. No. 7976, 2-4-1948.
[78] Directie Verre Oosten 450; *Sin Chew Jit Poh*, 17-6-1948.
[79] Directie Verre Oosten 450, 'Goods belonging to 50 commercial firms at Medan being detained by Dutch customs', *Nanyang Siang Pau*, 8-6-1948.
[80] "Threat to colony trade'; Indonesian on port closure', *Straits Times*, 17-6-1948, p. 7.
[81] 'Chinese decisions on barter trade', *Straits Times*, 6-4-1948, p. 7.
[82] Archief Consulaat-Generaal Singapore 1946-51, Singapore Cons. Gen. 1946-54 (Singapore), Map 24, Letter from P. Mijnarends (Consul) to the Secretary of State for Economic Affairs, X-B-3, 8529, 8-4-1948.

tions improved the situation considerably. Kwek Soan Loh pointedly noted that the inspection of cargoes at Tanjung Pinang was not any faster. In July 1948, it still required fourteen or fifteen days. This length of time caused heavy losses, he alleged, because crew had to be fed and paid, even though idle.[83] The Dutch response was conciliatory. Within a month of hearing about the complaint by Kwek, they investigated the delays and reported that there were plans to extend wharves and godowns at Tanjung Pinang. 'Common carriers', or those ships belonging to well-established firms, would be cleared faster than individual vessels engaged in private trade.[84]

In the monthly meetings of the Chinese Chamber of Commerce in Singapore, reports continued to arrive that the Dutch still raised obstacles in the inter-island trade, despite the trade agreement. Delegate Low Boh Tan complained that the Dutch seldom granted entry permits for exports to Indonesia. Vessels that were successful in their application for permits were invariably searched and legal action instituted against the *chinchew* and owners, ending in fines and confiscation of vessels. Another delegate, Ng Aik Huan, reported that restrictions on re-exports in Singapore caused heavy losses to merchants. Singapore was overstocked with goods, and unless these could be re-exported to Indonesia, business would suffer. He gave the example of milk. New brands of condensed milk were imported but could not find a ready market in Singapore. Meanwhile, permits for re-export were refused, resulting in the milk turning bad. The milk would have been bartered for the produce that was much needed by Singapore.[85]

The 23 March agreement also ignored one vital ingredient that was missing in trade exchanges during the pre-war period. The exchange rate between the Straits dollar and the Netherlands East Indies guilder was no longer stable. With the Dutch military operations against the Republic in July 1947 and the general insecurity for trade, the value of the NEI guilder was fluctuating widely, with a tendency to plummet down. The trade agreement of 23 March 1948 and the control regulations that followed similarly ignored the exchange value of the NEI guilder. As long as the NEI guilder remained stable, regulations and controls could be implemented, but the NEI guilder was falling in value. One month after the trade agreement was implemented, the official rate of exchange was $85 for one hundred NEI guilders, but on the black market, the guilder had fallen to a quarter of its value, such that $85 could buy four hundred NEI guilders.[86] To compensate for the fluctua-

[83] 'Petition to N.E.I. Consul-General; By Tribune staff reporter', *Malaya Tribune*, 19-7-1948, p. 3.
[84] 'Ship delays at Tandjong Pinang; By Tribune staff reporter', *Malaya Tribune*, 12-8-1948, p. 5.
[85] 'Inter-island trade talks; By Tribune staff reporter', *Malaya Tribune*, 30-4-1948, p. 2.
[86] An example of how actual currency fluctuations disadvantaged Indonesia can be found in the figures cited in the document entitled 'Betreft dollarrestitutie Singapore' (circa 1949), Directie Verre Oosten 336.

tion of the guilder's value, the Dutch therefore added a remedial measure to the trade agreement by insisting that Singapore merchants importing goods from Indonesia would have to make part payment in a hard currency.[87]

In view of the fluctuations, there were thus two exchange rates, an official exchange rate and a black market rate. The official rate was set by the local foreign exchange control in Singapore following the quotations of the Bank of England. It consistently valued the Java guilder much higher than the black market value. In some respects, this difference would not have mattered since there were certain goods that Singapore traders must buy from or sell to the Dutch, and for these transactions, the official rate had to be used. Moreover, in the overall settlement of accounts, the Dutch themselves had to make good their purchases from Singapore at their own quoted rate. But there was a catch. The Dutch had a separate arrangement for foreign exchange control. For them, the official rate was good only for approved transactions. For non-approved transactions, the black market rate was applied. This arrangement worked to the detriment of the Singapore traders, who would rather use the black market rate in all dealings.[88]

With all these difficulties, the trade agreement was in need of a major public relations exercise to convince traders that it was practical and workable.

A trial run (Hong Thong)

So, to convince the Chinese traders in Singapore to support the barter book system, the Singapore Secretary for Economic Affairs proposed a series of official barter trade trials to Indonesia. The first trial to be organized was the voyage of the Singapore ship, the *Hong Thong*, to Pakan Baru. It was expected to carry more than $100,000 worth of foodstuffs, textiles, soap, and sundries. It would call at Tanjung Pinang for Dutch inspection of the cargo on its outward and inward voyages. In this trial, the *chinchew* would be shown the best way to value the imports and exports. According to the Assistant Secretary for Economic Affairs (R. Oliver), it was hoped that the value of the return cargo from the trial run would balance with the value of goods sent. The success of the trial run would then form the basis for subsequent barter trips, and this would in turn encourage Dutch authorities to open up more closed ports to Singapore traders.[89]

The trial run began with cautious optimism. The *Hong Thong* left Singapore

---

[87] 'Hard currency payment for goods from N.E.I.; By Tribune staff reporter', *Malaya Tribune*, 28-4-1948, p. 8. A brief account of the early fluctuations in currency exchange involving the NEI guilder, Japanese army notes, and the rupiah can be found in Twang 1998:152-77.
[88] 'Foreign exchange control in the colony II: fixing the value of the Java guilder; By W.T.K', *Straits Times*, 22-2-1950, p. 6.
[89] 'First barter trade ship sails; NEI-bound with $100,000 cargo', *Straits Times*, 29-7-1948, p. 7.

on 28 July 1948, and in fact carried a cargo of $180,000 worth of textiles, foodstuffs, and sundries,[90] far in excess of the original estimate. The ship also carried letters of introduction from Oetoyo. It cleared Dutch inspections at Tanjung Pinang, after some disputes. Oetoyo accused the Dutch authorities at Tanjung Pinang of removing seven hundred pickaxes from the *Hong Thong* cargo, but the Dutch issued a denial saying that the pickaxes were offloaded at Singapore as they were not the sort of goods allowed in the barter agreement.[91] When the ship reached Tanjung Uban, Dutch naval authorities prohibited nineteen passengers on the *Hong Thong* from continuing the voyage.[92]

At Pakan Baru, pro-Republican authorities rejected the part of the cargo consisting of biscuits, cigarettes, soft drinks, and liquor, arguing that those were unnecessary luxury goods. The haggling over these goods resulted in a delay of twelve days. There was no difficulty, however, of bartering rubber with the Indonesians, and the *Hong Thong* eventually returned with 82 tons of Republican rubber. Needless to say, the *Hong Thong* also experienced delays at both Pakan Baru and Tanjung Pinang.[93]

The first trial run was sufficiently encouraging to warrant the organization of a second. Twenty-eight Chinese firms chartered the *Hong Soon* and this time, the destination was the Sumatran Republican port of Rengat. Zain of Indoff expressed the hope that this second voyage would be more successful than the first.[94] The ship returned to Singapore with $300,000 worth of rubber and copra, but before two more voyages could be organized, the Dutch closed the port to shipping because shore batteries had fired on navy ships.[95]

Thus ended the barter trial runs. Individual ships[96] continued to trade, but the trade ended soon when the Dutch launched their second military action a few months later in December 1948, and all trading operations ceased. Chinese traders were advised by the Singapore Department of Economic Affairs to consult the agency first if they wanted to trade with the Republican ports of Sibolga, Pakan Baru, Jambi, and Rengat.[97]

---

[90] 'Indonesians reject barter ship cargo', *Straits Times*, 28-8-1948, p. 4. The actual value of the cargo varied. According to another report, the cargo amounted to $150,000 ('19 in ship turned off by Dutch', *Straits Times*, 12-8-1948, p. 5).
[91] PG 304, Persconferentie mr Oetoyo, Aneta No. 1059, 31-8-1948. See also Nasution (1991b: 462-63), which described the offloaded items as *cangkul* and not pickaxes.
[92] '19 in ship turned off by Dutch', *Straits Times*, 12-8-1948, p. 5.
[93] 'Indonesians reject barter ship cargo', *Straits Times*, 28-8-1948, p. 4. See also PG 304, Persconferentie mr Oetoyo, Aneta No. 1059, 31-8-1948; and PG 166, the undated report – 'confidentially learned from the captain of the "Hong Thong"'.
[94] 'Second barter trade voyage', *Straits Times*, 4-9-1948, p. 7.
[95] 'Gunfire at Rengat halts barter trade', *Straits Times*, 21-10-1948, p. 2.
[96] 'Sumatra barter prospect', *Straits Times*, 7-12-1948, p. 4.
[97] 'Warning on Sumatra trade', *Straits Times*, 21-12-1948, p. 7.

Tackling the complaints of the Singapore Chinese

While efforts were being made to reach workable barter solutions with the Dutch, the British authorities in Singapore also tried to mediate between the Dutch and the local Chinese to resolve other differences. One of the chief sticking points was the issue of compensation for the seized Chinese vessels. Negotiations were conducted between 15 February and 19 June 1947. The British Secretary and Assistant Secretary for Economic Affairs acted as facilitators, but the Dutch were not to be pressured. The Chinese themselves were divided. Among them were those who were relatively indifferent because they were not badly affected by the Dutch blockade and other regulations.[98] The Chinese representatives negotiating with the Dutch on the issue of compensation were indeed a mixed lot. They included the SOCIEA, the Motor Boat Vessels Association, the Protection Committee (set up by the Singapore Chinese Chamber of Commerce), and the Federation of China Relief.[99]

The negotiations yielded indifferent results. Against the threats of retaliation by Tan Kah Kee, Van Mook was prepared to adopt a conciliatory approach. The negotiations started on an optimistic note. Very quickly, on 27 February 1947, agreement was reached to resume business and communications links between the Singapore Chinese and Indonesia. The Dutch even promised to compensate the family of a Chinese victim who had been shot by the Dutch marines, paying an amount of $12,000. However, this was about the only satisfactory result of the negotiations. The initial progress made was marred by more threats of boycott action in the middle of March 1947 if the Dutch did not pay compensation at the rate demanded for the seized rubber stocks from Chinese ships. The bargaining over compensation went as follows: Kwek Soan Loh submitted claims amounting to $5 million, based on the price of rubber at about $40 per kilogram. The Dutch made a counter-offer of $17.40 per kilogram, because this was the price paid by Singapore merchants to Indonesians in Ceribon. Kwek pointed out that Singapore merchants had to pay a forty per cent tax to the Indonesians as well as freight and handling charges, all increasing the cost two or three times.[100] Meanwhile, as the negotiations continued, more incidents of seizures occurred (Nasution 1978a:302-3).

Throughout the negotiations lasting four months, the Chinese showed their anger. Incensed by what they considered as continued arbitrary Dutch

---

[98] Archief Consulaat-Generaal Singapore 1946-51, Map 9, Singapore Cons. Gen. 1946-54 (Singapore), *Nan Chiau Jit Pao,* Editorial: re negotiations with Dutch, 21-6-1947.
[99] Archief Consulaat-Generaal Singapore 1946-51, Map 9, Singapore Cons. Gen. 1946-54 (Singapore), Chinese Importers and Exporters Association dissatisfied with Dutch will take drastic steps to deal with Dutch: indignant at Dutch for breach of promise, 13-6-1947.
[100] 'Dutch delay settling $5 million demand; By Tribune staff reporter', *Malaya Tribune,* 6-6-1947, p. 6.

actions, the president of the Chinese Chamber of Commerce (CCC), Lee Kong Chian, served the reminder that the Chinese in Singapore were obliged to observe British law and regulations only.[101] The Dutch explained that patrol boats had been instructed to perform checks with the least possible delay to *bona fide* shippers, although it would take some time before the orders could be implemented efficaciously.[102] However, they were prepared to pay compensation for the seizure of six Chinese vessels[103] that had been detained unjustifiably and their cargo seized, but coupled the offer with the demand that the CCC issue a written notice persuading its members to observe Dutch regulations governing import and export.

In the end, it was the Singapore colonial authorities that advised the Chinese not to launch any boycott or strike measures against the Dutch and urged them to obey Dutch regulations.[104] A letter from the Secretary for Economic Affairs to the chairman of the Chinese Chamber of Commerce in Singapore on 9 June 1947 also made clear that the British official position endorsed and recognized Dutch policies.[105] The British also stressed that any claims for compensation would only be supported if the British government was satisfied that claimants had followed all regulations, adding that obeying Dutch regulations would benefit the Chinese community in Southeast Asia in the long run. It was also emphatic that compliance with those regulations would not result in suffering or undue interference.[106] The Chinese negotiators caved in to British pressure and accepted the Dutch offer. As the Chinese leader, Lee Kong Chian, said on 10 June 1947, 'We are living in British territory and naturally cannot disagree with the British'.[107]

[101] Archief Consulaat-Generaal Singapore 1946-51. Map 9, Singapore Cons. Gen. 1946-54 (Singapore), Press Release 28-6-1947, CCC decides to observe regulations locally: will not issue notice to the effect to merchants in other places.
[102] Archief Consulaat-Generaal Singapore 1946-51, Singapore Cons. Gen. 1946-54 (Singapore), Map 9, Letter from P. Mijnarends, Consul, to the Secretary for Economic Affairs, K4/15320, 25-7-1947.
[103] Archief Consulaat-Generaal Singapore 1946-51, Map 9, Singapore Cons. Gen. 1946-54 (Singapore), 20 June release to all papers, Committee for negotiations with Dutch decides to demand compensation in cash.
[104] Archief Consulaat-Generaal Singapore 1946-51, Map 9, Singapore Cons. Gen. 1946-54 (Singapore), Press release, 28-6-1947, CCC decides to observe regulations locally: will not issue notice to the effect to merchants in other places. See also Archief Consulaat-Generaal Singapore 1946-51, Map 9, Singapore Cons. Gen. 1946-54 (Singapore), letter T. van der Gaast (Economic Affairs Branch, Colonial Secretary's Office), to M.F. Vigeveno, Consul-General, CSO 10218/47, 26-6-1947.
[105] Archief Consulaat-Generaal Singapore 1946-1951, Map 9, Singapore Cons. Gen. 1946-54 (Singapore).
[106] Archief Consulaat-Generaal Singapore 1946-51, Map 9, Singapore Cons. Gen. 1946-54 (Singapore).
[107] Inventaris van de archieven van her Consulaat-Generaal te Singapore, 1945-54, Ministerie van Buitenlandse Zaken (MBZ) 211.

The mode of compensation was established when the Dutch proposed how they were to deal with the group of six Chinese vessels. The Dutch offered to pay half a million guilders in cash. Alternatively, the six ship owners could form a special *kongsi* that would be allowed special privileges to trade and recover the profits it had lost as a result of the detentions and seizures.[108] There were other variations of this non-cash offer of compensation.[109] It was a testimony of how Chinese ship owners mistrusted the Dutch that they rejected the second mode of compensation and voted overwhelmingly to accept the cash compensation.[110] Better to cut losses than to try to recoup the investment!

Indoff trade regulations

Official Republican measures to control the trade lagged behind those of the Dutch, perhaps indicating the time needed for the Indonesians to get their act together. Indoff also tried to set up its own shipping company to bring in imports from Indonesia, but these efforts turned out to be a fiasco because of lack of experience. It all began with a meeting between Sjahrir and an old acquaintance, Major West, who was then working in the liaison office of the British Military Administration in Singapore. West suggested that the Republican government buy two boats to start a shipping company for trade with Sumatra. The boats turned out to be a bad investment because they were too expensive to maintain. Indoff decided to sell them to cut losses.[111]

Indoff also tried to muscle into the existing trade networks between Singapore and Indonesia. In this respect, it thought it held an advantage because its official status allowed it to conclude agreements with other local authorities like those at Rengat, Tembilahan, and Pakan Baru to bring some semblance of control.

Generally, these agreements embodied the following conditions. Only ships calling at Indonesian ports with introductory letters issued by Indoff would be loaded. The goods to be transported to Indonesia would be checked

---

[108] Archief Consulaat-Generaal Singapore 1946-51, Map 9, Singapore Cons. Gen. 1946-1954 (Singapore), Letter from the Secretary for Economic Affairs to the Singapore Chinese Chamber of Commerce Chairman, 9-6-1947; '$500,000 compensation; Dutch offer to Chinese will not be in cash; By Tribune staff reporter', *Malaya Tribune*, 10-6-1947, p. 5.
[109] 'Dutch offer local Chinese free NEI trade; Blockade may be lifted also', *Malaya Tribune*, 13-6-1947, p. 1
[110] Archief Consulaat-Generaal Singapore 1946-51, Map 9, Singapore Cons. Gen. 1946-54 (Singapore), 20 June release to all papers, Committee for negotiations with Dutch decides to demand compensation in cash.
[111] PG 385, Further interrogation of Dr Oetoyo by officers of HM Customs, Singapore, 4-11-1948.

in Singapore as to whether they were beneficial to the population. Luxury goods like cigarettes and wine were not permitted. Allocation of cargo space would be determined in Singapore.[112] All these conditions served to promote the role played by Indoff in barter trade, but in the free trade environment of Singapore, they were blatantly ignored or problems of enforcement surfaced.

Indoff trade regulations remained ineffective or were not observed. Indoff became a negligible player in the trade between Singapore and Indonesia to the extent that when the British and the Dutch signed their trade agreement of 23 March 1948, the Republic of Indonesia was not a party. Indoff did not receive details concerning the trade agreement. Faced with a *fait accompli* in the form of published details splashed over the newspapers in Singapore, it merely issued a statement that the Republic of Indonesia was also interested in promoting normal trade between Singapore/Malaya and the territories under Republican control. The same statement reminded affected parties to comply with Republican regulations in Java and Sumatra. Only vessels with Indoff permits would be permitted to trade. It reiterated that normal trade had been hampered by Dutch regulations, causing substantial losses.[113] Despite the statement, the impression could not be avoided that there were two parallel and hardly connected systems of trade, one operated by the Dutch and the other operated by the Republic through Indoff. The Chinese traders in Singapore straddled the two and faced the challenge of handling the ambiguities of each.

Following the proclamation of control measures by the Dutch in March 1948, Indoff retaliated with their own set of regulations. Indoff reserved the right to inspect the kind of goods exported to Republican-held territories (similar to the right claimed by the Dutch). At the same time, imports from the Republic must be at least 75 per cent of the value of exports from Singapore based on Singapore prices.[114]

The twenty per cent levy

The most controversial and widely publicized measure of control was Indoff's attempt to impose revenue-generating levies on the trade between Singapore and Indonesia. These levies were of two main types. There was the provision (Article 5) in the trade regulations published by Indoff on 25

[112] PG 170(I), CGDN 413/I/III, Singapore, Report by Secretaris voor Speciale Diensten (S. van Hulst) to Procureur-Generaal bij het Hooggerechtshof van Indonesië, Batavia, 19-11-1948. See also an earlier report by S. van Hulst to Procureur-Generaal, 18-8-1948, Inventaris van de archieven van her Consulaat-Generaal te Singapore, 1945-54, Ministerie van Buitenlandse Zaken (MBZ) 220.
[113] 'Indonesian view of UK-Dutch trade pact', *Malaya Tribune*, 3-4-1948, p. 2.
[114] 'Indonesia trade ruling', *Straits Times*, 24-8-1948, p. 4.

August 1948 that 'For every licence issued in Singapore, one thousandth of the total worth of the goods exported shall be charged.'[115] Again, given the free trade environment of Singapore, any levies were anathema, but since this was almost equivalent to the payment for a licence, Indoff probably felt it had the right to impose fees.

More audacious was its decision (also in September 1948) to impose a levy of twenty per cent on the value of goods moved between Singapore and Sumatra. The levy first became a public issue when a local Chinese merchant filed a complaint at the SOCIEA. Sometime in July 1948, one of his vessels carrying a cargo of $1.2 million worth of rubber and copra was required to make an agreement before leaving a Republican port in Sumatra that twenty per cent of his cargo would be surrendered as tax to Indoff when the ship reached Singapore. When the ship arrived at Singapore, the complainant alleged that Indoff demanded $50,000 as tax, but after much bargaining, the sum was reduced to $5,000.[116]

The Indoff spokesman on this issue of the twenty per cent levy was Zain. Zain was opposed to the levy[117] but he was placed in a difficult position to rationalize it publicly. His response therefore read like a defence of the levy and a form of damage control. He denied that there was a twenty per cent *ad valorem* tax on goods entering Singapore from Republican ports. Merchants carrying those goods were merely required to sign an agreement with local authorities undertaking to deliver twenty per cent of the goods to Indoff or its agent. In return, the Republican authorities undertook to hold the value of the goods to the credit of the merchant until his return on his next trip to Indonesia. He would be reimbursed in goods on the next trip with no loss to himself. This arrangement was designed to promote a regular flow of trade between the Republic and Singapore. It would discourage fly-by-night traders and, of course, it would enable the Republic to earn urgently needed Straits dollars.[118]

Unused to paying levies of any kind in a free port, the fee raised the shackles of the traders. It was not difficult for the SOCIEA to get the support of the Colonial Secretary for Economic Affairs in Singapore to declare that the twenty per cent levy was entirely unjustified. The disapproval of the British

---

[115] PG 166, Letter 965A from S. van Hulst (Secretaris voor Speciale Diensten) to Procureur-Generaal, 25-8-1948.
[116] 'Traders to discuss Indonesian tax', *Malaya Tribune*, 22-9-1948, p. 6.
[117] Directie Verre Oosten 336, Letter from A.M.L. Winkelman (Consul-General Singapore) to Director of Directie Verre Oosten (T. Elink Schuurman), VIII-C-3, No. 26298/362.
[118] 'Indonesian warning to Singapore traders; By Tribune staff reporter', *Malaya Tribune*, 24-9-1948, p. 5. On Zain's defence of the levy, see memo concerning informal meeting with Mr Zain on Thursday, 7-10-1948 (Raffles Hotel) written by R.J.C.M. Schreemann (Assistant Trade Commissioner, Netherlands Consulate-General Singapore) on 12-10-1948, Directie Verre Oosten 336.

colonial authorities, however, was expressed in less direct language. They declared that 'The Singapore government can make no allowance for any payment of 'tax' or 'levy' to third parties as far as trade between Singapore and Sumatra is concerned. Furthermore, the Government is determined that there shall be no interference in the straight dollar-for-dollar trade with Republican Sumatra.'[119] In fact, it was not impossible that the Singapore authorities – A. Gilmour (Secretary for Department of Economic Affairs, April 1946-1953) and T. van der Gaast (Gilmour's second-in-command) – encouraged the Chinese traders to protest the levy. The levy aside, local Chinese traders, however, were prepared to comply with any requirements for documentation.[120]

According to the account given in *Rahsia perdjuangan* (1948:129), Indoff denied that the levy of twenty per cent was a tax but only a deposit to ensure that traders continued to trade with the Republic. But this denial sounded hollow because Indoff was depending on this 'deposit' to generate revenue for itself.

Official levies were well and good, but their implementation was quite another matter. Right at the start, in early September 1948, a trader refused to pay the twenty per cent levy. Soedjati arrived in Singapore from Lampung (South Sumatra) with fifty tons of pepper and refused to pay. Instead, he sold his goods to a firm called Ban Heng Liong located at Raffles Place.[121] In another account, an Indonesian chief clerk or *chinchew* (by the name of Kadir) of a Chinese ship, the *Hong Ann*, was only asked to pay ten per cent instead of the usual twenty. And Kadir refused to pay even this discounted levy.[122]

The kind of control exercised by Indoff over the activities of Chinese traders was never uniform and varied from case to case. Several instances will illustrate the inconsistencies. In one case, the Singapore ship *Hong Tah* applied to Indoff for a permit to proceed to Jambi with cigarettes and wine valued at $60,000, together with textiles and foodstuffs. Indoff stepped in and prevented the ship from leaving with the cigarettes and wine,[123] presumably because such goods were not essentials. In another case, the *Wah Chang* arrived in Singapore from West Sumatra carrying coffee, rubber, and other commodities. It had been previously arranged that the *Wah Chang* would surrender twenty per cent of its cargo to Indoff, but upon arrival, the owner of the cargo alleged ignorance of the said agreement. The result: Indoff had to contest the allegation. In a third instance, ships coming to Singapore from Jambi were known to adhere to Indoff regulations that twenty per cent of the cargo would

---

[119] 'Trade 'tax' ignored', *Straits Times*, 20-11-1948, p. 4.
[120] PG 304, Report by informant, 17-8-1948.
[121] PG 168, CGDN, No. 175-48, Singapore, Report by J.W.J. de Haas, 15-10-1948.
[122] PG 558, CGDN, No. 13-49, Singapore, By R.W. van Lier, 17-1-1949.
[123] PG 304, Report by informant, 17-8-1948.

be retained as payment of tax.[124] But even this practice was soon dropped, and it was reported, on 10 March 1948, that the export levy for goods leaving Singapore for Jambi would be lifted.[125] The reasons were unclear. A fourth instance was even more interesting because it cast suspicion on the consistency with which Indoff applied its own regulations. According to a report in the *Malaya Tribune* of 22 September 1948, a Singapore Chinese merchant was required by Indonesian authorities to pay twenty per cent of the value of his cargo as tax to Indoff in Singapore. His ship was leaving one of the Republican ports in Sumatra with a cargo of $1,200,000 worth of rubber and copra. When the ship arrived in Singapore, Indoff demanded $50,000, but after bargaining, the amount was reduced to $5,000. Indoff's opponents, like the PI, seized upon this 'discount' to discredit Indoff. To them, it was an example showing that Indoff had cheapened Republican authority implied in a levy of this kind. Zain at Indoff explained that there was no bargaining. The $5,000 was only an instalment payment. Zain conceded that it was a mistake not to have clarified the point earlier so that the *Malaya Tribune* would not have given the wrong impression to its readers (*Rahsia perdjuangan* 1948:130-2). Another ship, the *Wah Chang* from Singapore, left Padang in West Sumatra carrying coffee and rubber after agreeing to pay twenty per cent of each category of cargo to Indoff upon its return to Singapore. Once there, the cargo owner professed ignorance when Indoff officials came to collect their due.[126]

Chinese counter-measures

Squeezed by the Dutch and somewhat inconvenienced by Indoff, Chinese traders had to resort to counter-measures. They were not totally defenceless. Before listing the actions taken, it would be useful to start by explaining the motives behind the Chinese interest in continuing trade activities despite the difficulties.

The profit motive

Obviously the primary motive of Chinese traders in their dealings with Indonesians was profit. Profit was so important that the Chinese would not hesitate to circumvent legalities in order to earn their livelihood. This suited the Indonesians very well. Thus, notwithstanding their profit motive, there was a convergence of interests between Indonesian freedom fighters and

---

[124] PG 304, Report by informant, 17-8-1948.
[125] PG 168, CGDN, No. 70-48, Report by S. van Hulst, 18-3-1948.
[126] Inventaris van de archieven van het Consulaat-Generaal te Singapore, 1945-54, Ministerie van Buitenlandse Zaken (MBZ) 220, Letter from S. van Hulst to Procureur-Generaal, 18-8-1948.

Chinese businessmen.

The notion of profit, however, must not be viewed only in money-grubbing terms. Often, there were whole careers and financial structures at stake, painstakingly built up by individuals who rose from rags to riches, risking their lives and necks in the process. A typical example was Kwek Soan Loh, mentioned above as chairman of the SOCIEA. Before the outbreak of the Second World War in the Pacific, Kwek had worked for a couple of years as the Chinese chief clerk (*chinchew*) of the Chinese-owned steamer *Senang*, plying between Singapore and Palembang. During the Japanese occupation, he started a brokerage business on his own. Later, he became secretary of the Overseas Chinese Union, a Japanese-sponsored local Chinese organization. This organization was recognized as a channel whereby Chinese concerns were conveyed to the Japanese government. At war's end, Kwek established his own export and import agency, the Hock Hoe Trading Company, headquartered at 37 Philip Street in Singapore, dealing in Indonesian rubber. Meanwhile, he organized the SOCIEA at 76 Robinson Road. The association was independent of the Chinese Chamber of Commerce, having its own executives, funds, and membership. Its members were drawn from those trading in Indonesian produce, principally estate rubber, tobacco, tea, and sugar. Many of them had taken advantage of the Japanese occupation to amass wealth that was then invested in the import industry with offices in Singapore after the war. Others had pre-war business connections with Indonesia or had resided there before the war.[127]

Profit and survival – these were powerful forces in the free enterprise environment of Singapore. Given those conditions, it would be difficult to control trade with Indonesia. The flow of goods tended to follow market forces, and these seemed impervious to artificial intervention. This had also been the experience some twenty years ago, when Malaya was restricting rubber production under the Stevenson Scheme in the 1920s but the then Netherlands East Indies was not. As a result, there was a highly profitable smuggling trade from the western coast of the Malay Peninsula to the eastern coast of Sumatra, where rubber could be sold freely.[128] The lesson to be learnt was that trade followed wherever there were viable opportunities.

The extent of actual profit realized varied considerably, but the absolute amounts of money that could be made were sufficient to arouse the interest of various parties – and not only the Chinese. It was common knowledge that $100 worth of piece-goods could be sent from Singapore to an Indonesian port in Sumatra and the trader could return with $500 worth of rubber in exchange. This worked out to a whopping five hundred per cent profit, at

[127] Archief Consulaat-Generaal Singapore 1946-51, Map 5, Singapore Cons. Gen. 1946-54 (Singapore), Singapore Overseas Chinese Importers and Exporters Association.
[128] 'Blockade by the Dutch', *Straits Times*, 8-3-1947, p. 4.

VII Commercial relations, or the 'Singapore squeeze'

least at face value. The Dutch were particularly incensed by the magnitude of the amount drained away. Indonesian leaders like Sjahrir were also uncomfortable because he suspected huge profits flowed to Chinese coffers in Singapore. Sjahrir told the British consul-general in Batavia that the Republic had 'done very badly in their deals with Singapore merchants'.[129] He was not the only one who held such thoughts. Even local Malay community leaders in Singapore entertained the same suspicions.[130]

Of course Chinese traders in Singapore operated at an advantage. Commissions were factored into prices without the knowledge of the counterparts in Indonesia. In some cases, goods fetched high prices in Singapore but the Indonesian party was not told of the selling price till it had fallen (Twang 1998:208).

However, matters were not that simple or straightforward. Shipping charges were high, reflecting the extra payment for risks involved. Also, the prospect of large profit margins obscured the fact that a process of capital flight to Singapore was taking place. Chinese merchants with interests in Sumatra were sending their produce to Singapore and banking the sales proceeds there. In turn, Singapore merchants were taking what goods they could get out of Singapore's godowns, exchanging them in Indonesian territories as profitably as possible, and then retaining the proceeds in Singapore. To the Chinese, the Dutch were merely making a big fuss. The Chinese were, in fact, arguing that the Dutch were swimming against the tide of free trade. After 1945, the trade with Indonesia was no different from the trade before 1942. It was all barter, especially since banking facilities and exchange controls were missing in many areas. Indonesia was facing an acute shortage of piece-goods and manufactured goods that Singapore could supply. Finally, of course, turmoil reigned even as the Dutch were trying to reimpose their former authority and the cost of taking risks was a factor in pricing.[131]

Any evaluation of the profits earned by the Chinese must also take into consideration the trade trends that had long existed between Singapore and Indonesia from the latter's colonial period onwards. Singapore's imports from the Dutch islands historically had always been more than its exports in the reverse direction. The trade figures in Table 1 for the periods before and after the Pacific War attest to this statement:[132]

---

[129] FO 810/4, Telegram from Mackereth to Foreign Office, Mo. 56, 23-1-1947.
[130] Directie Verre Oosten 568, Report by R. Moehtadi and R. Djajadikoesoema on mission (24-6-1948 to 5-7-1948) to Singapore and Kuala Lumpur to evaluate opinion about Indonesian federalism, 8-7-1948.
[131] 'First things last', *Straits Times*, 12-3-1947, p. 4; 'Singapore and the N.E.I.', *Straits Times*, 13-3-1947, p. 6.
[132] 'First things last', *Straits Times*, 12-3-1947, p.4; 'Singapore and the N.E.I.', *Straits Times*, 13-3-1947, p. 6.

Table 1

Year	Imports from N.E.I. (in dollars)	Exports to N.E.I. (in dollars)
1935	147,825,000	33,502,000
1936	161,220,000	32,951,000
1937	220,054,000	34,757,000
1938	147,822,000	36,858,000

Source: *Straits Times*, 12-13 March 1947.

Similar data for the period October 1946 through January 1947 show that the post-war trade situation was fast reverting to the pre-war position, wherein imports from Indonesia far exceeded exports in the reverse direction. The figures in Table 2 show this trend:

Table 2

Month	Imports from Indonesia (in dollars)	Exports to Indonesia (in dollars)
Oct 1946	19,433,000	3,561,000
Nov 1946	15,182,600	2,330,000
Dec 1946	15,758,000	3,012,000
Jan 1947	14,230,000	3,271,000

Source: *Straits Times*, 12-13 March 1947.

Furthermore, it had always been a trend for imports to exceed exports in Singapore's trade with Indonesia. Within Singapore circles, it was therefore felt that the Dutch were being unduly concerned about an outflow of specie to line the pockets of Chinese traders. Seen in this light, Dutch control measures were both unreasonable and inconvenient.

Threats to boycott

The gut reaction of some Chinese groups was to organize boycotts against the Dutch. It will be appropriate to provide an account of the threats adopted by the Chinese since the time when the Dutch counter-measures began to bite.

Sixty persons representing Chinese traders, labour, and trade unions affected by the vicissitudes of inter-island trade held a meeting in December

1946 at the Ee Hoe Hean Club (a meeting place for leading Chinese merchants in Singapore). They decided to form a committee to back the protests made by the Chinese Chamber of Commerce over the seizures of Chinese vessels and detention of cargo, and demand for compensation and their immediate release.[133]

Another major leader in these endeavours must have been the Singapore Chinese tycoon, Tan Kah Kee. Tan began his anti-Dutch activities as early as 4 February 1947, when he chaired a meeting sanctioning the boycott of Dutch ships by refusing to load or unload them. Using the overseas Chinese network, telegrams were sent to Hong Kong and Swatow (China) requesting that, in view of the boycott, goods should not be transported to Singapore on Dutch ships. With the framework of a boycott in place, Tan got down to details, for example how to support the workers whose income would be affected by the boycott.[134] Tan's plans included collecting monthly contributions towards the total costs of supporting a boycott. He estimated that forty per cent of the expenses would come from the SOCIEA, thirty per cent from owners of the vessels detained by the Dutch, and the remaining thirty per cent from Palembang Chinese merchants.[135]

Tan explained that the Chinese were increasingly anti-Dutch, especially after a ceasefire had been concluded in 1947, because they had expected the entire eastern coast of Sumatra to be opened for trade. It turned out that the coast in question remained closed from Jambi southwards. Also, strict visa regulations enforced in Dutch-controlled cities in Indonesia dismayed Chinese traders. Some applicants for visas had to wait six weeks or longer.[136]

Chinese seamen set up the Singapore Coastal Labourer's Indonesian Aid and Anti-Dutch Committee in 1947 with the aim of persuading harbour employees, including those of Indonesian origin, to put down their tools. This was never effective because there were always Indian and other Chinese labourers willing to replace them.[137] If there were initial successes, it was because the boycott against Dutch ships coincided with a period when there was sufficient demand for labour on other ships. Dutch ships that anchored out at sea and not near the docks were not hindered by the boycott and they were given the usual attention by Chinese labourers. (Workers on the docks

---

[133] 'NEI trade boycott threat', *Straits Times*, 27-12-1946, p. 1.
[134] PG 169 (I), Tweewekelijksche Politiek Overzicht der Residentie Riouw over de periode 1 t/m 15-2-1947, Singapore, 16-2-1947, by P.A. van der Poel, Commissaris van Politie I.
[135] 'Blockade by Dutch defended', *Straits Times*, 20-3-1947, p. 1.
[136] RRI 551, Tweewekelijksche berichtgeving van de Residentie Riouw over de periode 1 t/m 15-8-1947, By J. van Waardenburg, Resident, Tandjong Pinang, 28-8-1947.
[137] PG 173, Rapport van den Inlichtingendienst der Algemeene Politie (Singapore) by S. van Hulst (Commissaris van Politie II), No. 505GE, 7-8-1947.

were mainly of Indian and Malay origin.)[138]

It is also worthy of note that the chairman of the Chinese Chamber of Commerce, Lee Kong Chian, did not support boycotts or strike actions against the Dutch.[139] Moreover, the management of the Singapore Harbour Board tended to frown on such acts of boycott. They were considered detrimental to Singapore as a transit port.[140] A boycott could also result in undesirable retaliatory measures employed by the Dutch against Chinese traders operating in Indonesia. In a sense, there was a hostage issue here.

A meeting to decide on strike action held on 14 August 1947 confirmed the lack of unanimity among the various types of workers on the docks. The Singapore Harbour Board Workers Union voted for a boycott of Dutch ships. Its decision was to some extent the result of lobbying by Bizar Ahmad, chairman of the Indonesian/Malay section of the Singapore Federation of Trade Unions. Also, there was work on other ships available at that time so that the boycott of Dutch ships alone did not cause severe hardship to labourers.[141] However, the Lighter Workers Union (representing coolie labourers who loaded and unloaded ships at anchor) and the Steamship Loaders and Unloaders Union decided against a boycott.[142]

There were sound reasons why important Chinese leaders and entrepreneurs like Lee Kong Chian and the British authorities in Singapore frowned on any proposals of boycott against the Dutch. The signing of the Linggajati Agreement (March 1947) was expected to result in a trade boom in Singapore because large amounts of goods lay ready for despatch. Patience was needed to wait for the upturn. Boycotts of Dutch ships were also decisions of major importance for the welfare of labourers involved, and there was some reluctance to proceed for that reason. It was estimated that a boycott would cost $400,000 to tide over the difficulties faced by labourers who would be deprived of work. This money was not easily available, especially when there were no obvious advantages for labourers to enjoy as a result of the boycott.[143] Lee Kong Chian thus declined to be associated with public pro-

---

[138] PG 169 (I), Halfmaandelijksche berichtgeving van den vertegenwoordiger der Algemeene Politie van Nederlandsch-Indië te Singapore over de periode van 1-8-1947 t/m 17-8-1947, No. 518A, Singapore, by S. van Hulst, Commissaris van Politie II, 19-8-1947.
[139] PG 173, Rapport van den Inlichtingendienst der Algemeene Politie (Singapore), No. 495GE, Singapore, by S. van Hulst, 30-7-1947.
[140] PG 173, Rapport van den Inlichtingendienst der Algemeene Politie (Singapore), No. 521GE, Singapore, by S. van Hulst, 23-8-1947.
[141] PG 173, Rapport van den Inlichtingendienst der Algemeene Politie (Singapore), No. 511GE, Singapore, by S. van Hulst, 13-8-1947.
[142] PG 173, Rapport van den Inlichtingendienst der Algemeene Politie (Singapore), No. 516GE, Singapore, by S. van Hulst, 16-8-1947.
[143] PG 169 (I), Tweewekelijksche berichtgeving der Residentie Riouw over de periode 6-3-1947 t/m 31-3-1947, Singapore, By P.A. van der Poel, Commissaris van Politie, 31-3-1947.

tests of a high profile, although this did not mean that he refused support to counter-measures. For example, he endorsed a meeting in Singapore with representatives from various places in Sumatra (Bagansiapiapi, Indragiri, Selat Panjang, Pakan Baru, Siak, Tunggal, Bengkalis) to discuss measures to be taken in negotiations with the Dutch concerning the blockade. The meeting established an executive body chaired by a businessman, Lee Chao Ching, from Selat Panjang.[144] Lee Chao Ching was a representative of the Chinese Chamber of Commerce in Selat Panjang.[145]

Still, with the threat of a boycott hanging over their heads, the Dutch decided on the prudent measure of sending a delegation to soothe the ruffled feathers of the Chinese traders. In February 1948, P.A. Ursone, senior adviser at the Department of Economic Affairs in Batavia, arrived in Singapore. He said all the right things. He assured the Chinese traders that they could expect more trade in the future. However, this trade would continue to be governed by foreign exchange and other import and export regulations. Ursone tried to discount the 'blockade' as exaggerated. These were no more than normal checks on shipping, he said. Ships could trade anywhere provided the necessary permits were obtained first.[146] But if the aim was to regain the confidence of Chinese traders, Ursone failed. As a lawyer, he overemphasized the colonial government's legal duty on behalf of absentee estate owners whose properties had fallen into the hands of the Republic. He was not inclined to step beyond the legal limits of what the Dutch could offer.[147]

If protests and boycotts did not work, the only option left for the Chinese was to operate within the Dutch regulations. Provided some of the more distasteful practices were amended, the Chinese were still prepared to countenance the environment of rules and conditions. A set of proposals submitted by the SOCIEA[148] revealed the most objectionable aspects of the Dutch control regulations that they wanted to have amended. There were two of these.

a. The delays caused by inspections. The SOCIEA recommended that ships should not be required to call en-route for inspection. Instead, marine authorities could carry out inspections at the destination ports. In response to this recommendation, the Dutch replied that there were insufficient customs officers to be appointed at each port.[149]

[144] PG 171, *Nan Chiau Yit Pao*, 31-10-1947.
[145] PG 171, Letter 222d, dated 30-10-1947, from S. van Hulst to Onderhoofd der Algemene Recherche, Batavia.
[146] 'Future of trade with Netherlands East Indies', *Straits Times*, 19-2-1948, p. 7.
[147] FO 810/10, Telegram from Governor of Singapore to Secretary of State for Colonies, No. 153, 22-2-1947.
[148] 'Dutch "red tape" hinders colony, N.E.I trade; By Tribune staff reporter', *Malaya Tribune*, 10-2-1949, p. 8.
[149] 'Barter trade with Sumatra to end', *Malaya Tribune*, 18-2-1949, p. 5.

b. The balance between exports and imports. Under the barter trade conditions current in 1948, a merchant was required to obtain goods from a barter port to the extent of value of his imports there. If for any reason, he was unable to obtain the full value in kind of cargoes he had sent there, then the balance was credited against a subsequent trade deal. Merchants felt the system often tied up capital that could be usefully deployed to obtain goods from other ports. The SOCIEA therefore recommended that the balance of cargo values for each port be amended. This was unlikely to find favourable reception by the Dutch. The condition had been imposed to promote long-term trade and discourage one-off trading ventures.

The situation in 1948 was not better than the one in 1945-1946. In fact, given the proliferation of rules and regulations, the conditions of trade had worsened. From the hindsight of history, we know that the Indonesian struggle was to be successfully concluded soon, in 1949, but the bleak situation in 1948 provided no clues of this impending result. The Singapore connection yielded no results as far as legal trade was concerned. The connection's demise will form the subject of the concluding chapter.

CHAPTER VIII

Conclusion
Curtains for the Singapore connection

The termination of the Singapore connection loomed large with the Second Military Action launched by the Dutch in December 1948 and ending in January 1949. With the Dutch in a better military position to break the Singapore connection, it meant that the Indonesians, and Indoff in particular, were left stranded. Trade, normal or illegal, between Singapore and Indonesia came to a standstill.

The Second Military Action was also a last hurrah for the Dutch. Diplomatically, it was a major disaster as world opinion condemned the Dutch, and in fact, the military action made it possible for Indonesia to advance towards independence, albeit within a federal state structure. And with independence, was there further need for a Singapore connection?

This conclusion examines the decline in trade connections between Indonesia and Singapore in 1949, followed by the fate of Indoff, or rather, the transformation of Indoff's role within an independent Indonesia.

The trade downturn in 1949

The problems in trade relationship, the disputes and differences described in earlier chapters, all receded into the background when the Dutch launched their Second Military Action in December 1948. It was not possible to speak of a relationship if trade itself faced the danger of extinction as a result of the military operations.

Decline in Indonesian exports

The retreating Indonesian military applied a 'scorched earth' tactic. This left Chinese traders from Singapore reluctant to send barter ships to Sumatran ports for fear that they would not be able to bring back sufficient indigenous produce.[1]

Part of the trade downturn could also be attributed to the fact that various regions in Sumatra were reportedly empty of produce, accumulations having been worked off while little new produce was coming as a result of the unsettled conditions.

As a result, the Dutch promise of more trade after an effective military action did not materialize. Far from experiencing an upswing in trade volume, Singapore Chinese traders experienced starting March 1949 a slump in the export of all lines of consumer goods, including textiles and hardware. Imports from Sumatra, mainly pepper, copra, and rubber, also decreased.[2]

Ports reopened but danger and insecurity continued

Towns that were previously under Republican control and thriving on the trade with Singapore suddenly found their economic lifeline cut off. In Jambi and Pakan Baru, Dutch military actions against Republican forces left the Chinese in those two towns destitute. It was reported that in Jambi, eight hundred of the total Chinese population of 1,500 had their homes destroyed. According to another source, about two hundred Chinese were streaming into Singapore as refugees. Their compatriots in Singapore were quick to respond. A meeting of the SOCIEA decided to raise $100,000 for relief purposes to assist the Chinese in those two towns.[3] Chinese-owned ships sailing off Sumatra were gunned and their crew killed.[4]

Such treatment received at the hands of the Dutch would have alienated Chinese traders. The Dutch moved quickly to show that their military action was beneficial to trade in general. Former Republican ports that had previously been closed by the Dutch blockade were now reopened for barter. These included Rengat, Pakan Baru, Jambi, Bengkalis, Bagansiapiapi, Telukbitung, Priaman, Bencoolen, Krui, and Sibolga.[5] By January 1949, more ports had reopened, a sign that the Dutch were consolidating their military control over Republican towns.[6]

---

[1] 'Singapore traders won't barter with Sumatra', *Malaya Tribune*, 20-1-1949, p. 8.
[2] 'Move to extend Barter Trade', *Straits Times*, 4-4-1949, p. 5.
[3] '"Mercy" ships plan; Colony help to Sumatra', *Straits Times*, 7-1-1949, p. 6.
[4] 'Dutch statement on gunned ship', *Straits Times*, 8-1-1949, p. 7; 'Captain tells of air attack; 9 men died as Dutch gunned ship', *Straits Times*, 10-1-1949, p. 1.
[5] 'Sumatra ports open for barter', *Straits Times*, 13-1-1949, p. 3.
[6] 'Sumatra ports open for barter', *Straits Times*, 13-1-1949, p. 3.

Enforcement of shipping regulations

However, the Chinese soon realized that the reopening of ports did not lead to unconditional trade. For one, the Dutch banned Republican-registered ships from entering those ports. This was a major blow for the trade with Sumatra as it immediately affected about two hundred vessels of between 25 to 75 tons. Most of these ships had been constructed in Singapore during the Japanese occupation or the British Military Administration. Many of the ship owners had sought registration with the Republican authorities because they were not prepared to upgrade their vessels to international standards of seaworthiness.[7]

The issue of seaworthiness was not new. As early as 23 October 1946, the Merchant Shipping Ordinance in Singapore required small vessels plying between Singapore and the neighbouring islands (including Java and Sumatra) to employ qualified shipping masters and engineers, besides being properly certified as seaworthy by the surveyor-general of ships. As a result, 1,500 vessels were marooned in the inner roads of Singapore harbour, Crawford Bridge, Beach Road, Rochor River, Rochor district, and Boat Quay.[8] This would affect the crew, the firms that owned the vessels, their employees, and everyone's dependents.[9] This initial brush with the maritime regulation was averted when Gilmour, Secretary of the Department of Economic Affairs, realized how impractical it was to implement the ordinance. He arranged to sign permits allowing the vessels to operate without complying with the ordinance. But it was only a temporary reprieve. The vessels were still placed on a schedule for repairs over a period of eighteen months or more. Meanwhile, it was a miracle that no ships sank on account of their not being seaworthy (Gilmour 1973:9-10). The use of ramshackle boats was a carry-over from the Japanese occupation, when makeshift arrangements were tolerated. As war conditions were alleviated, vessels were subjected to more stringent checks. By May 1948, the registry of shipping in Singapore issued the restriction that small vessels could not sail to North and West Sumatra during the monsoon season from April to October.[10] Also, once the Dutch were ready to enforce stiffer regulations, as they were after December 1948, the owners and crew of the vessels would have to upgrade to accepted standards.

---

[7] 'Dutch ban Republican vessels', *Straits Times*, 14-2-1949, p. 5.
[8] '1500 vessels tied up in Singapore waters', *Malaya Tribune*, 21-11-1946, p. 3.
[9] 'Thousands here face destitution if merchant shipping act is enforced', *Malaya Tribune*, 11-11-1946, p. 6.
[10] 'Island trade hard hit; By Tribune staff reporter', *Malaya Tribune*, 8-5-1948, p. 2.

More stringent enforcement of checks on shipping

By the time of the Second Military Action, the Dutch navy had also grown from strength to strength compared to the early days after the Japanese surrendered. Ships caught bartering with Republican-held ports ran the risk of being sunk. This happened to the Singapore motor vessel, the *Kian Peng*. Without warning, it was strafed by Dutch fighter aircraft off Pakan Baru near the Sumatra coast on the last day of 1948. The stern of the ship was set ablaze and the captain gave the order to abandon ship. Chinese traders protested that the ship was carrying legitimate cargo. When asked to comment, Admiral Pinke, commander of the Dutch navy, said all ships sailing in Republican waters were at risk,[11] but the Netherlands consul-general admitted the *Kian Peng* tragedy was a 'mistake'.[12]

The *Kian Peng* was not the only ship to be strafed. The *Soon Hin Lee* suffered a similar fate in Sumatran waters. It left Singapore with a cargo of general merchandise and headed south for Karimun island. Next day, with the proper clearance, the ship sailed north for Sumatra. While on this voyage, the ship encountered rough weather and took shelter at Tanjung Ledang, where it remained till 30 December 1948. On that afternoon, Dutch planes strafed the vessel. Some crew escaped by jumping into the sea, but the captain and the supercargo were killed. The Dutch then towed the ship to deeper waters. It was doused with petrol and set on fire, without first removing the dead bodies.[13]

More effective control over the seas also meant that the Dutch could cease their checks on shipping previously carried out at Tanjung Pinang if they were proceeding to the Indonesian ports in Sumatra.[14]

Trade through banks, not barter

The more stringent checks were only the first nail in the coffin that ultimately sealed the fate of the barter trade with Sumatra. As the Dutch tightened

---

[11] 'Captain tells of air attack; 9 men died as Dutch gunned ship', *Straits Times*, 10-1-1949, p. 1; 'Chinese furious over sinking; Dutch action "unjust and unpardonable"', *Malaya Tribune*, 7-1-1949, p. 1. The Dutch paid compensation to the crew of the *Kian Peng* but there was no resolution on the amount to be paid for the ship. It was believed that the Dutch were dragging their feet so that with the expected formation of the United States of Indonesia, their liability would cease. 'Kian Peng – no settlement yet', *Straits Times*, 21-3-1950, p. 5.
[12] 'Dutch consul admits plane attack; Kian Peng tragedy a "mistake"', *Malaya Tribune*, 12-1-1949, p. 1.
[13] 'Dutch planes gun Singapore ship; Three dead; Wreck burned with bodies still aboard', *Malaya Tribune*, 7-1-1949, p. 8.
[14] 'Tanjong Pinang trading control finished', *Straits Times*, 23-3-1949, p. 8; 'Indonesian traders need not call at Tanjong Pinang', *Malaya Tribune*, 4-1-1950, p. 1.

control over the ports in Sumatra, barter was disallowed and traders were required to use bank transactions as required by the trade agreement of 1948. No longer could trade be conducted informally and freely as understood by the Singapore Chinese. The use of banking facilities meant conformity with import and export and foreign exchange regulations imposed by the Dutch, as well as similar regulations in Singapore.[15]

Under the system, Singapore merchants trading with Indragiri, Rokan, Telukbitung, Jambi, Sibolga, Bagansiapiapi, Pakan Baru, Bengkalis, Siak, and Selat Panjang – all ports where Dutch authorities had some semblance of control – were only allowed to import forty per cent of the value of the cargo exported. The balance value of the excess shipments must be paid into a local bank designated by the Dutch consulate in Singapore. Such payments would be credited in local currency to the exporter in Sumatra.[16] Then there was the question of the flow of foreign exchange between Singapore and Sumatra, which was one of the principal reasons for the launching of the Second Military Action by the Dutch in December 1948. The Dutch had been concerned that barter trade with Singapore provided only consumer goods and foodstuffs (except rice) for Indonesia in general and for Sumatra in particular. In this trade, the foreign exchange that was earned was one-sidedly in favour of Singapore, as little or no foreign exchange accrued to Indonesia to pay for capital goods, like machinery, and rice. Once the Dutch regained control over more extended parts of Sumatra, they were able to keep strict control on trade with all countries in order that Indonesia could earn the foreign exchange it needed. Such controls included the banking arrangements mentioned above.[17]

By 1949, these stringent foreign exchange regulations had damaging consequences on trade in Singapore. Singapore traders were required to pay with American dollars for Indonesian goods that were transhipped at Singapore on the way to other destinations. For example, if a Singapore trader purchased pepper from Indonesia for transhipment to France, he had to ask the French client for payment in American dollars. However, if the French client ordered pepper direct from Indonesia, he could pay in Dutch guilders. To Singapore traders, this seemed to be a measure designed to kill their role as brokers. The days were now numbered when a trader in Singapore could buy in the cheapest market the cheapest goods and tranship to any port where he could find a buyer.[18]

15 'Move to extend barter trade', *Straits Times*, 4-4-1949, p. 5; '$1,500,000 barter cargo from Singapore', *Straits Times*, 18-2-1949, p. 1.
16 'Indies trade: Govt wants more facts', *Straits Times*, 10-6-1948, p. 6; 'Cash and barter with Rhio', *Straits Times*, 20-6-1949, p. 5.
17 'Answers in Batavia', *Straits Times*, 20-6-1949, p. 4.
18 'Are we killing entrepot trade?', *Straits Times*, 7-5-1949, p. 9.

A subcommittee of the Singapore Chamber of Commerce described these conditions for normal bank-to-bank trading between Singapore and Sumatra 'unrealistic'.[19] A merchant trading at Lampung and Sibolga, where barter trading had been suspended because banking facilities had become available, complained that he had difficulties verifying letters of credit because banking services were not up to scratch. A further complication was the lack of cable facilities. The Netherlands consul-general denied the allegations, arguing that the Escompto Bank and the Netherlands Indies Commercial Bank were operating smoothly in Telukbitung (Lampung), Sibolga, and Jambi.[20] Singapore Chinese merchants therefore sought the resumption of the pre-war system of barter trade with certain Indonesian ports on the supercargo basis under the supervision of the Chinese Chamber of Commerce. Trading ports that formerly practised barter were unfamiliar with trade-through-banks because banks had not existed there before the war. SOCIEA claimed that Indonesian merchants had very few opportunities to make reciprocal arrangements with banks in Singapore. In its plea for the re-establishment of the barter system, it argued that Chinese traders were more used to good relations and harmony as traditional methods of trade as opposed to formal systems based on banks. Such methods had stood the test of time and 'there must be something in methods which have proved so successful for centuries'. Anything other than barter would mean 'inevitable and recurring difficulties of currency controls, export and exchange control and regulations and rules that would have to be changed as soon as they are made'.[21] The recommendation was to revert to the old barter system in which any trader in Indonesia could freely export produce to Singapore amounting to the value of say $100 in exchange for imports from Singapore to the value of $85. It was this margin that kept the whole barter business in Singapore going. Singapore merchants trading with Indonesia in turn bought their export goods from Chinese and Indian dealers, who in turn bought from British and other European importers. That was the essence of a flourishing entrepot trade.[22]

Diversion of trade from Singapore

Another cause of the downturn must also have been the attempts by the Dutch to divert trade away from Singapore. One such attempt was that a rubber quota for export to Singapore was slapped on Palembang. Singapore ships

[19] 'To discuss trade problems', *Straits Times*, 5-4-1949, p. 7.
[20] 'Reopen NEI barter trade, [Chinese] consul says', *Malaya Tribune*, 8-3-1949, p. 9.
[21] 'New move for barter trade revival', *Malaya Tribune*, 2-6-1949, p. 6.
[22] 'Government refutes Singapore trade charges; No discrimination against colony', *Malaya Tribune*, 15-6-1949, p. 1.

were also discriminated against. They were sometimes ordered away from a wharf to make way for Dutch vessels.[23] For example, the Singapore vessel, *Hong Soon*, arrived at Rengat to discharge cargo on 16 April 1949. Two days later, its master was ordered to give up its berth in favour of the KPM vessel *Kota Nica*. It was not possible to obtain berth space again till 20 April.[24] Dutch authorities explained the incident by saying that there was a lack of wharf space and priority had to be given to the KPM and military services. In the case of the *Kota Nica*, the ship had to be serviced first or its normal schedule would be delayed.[25] All in all, trading conditions remained unsatisfactory and it was the barter trade conducted by small-scale Chinese traders (commonly called the 'bazaar' trade) that received the full blow of this downturn.

Unfavourable global trade environment

However, the causes of the trade downturn were diverse, not just local but also international. It was not only the Indonesian market that had closed for Singapore traders. The China market had also closed due to the civil war between communists and non-communists.

Another reason for the downturn was the conclusion of an agreement (February 1949) between the United Kingdom and the Netherlands providing for direct trade between Britain and Indonesia, bypassing Singapore. The agreement allowed Britain to ship thirteen million sterling pounds' worth of manufactured goods to Indonesia and to import eight million pounds' worth of copra, palm oil, and other raw materials for 1949. Singapore's position as entrepot was undermined by this direct trade, and made worse by the fact that the copra and palm oil were purchased at prices slightly below those in Singapore. As a result, stocks in Singapore piled up and dealers could not pay overheads.[26] This time, the chambers of commerce, representing all traders and not just the Chinese, protested to the governor of Singapore that the Dutch were discriminating against Singapore traders.[27] They wanted resumption of 'normal' trade.

But what was 'normal' trade? Attempts to establish the etymology of the word have produced the following results. Dr Gani, the Republican vice-

---

[23] 'Challenge to entrepot', Straits Times, 27-6-1949, p. 4.
[24] Directie Verre Oosten 117, Letter no. 23 in CSO 11772/49 from T. van der Gaast (Department of Economic Affairs Singapore) to Netherlands Consulate-General Singapore, 12-5-1949.
[25] Directie Verre Oosten 117, Letter no. 18258/ASCH.20/AE.20, from Algemeen Secretarie to Minister of Overseas Territories, 30-8-1949.
[26] 'Trade with Indonesia: protest over restrictions', *Straits Times*, 6-5-1949, p. 1. For a list of commodities to be traded between UK and Indonesia, see 'Development of Indies trade', *Straits Times*, 17-5-1949, p. 5.
[27] 'Trade with the Indies', *Straits Times*, 9-5-1949, p. 4.

premier, distinguished between 'normal' trade and barter, as evidenced from newspapers in 1946. When asked whether the Republic controlled trade between Singapore and Sumatra, he said: 'It is not normal trade – we barter with Singapore'.[28] A spokesperson from the Netherlands consulate defined normal trading as compliance with the rules and not trying to sneak back and forth with goods to be disposed of at four hundred or five hundred per cent profit. Normal trade also meant compliance with checks at stipulated ports on both outward and inward journeys.[29] The Netherlands consul-general thought that if the chambers of commerce referred to barter as 'normal', then unrestricted barter was abnormal. Barter should only be allowed in those areas where no banking facilities existed. The consul-general affirmed that Indonesia was merely applying sound trade principles: buying as cheaply as possible and selling to the highest bidder. Citing copra as an example, Indonesia could not sell the commodity to Singapore below world parity or far below the price Singapore sold copra abroad.[30]

Secretary for Economic Affairs Gilmour supported the Dutch response. He phrased it very bluntly.

> It was useless to sit back and say 'Look at the map and see the advantages of buying and selling through Singapore' unless prices were going to be really competitive and the colony was able to put up a case both to the distant consumer of Straits produce and the adjacent consumer of inducement goods, that this was the cheapest and most convenient market.[31]

There was some truth in the charge that prices of Singapore goods were high. A contemporary description of Bugis traders in Singapore noted that their prauws carried considerable cargo to Singapore, but after resting for about ten days, they returned home empty because Singapore goods were considered too expensive.[32]

Such protests by the chambers were brushed off easily. The downturn in Singapore would not receive the attention of the British government because Britain's trade with Indonesia (thirteen million pounds) was a very low figure compared to Singapore's exports.[33] It did not matter that the indifference of the British government to the problems faced by

[28] 'Flourishing Sumatra – Singapore barter trade', *Malaya Tribune*, 22-10-1946, p. 6.
[29] 'Dutch bid to end gun running; 80 vessels now held in Rhio; By Tribune staff reporter', *Malaya Tribune*, 8-10-1948, p. 1.
[30] 'Dutch deny trade discrimination; Same rules for all countries, chambers told', *Straits Times*, 9-5-1949, p. 5.
[31] '"Prove Singapore is best market" Gilmour's advice to preserve entrepot trade', *Straits Times*, 18-5-1949, p. 7.
[32] 'Macassar prahu season begins', *Straits Times*, 31-8-1949, p. 7.
[33] 'Man-in-the-street; A Singapore merchant on the colony's trade; By "Singapore merchant"', *Straits Times*, 10-5-1949, p. 6.

Singapore traders on account of alleged Dutch restrictions was also damaging Britain's economy. As the *Financial Times* (UK) pointed out, Singapore's entrepot trade with Indonesia was based on barter and one of the goods bartered was British brands of cigarettes. It noted a little-known fact: 'The trade is in the hands of Chinese and, as a result of their enterprise, it was easier quite recently to buy a packet of a well-known British brand of cigarettes in an obscure village of Sumatra than in Britain itself'.[34] The British brand was 'Players' cigarettes. Products from other countries would also be similarly affected, for example tinned milk, fruits, and tomato ketchup from Australia, as well as Indian cloth and matches from Hong Kong.[35] If Chinese traders from Singapore could not barter, Britain too would eventually suffer the consequences.

British colonial authorities and the trade downturn

The British authorities in Singapore were not always sympathetic to the complaints of Chinese traders regarding the ups and downs of trade cycles. Time and again, British officials stressed the need for Singapore to be competitive in order to attract trade. A chief grouse was the cost of dock services and these were not new problems suddenly emerging in 1949.

Gilmour had already voiced his concerns about cost. As early as the first quarter of 1948, he warned that Singapore's lighterage and handling charges were too high. They should be reduced, or the benefits of Singapore as a free port and the future of its entrepot trade would be jeopardized, he argued.[36] Gilmour was making his comments against the background of an industrial strike action at the Singapore Harbour Board for better working conditions, including full pay for sick leave, workmen's compensation, and free hospital treatment. He took the opportunity to point out that port workers already enjoyed extra rates paid for night work, Sunday work, and work during meal times. Workers were also given two free meals, housing, and free use of public utilities (like electricity and water). Yet, production per man was falling as workers were incited to go slow. In consequence, labour costs for cargo handling had increased 5.5 times over the pre-war level.[37] The Netherlands consul-general (A.M.L Winkelman) felt that Singapore's traders could not compete with their counterparts in Hong Kong and that the Dutch control regulations were used as the scapegoat to hide the real reason for the down-

---

34 'Chinese "ingenuity" in Indonesian trade', *Straits Times*, 16-5-1949, p. 6.
35 'Impressions of Indonesian rule; Malaya's western neighbour; From a special correspondent', *Straits Times*, 4-11-1946, pp. 4 and 6.
36 'Restoration of normal trade', *Straits Times*, 31-3-1948, p. 6.
37 'An entrepot warning', *Straits Times*, 6 May 1948, p. 6.

turn.[38] This partly explained why the Dutch so stubbornly refused to lift the trade restrictions.

This time, the complaints about the trade problems in 1949 from SOCIEA and other agencies were channelled through the Singapore Department for Economic Affairs to be conveyed to the Dutch. However, they did not even receive the support of Van der Gaast,[39] the deputy secretary at the department.[40] On the restoration of pre-war barter trade, he said that the old system provided Indonesia with only consumer goods and foodstuffs. There was evidence that Sumatra was overstocked with consumer goods although not with rice and flour. Under the new circumstances, what Sumatra needed was capital goods and foreign exchange to buy rice and flour. These could not be purchased from Singapore cheaply.

Van der Gaast also commented on one of the grievances of the Chinese merchants – that the Dutch were bypassing them. As Dutch authority was restored in Indonesia, products like copra, coffee, pepper, groundnuts, and tea were compulsorily sold to certain Dutch-managed purchasing centres and not to Singapore traders. In turn, the purchasing centres sold direct to Europe or the United States. The purchasing centres only sold to Singapore if better prices were offered, for example the recent release of two thousand tons of copra to Singapore. However, the sale was allowed only on condition that the copra was used by local oil mills and not re-exported. Van der Gaast explained that the purchasing centres operated like cooperatives, buying produce above the world market price when prices were low, and buying below the world market price when prices were higher. In this way, price fluctuations for the producer would be more even.

Indoff and the trade downturn

In the wake of this downturn in trade, Indoff had to scramble and try to introduce damage-control measures. One solution was to make arrangements with the Dutch on the establishment of 'corridors' to reach Republican territories in order that essential goods could still be sent to those areas despite the unsettled conditions.[41] Corridors to the Republican territories in Java and Sumatra allowing for the inflow of essential goods would also resolve many

---

[38] Directie Verre Oosten 85, Letter from A.M.L. Winkelman (Consul-General Singapore) to Minister of Foreign Affairs, No. 9276/X213, 2-4-1949.
[39] T. van der Gaast was a pre-war rubber broker. Originally hailing from the Netherlands, he became a naturalized British citizen. See Gilmour 1973:6, 19-20.
[40] 'Government refutes Singapore trade charges; No discrimination against colony', *Malaya Tribune*, 15-6-1949, p. 1.
[41] PG556, CGDN, No. 139-49, Singapore, Report by P.A. van der Poel, 22-10-1949.

of the problems arising from smuggling. Goods would be transported along predetermined routes. The principal proponent of the establishment of corridors was Zain.[42]

The Dutch were not prepared to allow such corridors to be established because they would mean a lifting of the trade controls of the Republic and that would be a great concession on their part.[43]

The plea for corridors was then taken up at Bangkok during a conference of the ECAFE (Economic Commission for Asia and the Far East) in March 1949 attended by Oetoyo.[44] By that time, the issue of corridors had become even more urgent. The fighting between the Dutch and the Indonesians after December 1948 had made communications impossible. Meanwhile, the International Emergency Food Committee had made allocations of twenty thousand tons of rice for Indonesia for the year 1949. Given the unsettled conditions, it was not possible to transport the rice. Oetoyo therefore pressed hard for the establishment of corridors, even if they were temporary in nature (Nasution 1979c: 462-3). This did not work and it was not till the end of 1949 when the Dutch, faced with the threat that the latest ceasefire would not hold unless they made the concession, agreed to Zain's proposal to set up corridors.[45]

While corridors were essential to the flow of trade, Zain was also interested to establish an importers-exporters organization to oversee the trading arrangements between Singapore and Indonesia. This body would discourage private trading by individuals that had plagued the entire network of relations between the two territories. One such individual was Hassan Basri, himself a director of the importers-exporters organization. He decided to embark on some private trading with the Saleh Abas Corporation by sending a ship to Pakan Baru to transport products out of the Republic, and approached Indoff for the necessary permits. It was Zain who confronted him and stressed that individual trading was not permitted. Zain himself was anxious that an organized trading operation be started to pre-empt any further attempts by individuals to start similar operations on their own. On 12 November 1949, an emergency meeting of Indonesian traders was held and it was agreed that capital of at least $25,000 would be accumulated for a trading venture to Pakan Baru. This scheme devised by Zain also had the aim of replacing non-Indonesian traders[46] who up till then had dominated all trade-related activities.

---

[42]   PG 556, CGDN, No. 119-49, Singapore, Report by P.A. van der Poel, 13-8-1949.
[43]   PG 380, Letter 3187-G-I, from P.A. van der Poel, Secretaris voor Speciale Diensten, to Procureur-Generaal, 4-11-1949.
[44]   PG 558, CGDN, No. 62-49, Singapore, Report by P.A. van der Poel, 30-3-1949.; 'Oetoyo pleads for an Indonesian "corridor"', *Straits Times*, 20-3-1949, p. 1.
[45]   PG 380, Letter 3187-G-I, from P.A. van der Poel, Secretaris voor Speciale Diensten, to Procureur-Generaal, 4-11-1949.
[46]   PG 558, CGDN, No. 147-49, Singapore, Report by P.A. van der Poel, 19-11-1949.

Zain wanted to promote a trade policy that would help the Indonesian people meet their immediate needs by bringing goods to them that were essential, thus drawing their support for the Republic. However, by 1949, the major players in the trade league no longer included Indoff, and Zain's clout was tenuous at best. With the end of the Second Military Action in January 1949, and the arrest of civilian authorities like Soekarno and Hatta, the remaining regions such as Aceh that were still independent had become a force to be reckoned with. Aceh, with its exports of rubber, sisal, and palm oil, was one region that could defy the rules of having to check in at Belawan or Sabang. And what was more important, exports from Aceh had, of course, become the main source of income to support the activities of Indoff.[47] Thus when Sinar Soeryapoetra, the head of the Blue Ribbon Shipping Company (an Aceh-based trading group), voiced views that were different from Zain's, it was not possible to ignore him altogether. Soeryapoetra emphasized the importance of defence and had the means to implement his plans independent of Indoff.[48] He supported the idea that profits from the export trade should be used for defence – a proposition that would receive serious support from an Aceh that treasured its independence.[49] The Blue Ribbon Shipping Company had ambitious plans. According to the indefatigable defender of Republican interests John Lie, there were about $1 million worth of goods in Aceh awaiting shipment.[50] But the fighting between the Indonesians and the Dutch made transport difficult. The Blue Ribbon Shipping Company was formed in part to meet this need. On its own, it tried to establish communication links between Aceh and the outside world. It proposed to purchase planes to fly to Burma and Siam.[51] It had also taken over the shipping interests of the Aceh Trading Corporation (ATC).[52] Without the support of Aceh, Indoff's authority would have been severely diminished; in the face of opposition by Aceh-based traders, Indoff could hardly implement its plans.

The issue of corridors at the ECAFE meeting was a measure of last resort as the Republic's foreign representatives in Singapore tried to salvage a very critical situation. The ECAFE meeting, held in March 1949 soon after the Second Dutch Military Action, was convened at an opportune time because representatives from many foreign governments attended and the meeting provided a platform for the Republic's voice to be heard. Oetoyo seized the occasion. The ECAFE meeting was turned into a heated discussion on the con-

[47] PG 556, CGDN, No. 119-49, Singapore, Report by P.A. van der Poel, 13-8-1949.
[48] PG 556, CGDN, No. 118-49, Singapore, 10-8-1949.
[49] PG 556, CGDN, No. 126-49, Singapore, Report by P.A. van der Poel, 7-9-1949.
[50] AS2 596, Republikeinse wapentransacties met het aangrenzende buitenland, Centrale Militaire Inlichtingendienst (CMI), Batavia, 31-10-1949.
[51] PG 556, CGDN, No. 111-49, Singapore, Report by P.A. van der Poel, 15-7-1949.
[52] PG 556, CGDN, No. 116-49, Singapore, Report by P.A. van der Poel, 2-8-1949.

flict between the Netherlands and the Republic. Oetoyo asked 'any and every' United Nations agency to help stop the destruction of the Republic, although it was the Republic that was adopting a scorched earth policy as the only form of viable resistance. During the discussions, the chairman interrupted Oetoyo twice to 'keep to economics and leave out the Dutch'. Oetoyo urged the ECAFE headquarters to send a fact-finding mission to survey the destruction, asserting that the Dutch were making Yogyakarta uninhabitable as a future administration centre. He alleged that Dutch measures made it impossible for the Republic to implement proposals long worked out at Yogyakarta. Oetoyo said: 'Only the physical success of our guerrilla fighting has kept the Indonesia issue to the fore and, if we had not fought like this, there would exist a very real danger that an overworked United Nations would have written Indonesia off as a problem already settled and no longer existing'. It was good publicity, but action on Oetoyo's proposal was deferred as other delegates outlined problems for rehabilitation of their own countries.[53]

The end of the 'Singapore squeeze'

The difficulties faced by Chinese traders were also a reflection of the tight control that the Republic faced after the Dutch expanded their control over both land and sea. Data on the Indonesian component of the trade was less easily available, but the difficulties borne by an entrepot trade that depended largely on Indonesian goods were very revealing. There was a time in the borderlands of Indonesia near Singapore that the entrepot trade made such big bucks in the early post-war period that the phrase 'Singapore squeeze' was coined to describe the trade. The squeeze did not last long. The final attainment of Indonesian independence from Dutch rule in 1949 changed the traditional position of Singapore to a much greater extent than realized by the Chinese traders. The new government in Jakarta now questioned whether the old connections were really necessary under the new dispensation. The Dutch were not the only authorities that wanted to earn hard currency by bypassing Singapore. The basic motive was to retain all the profits of the processing trade carried out in Singapore, and an independent United States of Indonesia would follow the same course of action. But Singapore traders were still operating under the illusion that circumstances had not changed. They thought all that was required was to revert to the *status quo ante*.[54]

Indeed, under whatever dispensation, there was space enough for Chinese traders to evade the regulations. In fact, the more complex the regulations, the more room could be found to accommodate smuggling. In a June 1949

[53] '"Stop Republic's destruction" – Dr Oetoyo', *Straits Times*, 31-3-1949, p. 2.
[54] 'The produce trade', *Straits Times*, 6-10-1949, p. 6.

report submitted by the Netherlands consulate to the Singapore Department of Economic Affairs, the traditional smuggling strategies of the Chinese traders were listed. The easiest way was to under-declare the values of goods to the consulate. After all, the officials from the consulate could only check the declared values of exported goods by sampling. Traders were expected to submit representative samples, but the consulate was able to cite a number of instances when deliberate falsifications could be documented.[55]

Smuggling, barter, entrepot exchange – these were the staple of traditional trade relations between Singapore and Indonesia during the nineteenth century and the first half of the twentieth century. Such methods of trading could not remain unchanged. The observations of the Netherlands consul-general in Singapore on the port's role as entrepot are relevant. He said in June 1949:

> Entrepot ports are a relic of a Middle Ages economy and must eventually disappear, if they do not have a hinterland [...]. Only if Indonesia returns to the conditions of the Middle Ages – which is possible but still not expected – shall Singapore do a 'roaring trade' for years. When Indonesia re-emerges, then Singapore shall [have] nothing to offer.[56]

The end of the Dutch-Indonesian conflict did not therefore mark the start of a new era in trade relations. Chinese traders and their business partners in Indonesia still clung to the hope that the old and profitable trade patterns and practices would be revived. True, the restrictive Dutch regulations of 1947 and 1948 were lifted, but the *status quo ante* was not restored. The barter trade with Aceh was stopped. In other parts of Indonesia where there no banks, for example Bengkalis, Selat Panjang, Siak, Sri Indrapura, Pakan Baru, and Bagansiapiapi, Singapore traders were only permitted to trade on the basis of thirty per cent barter and seventy per cent cash payment.[57] In fact, the impatience of Chinese traders was now redirected from the Dutch to the United States of Indonesia (USI). Kwek Soan Loh, who protested loudly and clearly against Dutch trade regulations, described the USI conditions of trade as a 'waste of time and expense'. Chinese trading firms in Singapore were now required to deliver the goods to buyers and receive payment. Such payments were then turned over to Indoff. Indoff retained seventy per cent of the payment and sent the balance to the seller. It was now a 70-30 system instead of the Dutch system of 60-40. Kwek claimed that the previous procedure allow-

[55] Directie Verre Oosten 336, Letter from C. den Hollander (Consulate-General Singapore) to Secretary for Economic Affairs, XVI-D-1/12668, 4-6-1949.
[56] Directie Verre Oosten 117, Letter VIII-A/14414/326 from A.M.L. Winkelman (Consul-General Singapore) to Minister of Foreign Affairs, 27-6-1949.
[57] 'Trade centre for Indies', *Straits Times*, 22-12-1949, p. 4; 'Barter with Indies ports', *Straits Times*, 10-2-1950, p. 4.

ing all importers to take charge of all their imports had been 'very satisfactory'.[58] It was a no-win situation for the Chinese traders. What about Indoff?

The end of Indoff's mission

By the middle of 1949, Oetoyo and Indoff were already suffering from a kind of diplomatic quarantine. Indoff's patron, Lord Killearn, had left Singapore in 1948 and the British authorities became more diplomatically correct in their attitude. Oetoyo found that he could still use his office to issue visas for Indonesian pilgrims travelling to the Middle East, but these visas were like one-way exit permits from Singapore. The pilgrim could not return to Singapore unless a British consulate in the Middle East was prepared to approve the necessary papers. Needless to say, the Indonesian pilgrims also found they could not return to Batavia since they had not applied for exit permits from the Dutch authorities in Batavia. They were thus stranded.[59]

As an organization, Indoff was reeling under the turbulence of the fighting taking place in Indonesia. Problems arose even months before the December 1948 military action. In September 1948, the abortive communist revolt in Madiun (Central Java) left no doubt that the Republic was entering a period of confusion plagued by internal disunity. Oetoyo visited Yogyakarta shortly after the revolt for consultations with his Republican superiors and found that the Republic was in dire straits. Under those circumstances, Oetoyo received instructions from the Yogyakarta authorities that Indoff should modify its role. A refocusing of duties was necessary. Oetoyo learnt that the foreign policy of the Republic 'must thus in the first place be directed' towards lifting the Dutch economic blockade (which had caused so much misery) in contrast to the attention given earlier to securing diplomatic recognition.[60] Indoff had to adapt accordingly. But even this narrower set of duties was difficult to execute. Cut off from Yogyakarta, left to fend for itself, starved of trade and the funds it could generate, Indoff was tested to the limits. Its pocketbook was hit really hard.[61] In February 1949, an unconfirmed report was even filed by the Dutch authorities that the Republican minister of finance and the prime minister had permitted department heads to use certain amounts of opium for the payment of services which could not be paid using a more legal form of reimbursement.[62] If the internal situa-

---

[58] 'USI trade system "waste of money"', *Straits Times*, 10-2-1950, p. 4.
[59] Directie Verre Oosten 568, 'Korte samenvattende beschouwingen reisverslag Mochtadi – Jafizham (Singapore – Kuala Lumpur, 9-31 May 1949)', report dated 15-6-1949, p. 19.
[60] *Officiële bescheiden*, XV:512, note 8.
[61] PG 558, CGDN, No. 53-49, Singapore, 17.3.49. By P.A. van der Poel, 17-3-1949.
[62] PG 377, Report by D. van den Dool, Batavia, Commissaris van Politie tweede klasse bij de Dienst der Algemene Recherche, 22-2-1949.

tion within the Republic was that hard hit, external organizations like Indoff could not be any better. As the financial position of Indoff deteriorated in early 1949, there were more and more reports about Oetoyo wanting to shift operations from Singapore. One solution was to make the Singapore Indoff a branch of the Penang Indoff.[63] Penang was the hope for the future. It still had a steady income available because the trade with Aceh proceeded apace, unlike the rest of Indonesia where military activities had prevented goods from leaving.[64] Another option was Delhi.[65] Oetoyo had in fact been looking towards India for assistance. In January 1949, he returned to Singapore after he had closed a loan agreement with the Indian government to help the impoverished Indoff.[66] There were also plans to send Oetoyo to India for a new posting[67] but it turned out that the immediate victim of the 1948 military action was not Oetoyo but Daroesman. Documents seized in the Yogyakarta archives implicated Daroesman in clandestine activities and it was time for him to be reassigned before an arrest warrant could be served on him.

Communist threats

The 1948 military action could not have come at a worst time for Indoff and other political organizations in Singapore. The proclamation of the Malayan Emergency to fight the communists in Malaya in June 1948 has already been mentioned. This was followed by the abortive September 1948 communist revolt at Madiun in Central Java. All these made British authorities very watchful of activities in Singapore of a political nature, especially those with foreign or international linkages. The documentation available suggests that Dutch authorities were on the alert for any evidence to prove that Republican sympathizers were allied with pro-communist organizations, whether these were the Indonesian Communist Party (PKI) or the Malayan Communist Party (MCP). Such linkages, if any, were not quite proven and although some messages indicating Republican-communist communication were intercepted, there was no conclusive proof. It is most likely that these messages were shared with the British authorities in Singapore as part of an informal Anglo-Dutch exchange of information. The Dutch benefited from this cooperation with the British because it enabled them to show how organizations like Indoff were taking actions that were dangerously close to illegal transactions. It was in this context that the Singapore police probably inter-

[63] PG 558, CGDN, No. 28-49, Singapore, By P.A. van der Poel, 9-2-1949.
[64] PG 558, CGDN, No. 33-49, Singapore, 16-2-1949.
[65] PG 558, CGDN, No. 23-49, Singapore, By P.A. van der Poel, 2-2-1949.
[66] PG 558, CGDN, No. 24-49, Singapore, By P.A. van der Poel, 3-2-1949.
[67] PG 558, CGDN, No. 28-49, Singapore, By P.A. van der Poel, 9-2-1949.

rogated Oetoyo about Indoff's involvement in opium smuggling and weapons transactions. But hard evidence was not available. The linkages between the Republic and the communists were also not proven conclusively.[68] But the general effect of all this information was that the British could no longer turn a blind eye to what was happening among the Indonesian community in Singapore (and Malaya). The 1948 political atmosphere therefore became more restrictive; the field of operations was increasingly narrowed; such conditions contributed inevitably to the weakening of attempts to advance the Republican cause in Singapore.

If there were any links, then most likely it was the communist movement in Sumatra that enjoyed support from fellow communists in Singapore and Malaya. On the eastern coast of Sumatra, a front organization known as the China Democratic League was influential in most residencies and especially Medan. The League also had supporters in Singapore.[69] Dutch authorities in Batavia also reported that there was communist infiltration from Singapore and Penang, accusing Indoff of facilitating the despatch of '500 to 600' young communists, most of them about 25 years old, and belonging to the former underground resistance that had fought the Japanese in Malaya. Upon arrival in Batavia, fellow Chinese would meet them and work would be arranged for them before they were assigned to infiltrate Dutch-controlled territories.[70]

Negotiations leading to independence

The negotiations that ensued from the 1948 military actions were collectively called the Round Table Conference and began on 23 August 1949 in The Hague. Sovereignty was finally transferred to Indonesia, though not in the form the Republic wanted. Instead of a unitary state under the Republic of Indonesia, a federal state (the United States of Indonesia, USI) was constructed, with independence bestowed on 27 December 1949.

Altogether, the period from mid-1948 onwards through 1949 was bleak. At the ceremony in Singapore to celebrate the transfer of power by the Dutch to the newly created United States of Indonesia (USI), the mood was one of

---

[68] Scattered references are available. See AS 2/867, Letter from Capt Muchtar, 'Kepala Pertempuran Tentara Divisi IX', Bukit Tinggi, addressed to Mr Zubir Iljas, Brevet Capt., Kuala Lumpur, No. 1176/kd/Rhs, 26-5-1948; AS 2/867, Letter from Dt. Padoeko Malim (de Hoofleider van de PKI Sectie Sumatra), Bukit Tinggi, addressed to St. Djanain, Kampong Bahru, Kuala Lumpur, No. 817/Rha/Bkt/48, dated 11-6-1948. This letter mentions the payment of $175,000 for arms and the promise to pay the establishment costs of a PKI branch in Singapore.
[69] AS 2/263, 'Indonesië en het communisme'.
[70] AS 2/263, Report from de Reg. Adv. voor Pol. Zaken, Batavia, to Algemene Secretarie, 5-6-1948.

restraint. Unlike the annual celebrations of 17 August, there were no flags except one flying at Oetoyo's residence and another at Indoff at Raffles Place. But everyone wore a red ribbon. The air was punctuated by restrained shouts of 'merdeka!' Prayers were held at the Sultan mosque. In his speech, Oetoyo stressed the need to roll up the sleeves and get to work. He said,

> Work and be silent – despite the great occasion [...] more work and less talk. It is up to the Indonesians in this colony to make greater efforts than they ever did before to protect their interests, cultivate the goodwill, and give full cooperation to the people of this country with whom they have established a sound reputation.[71]

It was a quiet mood. There were no flags because under a state of emergency, foreign flags could not be flown. This regulation was directed at communist China's flags although there was an escape clause that allowed exceptions.[72]

The last duties of Indoff's mission

One of Oetoyo's last official duties, a kind of sequel to the Dutch-Indonesian conflict, was to petition Singapore's governor for the extradition of Westerling, who fled to Singapore after capturing control of Bandung for several hours. There was one complication. The USI did not have any extradition treaty with Britain. However, the chief justice of the USI claimed that the USI succeeded to the Netherlands-Britain extradition treaty. But even if there were one, a court would have to be convinced that Westerling was not being sought for political crimes. A judge had to decide whether Westerling was a common criminal or a genuine rebel, in accordance with the law.[73] Governor F. Gimson rejected the petition saying there was no *prima facie* case against Westerling. There was little that Oetoyo could do. His only response was: 'I have heard nothing officially. More than that, I cannot say.'[74] As expected, Westerling was deported after the extradition hearings. A representative from the USI was present at the airport to ensure that Westerling departed for Holland as scheduled. It was just as well, because Westerling had spoken to the press about his intention to lobby for the creation of a world army that would intervene in conflicts like those between the Republic and the Netherlands. In fact, Westerling almost did not leave. The plane was taxiing

---

[71] 'Singapore Indonesians celebrate: no flags – but everyone wore a red ribbon', *Straits Times*, 28-12-1949, p. 7.
[72] For a minor controversy on flying foreign flags, see 'The Indian flag', *Straits Times*, 4-1-1950, p. 6.
[73] 'Unwelcome guest', *Malaya Tribune*, 3-3-1950, p. 4; 'Turko to be charged in court soon', *Malaya Tribune*, 7-3-1950, p. 1.
[74] 'Gimson refuses request for Turko', *Malaya Tribune*, 23-5-1950, p. 1.

down the runway to take-off when the captain decided there was insufficient boost in one of the engines. The plane returned to the landing apron for repairs. After two hours[75] it must have been a relief to everyone that the plane finally left Singapore with Westerling.

While the negotiations to transfer power went on, a big question mark hung over the future of the Indonesian operations in Singapore. Much would depend on the structure of the new state that would emerge from the talks.

When the Round Table Conference reached agreement, the Netherlands consulate in Singapore transferred its Indonesia Affairs Division to Oetoyo as representative of the USI. This division housed the previous Economic Affairs Department (Indonesia), the visa section, and the immigration office. Oetoyo was expected to move into his new office in the KPM Building, one floor above the Netherlands consulate, early in January 1950. Dutch officials formerly employed by the Netherlands consulate in this division would remain in service. Some were due to retire the following year but others might continue in employment.[76]

Meanwhile, rumours abounded in Singapore. According to one, Oetoyo would be replaced. He was to return to a senior post in the Ministry of Foreign Affairs.[77] Indeed, in November 1949, a note had been circulated within Indoff that major restructuring would take place when the USI was formed.[78]

Oetoyo did not remain in Singapore much longer. He was reassigned but he continued to serve the Republican Ministry of Foreign Affairs with distinction, including a stint in Australia[79] where Daroesman, his former Indoff colleague, joined him. He returned to Indonesia in 1954 or 1955 prior to reassignment to Latin America, but died before taking up his new posting.

The fate of the PKBI-PI

As for the PKBI-PI, prospects for its future were also in doubt. Already the July 1947 military action had severed its links with Palembang, and this was a serious blow because its financial viability was dependent on the sale of goods exported from that region.[80] From then on, the PKBI-PI was strug-

---

[75] 'Turko plans world army in S.E.A.; An unrehearsed thrill at the airport; By Tribune staff reporter', *Malaya Tribune*, 22-8-1950, p. 8.
[76] 'Dr Oetoyo takes over from Dutch', *Malaya Tribune*, 30-12-1949, p. 2; 'Dr Oetoyo's new office', *Malaya Tribune*, 4-1-1950, p. 2; See also PG 556, CGDN, No. 144-49, Singapore, Report by P.A. van der Poel, 9-11-1949.
[77] PG 556, CGDN, No. 140-49, Singapore, Report by P.A. van der Poel, 26-10-1949.
[78] PG 556, CGDN, No. 143-49, Singapore, Report by P.A. van der Poel, 5-11-1949.
[79] 'Oetoyo for Australia; Represent USI at Canberra', *Straits Times*, 16-3-1950, p. 5.
[80] RI 551, Tweewekelijksche berichtgeving der Residentie Riouw over de periode 16 t/m 31-8-1946, By J. van Waardenburg, Resident, Tandjong Pinang, 10-9-1946.

gling against all odds to survive. The end of the fighting and the transfer of sovereignty would further compound its difficulties because it would mean that old goals would have to be jettisoned to accommodate the new circumstances. The organization would have to be redefined to remain relevant. Tobing's own position within the PKBI-PI was also subject to strain. A meeting had been held on 21 February 1949 to discuss the replacement of Tobing. Tobing himself was not present and those attending were rather uninhibited in their views. There seemed to be a consensus that membership would increase if Tobing stepped down.[81]

Tobing was aware that there was opposition to his leadership and he decided to take measures to regain his position. He thought that one way out was to help the Indonesian Red Cross in Yogyakarta to raise funds.[82] By so doing, the PKBI-PI would acquire a new role, and perhaps a new lease on life. Since it was his idea, perhaps his involvement, if not his leadership, would be assured. This rearguard action was quite successful. Tobing managed to persuade his main challenger, Achmad Jafar, to join his side, but two other opponents, Hoetagaloeng and Ibrahim Siregar, resigned from their posts.[83] The ultimate fate of the PKBI-PI disappeared into historical oblivion. Until fresh data is unearthed, it is not possible to say what happened to the PKBI-PI after 1949.

Seen from the perspective of events, the Singapore connection ground to a halt at the close of 1949. With independence, there was no need to continue furtive operations against the Dutch. Business could be placed on a firmer and more transparent footing. In that sense, the Singapore connection was terminated. However, this study has also made allusions to the 'non-events' that permeated the Singapore connection – the passions, the dangers, the immorality and corruption, the sacrifices. Unlike the events and happenings of the Singapore connection, these 'non-events' did not reach a terminal point. They persisted and continued beyond 1949. The Singapore connection of 1945-1949 may have ended, but the connections with Singapore did not end. They continued through the 1950s up till today. Diplomats (the successors of Oetoyo), Indonesian (Chinese) businessmen, smugglers – all these continue to play their respective parts on the stage of Singapore. Their missions were different, but the passions and emotions did not change substantially. It is perhaps fitting to finish this chapter by encapsulating these 'non-events' in a fictional account of Indonesian operations in the Singapore connection that touches on all the issues mentioned in the earlier chapters.

[81]   PG 558, CGDN, No. 37-49, Singapore, By P.A. van der Poel, 22-2-1949.
[82]   PG 558, CGDN, No. 40-49, Singapore, By P.A. van der Poel, 25-2-1949.
[83]   PG 558, CGDN, No. 44-49, Singapore, By P.A. van der Poel, 2-3-1949.

VIII Conclusion

Mochtar Lubis' 'Maut dan Cinta' (1977)

The Singapore connection was a popular subject for Indonesians to write and reminisce about. There was room to discuss commercial relations, colonial policies, the responses and attitudes of various interested parties, diplomacy, and clandestine activities. It was history at its best. But a careful reader would have noticed that moral issues of the Singapore connection were hidden in the interstices. These were difficult to flesh out and substantiate, because the primary sources only occasionally alluded to them, and then largely in a clinical fashion, as if history were cold and objective and could not handle moral issues. Yet one conclusion that could be drawn from this study on the Singapore connection is that it consisted of people of flesh and blood, people with emotions and an awareness of right and wrong, sacrifice or personal gain, passion, duty, and neglect. To illustrate these moral issues, this concluding chapter will end with a discussion of a novel to show the extent of what is already known about the Singapore connection and what remains unfamiliar and uncharted territory.

This novel is entitled *Maut dan cinta* and its author is Mochtar Lubis,[84] the famous journalist-novelist who was active in the establishment of Antara in Singapore. The plot is set in the context of the speedboat operations to and from Singapore. It is a tale of intrigue, adventure on the high seas, love, passion, nationalism, and much more. The novel is dedicated to many people, among them Sjahroedin – the journalist from Antara. It is also dedicated to those who ran the blockade imposed by the Dutch.

The story's main character is Major Sadeli. An intelligence officer, he was sent to Singapore to investigate why another officer, Captain Umar Yunus, retained the proceeds of the sale of sugar that was given to him on consignment instead of returning the money to the rightful owners of the goods, in this case, the Indonesian government. When Sadeli found Umar Yunus, the latter was enjoying a luxurious lifestyle that included cavorting with a Chinese girl called Rita Lee. Umar Yunus was clearly a cheat. He had used the proceeds of the sugar transaction for personal gain whereas they were originally budgeted to pay for the Republic's external relations, and also to subsidize the purchase of medicine, weapons, or communications equipment. The story has a happy ending, however. Umar Yunus eventually came to his senses and even went on to serve his country gallantly.

In Singapore, the police were spying on Major Sadeli. Inspector Hawkins

---

[84] Lubis started writing the novel before the Gestapu coup of 1965 while he was detained in Madiun. He continued to work on it after his transfer to house arrest in Jakarta. After his release in May 1966, there was no time to carry on writing till a summer stint in the Aspen Institute, USA, as a scholar or artist-in-residence.

somehow got to know about Major Sadeli's mission. However, Hawkins did not obstruct Sadeli's movements, and in fact provided friendly advice to be careful about his Chinese contacts. As it turned out, some of the Chinese were treacherous.

Sadeli's other assignment was to purchase military equipment and ship it to the Republic. As he went about his business in Singapore, Bangkok, and Hong Kong, he established contact with several people who had access to weapons and communications equipment. The longer he worked at his job, the more it dawned upon him that there was only a thin line separating corruption and duty. The novelist draws a powerful scene to illustrate the moral dilemma facing Sadeli. There was a meeting between Sadeli and an influential Chinese businessman called J.C. Kwan-tok. Kwan-tok offered him a speedboat complete with crew to transport whatever goods to Indonesia and back. But he asked for seventy per cent of the proceeds. Sadeli smiled, and asked for time to consider. Then, as an additional inducement, Kwan-tok threw in an offer of women: 'Banyak gadis manis. Tuan boleh memilih!' Sadeli refused, but he sensed that if he wanted to be accepted in the world of business, Singapore-style, he would have to behave like these business-men. One day, it would be his turn to invite them for food and drinks, and dancing. He would also have to vacate his room in the hotel and move into a luxury house. How else could the world of commerce in Singapore have confidence in him if he continued to stay in a mere hotel room? In the end, what could be seen as corruption was only a business expense that was legitimate in every sense of the word.

At the same time as this personal moral conflict was tearing away at his insides, Sadeli also participated in discussions with other characters in the novel about the nationalist content of Indonesia's struggle against the Dutch. Although the views and opinions were definitely patriotic, the characters voicing them were ordinary people living in sin, with cabaret girls and dance hostesses. In the case of Sadeli, he even had furtive sexual relations with the wife of one of his contacts, and in the latter's own bedroom at that.

In the context of this study, the novel provides an important and relevant message. Many Indonesians were sent to Singapore on critical missions to gather intelligence, buy weapons, or smuggle goods. But no matter how important, they were like everybody else with their inherent strengths, weaknesses, secrets, and temptations. In short, the Indonesian struggle was also the business of ordinary humans. And, for this study, the Singapore connection was more than the sum total of events and participants.

The problem in studying the Singapore connection is how to represent this moral dimension of the struggle. Should the job be left to the novelist? It was easy enough to gather data to show that speedboat operations were successful or not. However, such data threw little light on the fear that must have weighed heavily on the minds and hearts of the speedboat crew as they tried to break the Dutch blockade. Similarly, it was relatively simple to establish that Indoff was financially weak, but what was it like to face destitution in a big city like Singapore, ruled by alien authorities who were not obliged to provide a safety net to meet contingencies?

So what was Indonesia's Singapore connection? More than half a century later, and with the hindsight of victory, it is not wrong to stress all those events in history that eventually contributed to the successful conclusion of Indonesian's struggle within the Singapore domain. Against the background of all those glorious events, the accusations of corruption fade into obscurity. The financial deprivations are hardly remembered. The sense of insecurity faced by Indonesians operating in Singapore without official papers is glossed over. And generally, the fear of being detained or interrogated by the Singapore Criminal Investigation Department is forgotten. Yet they formed a part of the history of the Singapore connection. It was a time of heroic achievements. But it was also a topsy-turvy world in which life was lived in emergencies. It was a time of confusion and bewilderment. The frustrations were legendary, although they might now appear to have been well worth the effort.

Bibliography

Abbreviations used for archival material

AS	Algemene Secretarie
CGDN	Consulaat-Generaal der Nederlanden
FO	Foreign Office (London)
PG	Procureur-Generaal
RI	Rapportage Indonesië

Archival

Algemeen Rijksarchief (now Nationaal Archief), The Hague
    Archief van de Algemene Secretarie van Nederlands-Indië
    Archief van het Ministerie van Algemene Zaken
    Archief van het Ministerie van Koloniën
    Archief van het Ministerie van Overzeese Gebiedsdelen
    Archief van de Procureur-Generaal bij het Hooggerechtshof in Indonesië (Overgekomen archief)
    Directie Verre Oosten
    Rapportage Indonesië

Ministerie van Buitenlandse Zaken, The Hague
    Archief van het Ministerie van Buitenlandse Zaken
    Archief Consulaat-Generaal Singapore, 1946-1951

Foreign Office, London
    FO 371 series
    FO 810 series

St Antony's College, Oxford
    Killearn Diary, 1946-1948

National Archives, Singapore
Oral history records
    Haji Badron bin Sainullah
    Haji Mohamed Sidek bin Siraj
    Haji Mohamad Sadli bin Mohamad

Published sources

Abdullah bin Malim Baginda
1967   'Our Baweanese people', *Intisari* 2-4:15-71.

Adams, Cindy
1965   *Sukarno, an autobiography as told to Cindy Adams*. Hongkong: Gunung Agung.

Anderson, Benedict R. O'G.
1972   *Java in a time of revolution; Occupation and resistance 1944-1946*. Ithaca/London: Cornell University Press.

Broek, Jan O.M.
1942   *Economic development of the Netherlands Indies*. New York: Institute of Pacific Relations.

Broersma, R.
1927   *Handel en bedrijf in Zuid- en Oost-Borneo*. 's-Gravenhage: Naeff.

Bung Hatta's answers
1981   *Bung Hatta's answers; Interviews Dr Mohammad Hatta with Dr. Z. Yasni*. Singapore: Gunung Agung.

Coast, John
1952   *Recruit to revolution; Adventure and politics in Indonesia*. London: Christophers.

Cheah Boon Kheng
1983   *Red star over Malaya; Resistance and social conflict during and after the Japanese occupation of Malaya, 1941-1946*. Singapore: Singapore University Press.

Cribb, Robert
1988   'Opium and the Indonesian revolution', *Modern Asian Studies*, 22:701-22.
1981   'Political dimensions of the currency question 1945-1947', *Indonesia* 31:113-36.

Chew, C.T. Ernest and Lee, Edwin (eds)
1991   *A history of Singapore*. Singapore: Oxford University Press.

Darusman, Suryono
n.d.   'Singapore and the Indonesian Revolution 1945-1950.' [Typescript.]
1992   *Singapore and the Indonesian Revolution 1945-50; Recollections of Suryono Darusman*. Singapore: Institute of Southeast Asian Studies.
1992   Interview in Jakarta, 20 March.

Djajadiningrat, I.N.
1958   *The beginnings of the Indonesian-Dutch negotiations and the Hoge Veluwe talks*. Ithaca: Department of Far Eastern Studies, Modern Indonesia Project.

Djen Amar
1963   *Bandung lautan api*. Djakarta: Dhiwantara.

Economisch weekblad voor Nederlandsch-Indië, 1946-1947

Een halve eeuw paketvaart
1941   *Een halve eeuw paketvaart, 1891-1941*. Amsterdam: DeBussy.

Ekonomisch beleid
1972-75   *Het ekonomisch beleid in Nederlands-Indië; Capita Selecta; Een bronnenpublikatie.* Edited by P. Creutzberg. Groningen: Wolters-Noordhoff. Four vols.
Entrepot trade
1945   *The entrepot trade of Singapore.* Singapore: British Military Administration, Department of Trade.
Gilmour, Andrew
1973   *My role in the rehabilitation of Singapore, 1946-1953.* Singapore: Institute of Southeast Asian Studies. [Oral History Pilot Study 2.]
Hatta, Mohammad
1981   *Mohammad Hatta; Indonesian patriot; Memoirs.* Edited by C.L.M. Penders. Singapore: Gunung Agung.
Homan, Gerlof D.
1983   'American business interests in the Indonesian Republic, 1946-1949', *Indonesia* 35:125-32.
Indonesian intentions
1964   *Indonesian intentions towards Malaysia.* Kuala Lumpur: Jabatan Chetak Kerajaan.
Indonesian Observer (Jakarta). Relevant issues.
Kahin, Audrey R. (ed.)
1985   *Regional dynamics of the Indonesian revolution; Unity from diversity.* Honolulu: University of Hawaii Press.
Kartodirdjo, Sartono
1982   *Pemikiran dan perkembangan historiografi Indonesia; Suatu alternatif.* Jakarta: Gramedia.
K'tut Tantri
1960   *Revolt in paradise.* London: Heinemann.
Lindsey, Timothy
1997   *The romance of K'tut Tantri and Indonesia; Text and scripts, history and identity.* Kuala Lumpur: Oxford University Press.
Lubis, Mochtar
1977   *Maut dan cinta.* Jakarta: Pustaka Jaya.
Malaya Tribune (Singapore), 1945-1950.
Memoar pejuang
1992   *Memoar pejuang Republik Indonesia seputar 'Zaman Singapura' 1945-1950.* Edited by Kustiniyati Mochtar. Jakarta: Gramedia.
Money, J.W.B.
1985   *Java, or how to manage a colony.* Reprint. [First edition London: Hurst and Blackett, 1861.]
Nasution, A.H.
1977   *Sekitar perang kemerdekaan Indonesia; Jilid 3, Diplomasi sambil bertempur.* Bandung: Disjarah-AD/Angkasa Bandung.
1978a   *Sekitar perang kemerdekaan Indonesia; Jilid 4, Periode Linggajati.* Bandung: Disjarah-AD/Angkasa.

1978b   *Sekitar perang kemerdekaan Indonesia; Jilid 5, Agresi Militer Belanda I.*
                Bandung: Disjarah-AD/Angkasa Bandung.
1978c   *Sekitar perang kemerdekaan Indonesia; Jilid 7, Periode Renville.* Bandung:
                Disjarah-AD/Angkasa Bandung.
1979a   *Sekitar perang kemerdekaan Indonesia; Jilid 9, Agresi Militer Belanda II.*
                Bandung: Disjarah-AD/Angkasa.
1979b   *Sekitar perang kemerdekaan Indonesia; Jilid 10, Perang Gerilya Semesta 2.*
                Bandung: Disjarah-AD/Angkasa.
1979c   *Sekitar perang kemerdekaan Indonesia, Jilid 11, Periode konferensi Meja
                Bundar.* Bandung: Disjarah-AD/Angkasa.

Officiële bescheiden
1971-96   *Officiële bescheiden betreffende de Nederlandse-Indonesische betrekkingen,
                1945-1950.* Edited by S.L. van der Wal, P.J. Drooglever and M.J.B.
                Schouten. 's-Gravenhage: Nijhoff/Instituut voor Nederlandse Geschiedenis. Twenty vols.

Palmier, Leslie
1962   *Indonesia and the Dutch.* Oxford: Oxford University Press.

Pelzer, Karl J.
1978   *Planter and peasant; Colonial policy and the agrarian struggle in East Sumatra, 1863-1947.* 's-Gravenhage: Nijhoff. [KITLV, Verhandelingen 84.]

Pluvier, Jan M.
1995   *Historical atlas of South-East Asia.* Leiden: Brill.

Rahsia perdjuangan
1948   *Rahsia perdjuangan Indonesia di Singapore.* Compiled by Sjamsudin
                Lubis. Documented by S.L. Tobing. Singapore: S.L. Tobing.

[Read, W.H]
1901   *Play and politics; Recollections of Malaya by an old resident.* London: Gardner, Darton.

Reid, Anthony J.S.
1969   *The contest for North Sumatra; Atjeh, the Netherlands and Britain, 1858-
                1898.* Kuala Lumpur: Oxford University Press, Singapore: University
                of Malaya Press.
1974   *Indonesian national revolution 1945-50.* Hawthorn, Victoria: Longman
                Australia.

Rowan, Roy
1949   'Guns – bibles – are smuggled to Indonesia', *Life Magazine*, 26 September, pp. 49-52.

Rush, James R.
1990   *Opium to Java; Revenue farming and Chinese enterprise in colonial Indonesia, 1861-1910.* Ithaca: Cornell University Press.

Said, Salim
1991   *Genesis of power; General Sudirman and the Indonesian military in politics,
                1945-49.* Singapore: Institute of Southeast Asian Studies, Jakarta: Sinar
                Harapan.

Samad Ismail
1987   *A. Samad Ismail; Journalism & politics.* Compiled and edited by Cheah
                Boon Kheng. Kuala Lumpur: Singamal.

Schiller, A. Arthur
1955   *The formation of federal Indonesia, 1945-1949*. The Hague/Bandung: Van Hoeve.
Schulte Nordholt, Henk
1996   *The spell of power; A history of Balinese politics, 1650-1940*. Leiden: KITLV Press. [Verhandelingen 170.]
Smail, John R.W.
1964   *Bandung in the early revolution, 1945-1946; A study in the social history of the Indonesian revolution*. Ithaca: Southeast Asia Program, Cornell University.
Straits Times (Singapore), 1945-1950.
Suryadinata, Leo
1995   *Eminent Indonesian Chinese; Bibliographical sketches*. Singapore: Institute of Southeast Asian Studies.
Sutter, John O.
1959   *Indonesianisasi; Politics in a changing economy, 1940-1955*. Ithaca: Cornell University. Four vols.
Travellers' Singapore
1994   *Travellers' Singapore; An anthology*. Compiled and introduced by John Bastin. Kuala Lumpur: Oxford University Press.
Twang Peck Yang
1998   *The Chinese business elite in Indonesia and the transition to independence, 1940-1950*. Kuala Lumpur: Oxford University Press.
Van der Kraan, Alfons
1980   *Lombok; Conquest, colonization and underdevelopment, 1870-1940*. Singapore: Heinemann.
Vredenbregt, Jacob
1964   'Bawean migrations', *Bijdragen tot de Taal-, Land- en Volkenkunde* 120: 109-39.
Westerling, Raymond ('Turk')
1952   *Challenge to terror*. London: Kimber.
Yong Mun Cheong
1982   *H.J. van Mook and Indonesian independence; A study of his role in Dutch-Indonesian relations, 1945-48*. The Hague: Nijhoff.
Zed, Mestika
1991   *Kepialangan, politik dan revolusi: Palembang 1900-1950*. [PhD thesis, Vrije Universiteit Amsterdam.]

Index

Abdoellah, Radji Hadji 46-7
Abdulrachman, Haji 10
Aceh 9-10
Ahmad, Abdoel 29
Airabu 124
Aminoellah 29
Antara 3, 40
Anwar A Moe'in (journalist) 27
Api 34
Arab Street 45
Asahan 9
Atjeh Trading Company 49
   A.K. Gani (founder) 49
   Penang 50
   relations with Indoff 50

Badan Pemberontak Indonesia Blakang Mati 34
Badan Pemberontak Kalimantan 34
Bagansiapiapi 176, 179
Baghdad Street 30
Bangka 101-2, 149
Bangka Straits 3
banking 154, 178-9
Banking and Trading Corporation (Djakarta) 50
Banking and Trading Corporation (Yogyakarta) 50
barter 47-8
   barter book system 154-7
Batak
   ethnic organization 35
   supporters 30, 33
Bawean 7, 53, 74
   migration to Singapore 53
   Persatoean Bawean Singapore 53
Beach Road
   entry point 2, 25, 102

Belawan 144
Bengkalis 8, 151, 176, 179
Billiton 101-2
blockade runners 45
Blundell, E.A. (Governor) 8
Boat Quay 102
British
   Chinese boycott 152
   relations with Dutch 82
   trade 182-3
Buleleng 8

Cavenagh, O. (Governor) 9
Change Alley 38
Changi 101
Chinchew 148, 159
Chinese
   boycott and measures against Dutch 150-1, 167, 170, 172-3
   commodities traded 51-2, 160
   complaints against Dutch 161-3
   Lee Kong Chian 172-3
   Ng Aik Huan 150
   seizure of ships 143-4, 148-9
   smuggling 52
   SOCIEA 51, 147, 161, 165, 168, 171, 173-4, 176, 180
   Tan Kah Kee 151, 161, 171
   Teoh Thiam Chong 151
   traders 51, 168-70
Chinese Chamber of Commerce 158
Cirebon 149
Clifford Pier
   entry point 2, 25-6
Coast, John 45
communists 190-1

Daroesman, Suryono

Biodata 43-4
Indoff 37
Mariam Bee 101, 123
opium 134-5
reassignment 190, 193
Deli 9
Djawatan Koeasa 46, 93-4, 97
Dutch
  boycott 173
  Chinese complaints 161-2
  Prisoners of war 58

Ee Hoe Hean Club 171
Emergency (1948) 22-3, 57
ethnic dimensions 76-7
  Minang 35
  Batak 35
  Sahata 35

Force 136 (Johore) 101, 123
Fox agreement 90

Gaast, T. van der 184
Gani, A.K. (Republican Governor of South Sumatra)
  pro-Republic 2, 33
  seizure of ships 146
  Singapore 78
  smuggling 108
  trade 182
Gaus, Mahyudin 54, 69-70, 75, 149
General Labour Union (GLU)
  strikes 29-30
Gerakan Angkatan Muda 34
Geylang Road 28
Geylang Serai 26, 28, 52
  anti-Dutch and anti-British activities 34
Gilmour, A. (Secretary for Economic Affairs) 104, 182-3
Gui Oh Nua 129

Haig Road 28
Happy World 28
Hassan (Governor of Sumatra) 38
Henderson Road 26
Hidoep Seresam 45
Hire, Carlton 116

Hiwarni 32
Hong Thong 159-60
Hung Hai 150
Independence Day
  celebrations (1946) 68-9
  celebrations (1947) 70
  celebrations (1948) 70
  celebrations (1949) 71
  Republic 191
Indoff
  antecedents 37
  choice location for Singapore 36
  corruption 87
  end of mission 189, 192
  formation 35-6, 37
  funds 88-91
  goals 41
  information 88
  levies 90, 164-7
  moral issues 87
  opium 76, 93
  relations with PKBI 67-8, 70
  relations with PKBI-PI 83-7
  rice 92
  trade 91, 163-4, 184-7
  United States 71
Indonesia
  Bersiap period 34
Indonesia Import and Export 49
Indonesian Tourist Pilgrim Association 34
Indragiri 179

Jambi 156, 176, 179
Japanese
  surrender 14
Javanese
  labourers 26
  support for Republic 53
Johor-Riau Empire
  past glory 31
Johore
  weapons caches 116, 123
Juliana camp 28

Kampong Glam 45, 69-70
  past grandeur 30-1
Karimoen 101

Kemadjoean Pemoeda Aman 34
Kengtung 116
Kesatoean Pemoeda Indonesia 34
Kian Peng 178
Killearn, M.W.L. 39
  departure 55, 189
  impressions of Oetoyo 56
  relations with Republic 56, 71
  rice 55-6
Koempoelan Kampong Geylang Serai 34
Koempoelan Pemoeda Indonesia 34
Koh Peng Kuan 95-6
Krui 176
K'tut Tantri
  Singapore 3
Kwek Soan Loh 147, 158, 161, 168, 188

Labuan Bilik 109-10
Langkat 9
Lee Kong Chian 162, 172-3
Lee Kwet Jin 127
Lie, John 122-3
Lien Ying Chow 148
Linggajati Agreement
  diplomatic missions 36
  impact on Singapore 19-20
  interpretations 19
  terms 18-9
Loebis, Tahir Karim
  espionage 136
  official presence in Singapore 38
  reconciliation efforts 31-2
Loh, Captain Joseph 101
Lombok 10

Malays
  support for Republic 24, 52
Malygin, W.P. 11
Margono Djojohadikoesoemo 140-1
Mariam Bee 101
Mawardi 3
Mecca 9
Mendelaar, J.J. (Resident) 149
Meoeraksa, Djohan 38
Middle Road 4
Military Action

First 20-2, 60-2, 71
  resistance 23
Second 22-3, 57, 63-5, 175-6
Mitchell, J.C. 10
Mochtar Effendi 54
Moekarto Notowidigdo 127-8
Money, J.W.B. 11-2
Mook, H.J. van
  Borneo and Great East 17-8
  negotiations 16
  relations with investors 20
  shipping control 146
Mountbatten, Louis (Supreme Commander of SEAC) 15, 54
Muntok 144, 148-9
Muslim Welfare Association 34

Namsoco
  business connections with Singapore 34
  relations with Antara 49
  relations with PKBI 49
  representing A.K. Gani 49
Nee Soon 26
Netherlands-Indonesia Union 22
Netherlands Consulate
  duties 58-9, 193
  S. van Hulst (Secretary for Special Services) 35
  trade downturn 182
  Utusan Melayu 59
Ng Aik Huan 150, 158
Noerdin 29
Noesantara Agency 49
  T.K. Loebis (founder) 49
North Bridge Road 44

Oesaha Baroe 49
Oetomo (Ministry of Information)
  departure 40
  disagreements with Oetoyo 40
  Indonesian Information Service 39
  secondment 38
Oetoyo Ramelan
  biodata 41-2
  Hong Thong 160
  Killearn 42, 82-3

official presence in Singapore 38
opium 133-4
reassignment 190, 193
Republican policies 82
Sjahrir 42
United States of Indonesia 192
welfare 73-74, 75, 81
opium
Batavia supplies 127
prices 128
smuggling 6-7, 127-9

Pakan Baru 151, 159-60, 176, 179
Palang Merah Indonesia 34
Palembang 2, 149
Pasir Panjang
entry point 2, 25
smuggling 110
passports 2, 71, 74-5, 79, 110, 189
proper documents 3-4, 27, 52
recognized by British 2
Peheman 34
Perkabim
formation 30
funds 31
Persatoean Indonesia
choice of name 33
formation 33
Philippines 116
pilgrims 9
Pinke, Admiral A.S. 145-6
PKBI
formation 28
funds 31
relations with Indoff 67-8, 70
labourers 28-9
new 30-1
see also Tobing, S.L.
PKBI-PI 72-3
espionage 137
fate 193-4
Indoff 83
Martinus Indra 83-4
weapons 126
Pluto 9
Porkas, Haris 4-5
Priaman 176

Raffles Place 40
Rengat 176
Renville
negotiations 22
Restaurant Kita 44-5, 70
Riau
Abdoellah, Radja 94-5
anti-sultanate camp 97
Djawatan Koeasa 93-4, 97
Persatoean Melayu Riouw Sedjati 98
restoration of sultanate 21-2, 46, 90-8
Utusan Melayu 94
rice 55-56
Rochor area
entry point 2
Roekoen Agawi Santoso 34
Rokan 179
romusha 27
Roura, Edouard 10

Sa'adon bin Jubir 54
sailors 28
Salim, Hadji Agoes 18, 78
Samad, Abdul
pro-Republican 37, 54
relations with Republican leaders 54
Utusan Melayu 54
Selamat, Oemar 37, 125
Selat Panjang 110, 151, 179
Semarang 150
Serdang 9
SERTA (Sarikat Rahasia Tanah Air)
organization 35
shipping 144-9
British mediation 152
boycott 148, 150-1
checks 177-8
Dutch regulations 149-50, 153
seaworthiness 177
seizures 143-4, 148-50
Siak 8, 179
Siak river 110
Sibolga 176, 179
Siglap 70
Simandjoentak, Herman 29
Singapore
anti-Dutch activities 7-11

barter 188
crime 27
El Dorado 26-7
fistfights 28
information gathering 11-2
labour recruits 26
merantau destination 25
Singapore connection 1, 11, 41, 175
trade 139, 140-2, 175, 187-8
Sjahrir, Soetan
   Killearn 79
   negotiations 17-8
   Oetoyo 42
   Prime Minister 16
   Singapore 71, 78-9
Sjahroedin
   Antara 40
   biodata 2-3, 27
Sjarikat Dagang Tapanoeli 51
smuggling 102
   Borneo 112
   bribery and corruption 113-4
   by air 115
   Chinese firms 107-8
   commodities 102-3
   contraband 102, 110
   East Indonesia 114
   Environment 103
   Jambi 109
   Japanese Occupation 102
   Kampong Laut 109
   Labuan Bilik 110
   modus operandi 108
   Muara Sabak 109
   Netherlands navy 106
   Pakan Baru 110
   Palembang 108-9
   Pasir Panjang 110
   Pemangkat 113
   Port Swettenham 110
   Pulau Pisang 110
   Pulau Rangsang 110
   Riau archipelago 111
   sectors 108-14
   Selat Panjang 110
   shipping regulations 105
   Siak river 110
   Singkawang 113
   smugglers' profile 107, 109-11
   Sungai Apit 110
   surplus military stores 104, 118
   surveillance 115
   Tanjung Pinang 108-10, 116
   vessels 1034
Soekarno 37
Soon Hin Lee 178

Soumokil, C.R.S. (Minister of Justice, East Indonesia) 114
Straits dollars 106
sugar 101
Sultan mosque (Arab quarter in Singapore) 27
Sumatra Banking and Trading Corporation (SBTC) 50

Taharoeddin, Ahmad
   leader of Minangs 30, 44
Tambunan and Company, E. 51
Tan Kah Kee 151, 161, 171
Tanjong Katong 28
Tanjung Balai 144
Tanjung Pinang 144, 156, 159-60
Tegal 3, 11, 101, 150
Telukbitung 176, 179
Teoh Thiam Chong 151
The Toan Huat 6-7
Tibang (shahbandar) 9
Tjioe Men Leong 127
Tobing, S.L. (PKBI President)
   biodata 29
   mass meetings 32
   red and white symbols 32
   relations with Oetoyo 68
tongkang 47, 91
Trade 91
   balance 48-9
   banking 154
   barter book system 154-5
   blockade 62-3, 147, 151
   downturn 175, 180-8
   Dutch regulations 142-4, 146, 149-50, 158, 161-3, 167
   exchange rate 158
   Hong Thong trial run 159-60
   rice 92

Second Military Action 176

United States of Indonesia 22-3
Ursone, P.A. 173

Vigeveno, M.F. (Netherlands Consul-General) 56

Waterloo Street 26
Wen, Tony 128, 130-2
Weapons
  acquisition 26, 47-8
  Airabu 124
  China – Hongkong 124-5
  Emergency 120-1
  explosives 27
  Indoff 119-21
  Mariam Bee 101

modus operandi 118-9
prices 119
traders 116-8, 122-6
Westerling, R.P.P. 4-5, 192
Wilhelmina camp 28
Wilson, Adam 8
Winkelman, A.M.L. (Netherlands Consul-General) 183
Wirohardjo, Saroso 44

Zain, Zairin 84
  barter book system 156
  biodata 43
  Hong Thong 160
  levy 165
  Oetoyo 43
  trade 185-6
Zubir Said 54

www.ingramcontent.com/pod-product-compliance
Ingram Content Group UK Ltd.
Pitfield, Milton Keynes, MK11 3LW, UK
UKHW041959230426
12048UKWH00008B/424

9 789067 182065